The Superintendent of the Future

Strategy and Action for Achieving Academic Excellence

Robert R. Spillane, BA, MA, PhD

Regional Education Officer
U.S. Department of State
Washington, DC

Paul Regnier, BA, MA, PhD

Coordinator, Community Relations
Fairfax County Public Schools
Fairfax, Virginia

AN ASPEN PUBLICATION®

Aspen Publishers, Inc.
Gaithersburg, Maryland
1998

Library of Congress Cataloging-in-Publication Data

Spillane, Robert.
The superintendent of the future:
strategy and action for achieving academic excellence/
Robert R. Spillane and Paul Regnier.
p. cm.
Includes bibliographical references and index.
ISBN 0-8342-1097-5
1. School superintendents—United States—Case studies.
I. Regnier, Paul. II. Title.
LB2831.72.S65 1995
371.2'011—dc21
98-6789
CIP

Orders: (800) 638-8437
Customer Service: (800) 234-1660

About Aspen Publishers • For more than 35 years, Aspen has been a leading professional publisher in a variety of disciplines. Aspen's vast information resources are available in both print and electronic formats. We are committed to providing the highest quality information available in the most appropriate format for our customers. Visit Aspen's Internet site for more information resources, directories, articles, and a searchable version of Aspen's full catalog, including the most recent publications: **http://www.aspenpub.com**
Aspen Publishers, Inc. • The hallmark of quality in publishing
Member of the worldwide Wolters Kluwer group.

Editorial Services: Nora Fitzpatrick
Library of Congress Catalog Card Number: 98-6789
ISBN: 0-8342-1097-5

Printed in the United States of America

1 2 3 4 5

To the thousands of teachers, school administrators, and other public school workers with whom we have worked; to the thinkers and scholars whom we have read and talked with—all of you have taught us to be clear, thoughtful, practical, and intellectually independent.

And to Gerry and Ana, *sine qua non.*

Table of Contents

Contributors

Dolores Boylston Bohen, MEd
Assistant Superintendent
Department of Communications
Fairfax County Public Schools
Fairfax, Virginia

Andrea D. Clements, PhD
Assistant Professor
Human Development and Learning
College of Education
East Tennessee State University
Johnson City, Tennessee

Jacqueline P. Danzberger, BA
Director, Governance Programs
Institute for Educational Leadership
Washington, DC

Denis P. Doyle AB, MA
President
Doyle Associates
Chevy Chase, Maryland

Gioia Caiola Forman, AAS, BS, MA
Director of the Office of Security and
   Risk Management Services
Fairfax County Public Schools
Fairfax, Virginia

Louis Grumet, BA, JD, MPA, CAE
Executive Director
New York State School Boards
   Association
Albany, New York

Marlene C. Holayter, MA, EdD
Superintendent
Shoreline Public Schools
Shoreline, Washington

Michael S. Radlick, BA, MA, PhD
Director of Educational Technology
Open Systems Technologies
Clifton Park, New York

Paul Regnier, BA, MA, PhD
Coordinator, Community Relations
Fairfax County Public Schools
Fairfax, Virginia

Rosemarie V. Rosen, BA, MS
Executive Director
New York State Public Employment
   Relations Board
Albany, New York

Robert R. Spillane, BA, MA, PhD
Regional Education Officer
U.S. Department of State
Washington, DC

J.E. Stone, EdD
Professor, Licensed Psychologist
College of Education
East Tennessee State University
Johnson City, Tennessee

Preface

Practical men, who believe themselves to be quite exempt from any intellectual influences, are usually the slaves of some defunct economist. Madmen in authority, who hear voices in the air, are distilling their frenzy from some academic scribbler of a few years back.

John Maynard Keynes, *The General Theory of Employment, Interest, and Money*, 1936

Keynes was not only right about politics and economics; his comment can be applied to many other fields, including education. As school administrators, we are, indeed, practical people, but we are not exempt from intellectual influences. Our practical actions rest on ideas, and usually these ideas are the product of a defunct educational writer or on some academic scribbler of a few years back. Unearthing, analyzing, criticizing, and rethinking these ideas should be a high priority for those of us with practical responsibilities. The ideas of the past, which have motivated our actions in the past, are not always good ideas for the future. In fact, some of these ideas of the past were never too good to begin with.

We wrote this book so that school superintendents and those who aspire to this office will have a guide to thinking and rethinking what they do, and why—"why" being the ideas that motivate what we do. Both of us have seen many changes—in ideas, goals, environments, and structures—in public education over the past 20–30 years. Especially in the last 15 years, these changes have reached a point at which the future of public schools as we know them is in doubt. We are also strong advocates of public schooling, and we therefore want all the players in the public education enterprise—especially superintendents—to get involved in the comprehensive rethinking without which public schooling will be at risk.

Unfortunately, superintendents have not been prominent in the rethinking of the past 15 years. While politicians and pundits have developed, publicized, and legislated new ideas, superintendents have continued their practical work with actual students in actual schools in actual communities. We hope that this book will help superintendents to become part of the ongoing dialogue about the future of public education—a dialogue that is likely to substantially affect the school systems they will be superintending in the twenty-first century.

Becoming part of this dialogue means linking practical matters with a critical discussion of ideas. This requires practical people who no longer believe they are exempt from intellectual influence and yet are not slaves of some defunct educational writer. It requires superintendents who can knowledgeably and critically examine the ideas that are part of their profession's conventional wisdom, as well as the ideas that are offered in contradiction to that wisdom.

We, along with the other authors of this book, have tried to make that connection between the practical and the intellectual in ways that will make sense to people who are daily inundated with practical problems and issues. The idea is to be able to think one's way through the problems and issues without falling back on the unexamined beliefs that have often made it easier to make decisions in the past.

The Superintendent of the Future will be a Thinking Person's Superintendent and a reflective, broadly learned, person of affairs. To resurrect an often misused term, the superintendent of the future will be a Renaissance Man (in which "man" includes both genders) a person comfortable both in the world of practical affairs and in the realm of ideas. We hope that this book will help today's superintendents, and those who aspire to that office, to become tomorrow's.

Robert R. Spillane
Paul Regnier

CHAPTER 1

This Is Now; Then Is Then

Robert R. Spillane and Paul Regnier

In the view of many literary critics and in the tradition of Western literature (beginning at least with Homer), a narrative should begin "*in media res*"—or "in the middle of things." In this tradition, this book begins with a day in the life of a superintendent toward the end of the twentieth century. This is now.

A DAY IN THE LIFE ...

7:30 a.m.

I arrive for breakfast at the Tower Club, a posh business club where the elite of Fairfax County meet to eat. This is a breakfast meeting I have every few months with my Business and Industry Advisory Council (BIAC). Making sure that there is two-way communication between the school system and the business community is very important for any superintendent these days. This advisory council is broadly representative and particularly concerned with technology issues. The bottom line with them is that the schools continue to produce high student achievement so that businesses can lure employees to live and work in Fairfax County. The business community is a subset of the 70% of the population who do not have children in the schools but who do vote and pay taxes. It is crucial that they are involved in decision making and have a good understanding of what is going on in schools and what the school system is doing to improve student achievement. Perhaps more than any other group in the community, business people want to hear directly from the superintendent; they accept no substitutes. Much of what I do with this group is to answer their questions based on what they have heard in the rumor mill or read in the newspapers. Talking with them, I get a very good idea of community scuttlebutt. One of the most important things for a superintendent to keep in mind about the business community is that it is constantly changing. For instance, when I came here a dozen years ago, the Fairfax County business community was dominated by a few property developers; now it is dominated by high-technology companies and there are more of them than developers. The developers also had a clear financial interest in excellent schools—good schools sell houses and even rent office space. With the high-technology companies, the financial interest in excellent public schools is not so direct. What's in it for them is a question that one always needs to ask when dealing with any part of the community, and business is no exception. I came to the breakfast directly from home, and driving back to the office at 9 a.m., I call ahead on the car phone and find no immediate crises.

9:10 a.m.

Back in the office, I go through what's left of yesterday's mail, which takes an hour or more because I am interrupted by phone calls. The mail has already been sorted by a secretary, so I am only getting mail that, supposedly, I need to see. I always want to know what people in the community think is important enough to write the superintendent about, but often letters go to the appropriate office (e.g., the transportation office for a letter about school buses) to be answered. After that, I see the letter with the answer, which I sometimes change. The mail today includes requests for public appearances, parent complaints, and, also, parent commendations (sometimes there is a complaint and a commendation about the same thing—you can't please everyone all the time). I mark everything for response or action.

These days, there is a new type of mail to be dealt with—e-mail; after initially trying to go through all the e-mail myself, I have asked my administrative assistant to screen it. This is a very interesting form of communication with advantages over regular mail (e-mail is instantaneously delivered) and telephone calls (e-mail can be read and responded to on your schedule, not the caller's).

10:20 a.m.

I visit Stuart High School. I have a schedule of school visits, trying to visit at least one every business day, which is the only way that the people who work in each of our 200-plus schools ever get a sense that the superintendent cares about what happens in "my" school. Also, I get a much better idea of the atmosphere out there. What is the purpose of such a visit? Show the "flag," make contact with students and teachers, see the principal and find out directly what his or her major issues are, read to elementary school students or answer the questions of high schoolers (but you only have time to do one classroom). Greet every adult who works there (including custodians and lunch-room workers—who may give you a better idea than teachers of what is really going on).

11:00 a.m.

I am back in the office to meet with a group of parents who are concerned with the proposed new middle school report cards and grading system. This is a complicated issue that was not helped by the fact that it was inadequately explained to the middle school teachers and principals. The bottom line is that the parents need assurance that the proposed system will not be implemented until everyone (parents, students, and teachers) understands the basis for grading. This, as with most concerns of the community, is reasonable; too often educators view any opposition from the community as an attack on their professional judgment. Deciding which groups to meet with is a dilemma for a busy superintendent. Many issues can be dealt with at other levels, but if something is going to become a hot issue, the superintendent had better get a personal handle on it, and there is no substitute for a personal meeting. It is also important to be adequately briefed for the meeting. Know what the different positions are and what your staff is recommending. But sometimes, you get a perspective in the actual meeting that changes your mind. You also need to know what your options are as well as the quickest way to resolve the issue. Do you just listen and pass on the group's ideas to upper-level staff members, or do you try to work out a solution right at the meeting? In the case of the middle school grading controversy, I assured the group that the plan was back on the drawing board and that there would be ample opportunity for community comment before anything was implemented.

11:30 a.m.

The meeting over, I check phone calls that my secretary has been taking. I call back a school board chair in Florida who is checking on a superintendent candidate who used to work for me in Boston. A Fairfax County school board member has heard from a parent saying that at her school there are gangs, but the principal denies it; I tell her I will look into it and have Mary Ann, my administrative assistant, call the area superintendent to check on the school. There are gangs in some of our schools, and we need to be honest about this, but we also need to scotch rumors when they are merely rumors. The local all-news TV station, Channel 8, wants to interview me this afternoon about a group of parents who want inclusion of all handicapped students in neighborhood schools; I agree to a 2:45 interview in front of my office building. The assistant superintendent for financial services wants five minutes to explain why the difference between the school board's advertised budget for next year and the cap on the transfer of funds from the county board of supervisors has just been reduced by $5 million. I tell Mary Ann to send him upstairs. There is a call from a local congressman's office—the Impact Aid Bill (providing subsidies to school systems that educate military dependents) is coming up for a vote in committee. Can we get someone to brief the Hill staffer on our Impact Aid history?

11:50 a.m.

Carl, the assistant superintendent for financial services, comes in. The relatively warm winter means heating bills for the year are $5 million less than budgeted, reducing the budget gap for next year. But this kind of thing could go either way, and a few years ago everything went the wrong way. Do you budget straight up or leave a cushion? Either way, you have a potential credibility problem. I also tell Carl to call the Hill staffer, offering to brief her or the congressman on our Impact Aid situation.

11:55 a.m.

I meet with Roger, the assistant superintendent for facilities services. Some school board members are arguing for more renewals in the eastern (older) part of the county and others are arguing for more new buildings in the western (newer) part. Given a bond issue limited by the county's desire to maintain its AAA bond rating, choices need to be made—some old, some new, but nobody gets everything he or she wants. Of course, there are parents organized on both sides, and other people are trying to figure out how to overcome the facilities shortage without putting up as many buildings as needed to house all the students; most of these alternative plans (e.g., year-round schools that stagger vacation times throughout the year or drastic boundary shifts that would have students living in the newer part of the county riding buses for hours to get to schools in the older part) are pretty unpopular with parents. Putting together a list of bond-funded projects that will get the votes and satisfy as many constituents as possible is a problem. I look at Roger's list of projects, make some suggestions, and ask him to put the package together for school board consideration.

12:20 p.m.

I return phone calls in the car while I drive into Washington for lunch at the *Washington Post* with metropolitan-area superintendents. This is a good group with which to catch up on the rumors. Many of these are very large school systems, like mine (although none as large as Fairfax County). The luncheon speaker is Ben Bradlee, the retired *Post* editor who became famous during Watergate. What a *mensch*! He has lots of war stories and helps the superintendents to get out of our narrow focus and see some of the changes going on in the world at large.

1:30 p.m.

I call my office and return a call in my car driving from the *Post* to the office of Area III, one of the regions of Fairfax County, where I meet with the Area III principals. Issues for discussion include middle school grading, facility renewals, seventh-grade algebra, and focus schools. Will all schools eventually have to have some kind of special focus? The Disrespect Involving Students (DIS) program of the school board might require schools to have rooms where any teacher can send disrespectful students. How would these be staffed? Is it possible that next year's budget will cut some assistant principal positions as rumor has it? The new teacher-hiring technology is making it easier to hire better teachers (because we are hiring earlier); it's great to see an example of a technological application that clearly improves what we do.

2:15 p.m.

Back in my office, I am told that Bruce, the coordinator of student activities and athletics, wants to see me about a coach who is being accused of making inappropriate remarks to officials at a basketball game. Stories are already out in the press, and the coordinator is working with the principal on deciding what to do.

2:20 p.m.

Dolores, the assistant superintendent for communications, comes by to say the *Fairfax Journal* wants a quote from me on a bill in the state legislature that would give parents an "absolute right" to make all decisions about their children's education. I will not speak on this for attribution. Dolores also says the Channel 8 van is pulling into the parking lot. They will put up their uplink for the 2:45 interview.

2:30 p.m.

I read the *New York Times* for ten minutes. There is an article about anarchy in Albania (looks like Fairfax County will be getting more Albanian students—I wonder how many we have now). In President Clinton's speech on education in North Carolina, he is pushing testing for all students using comparable tests and is telling the Defense Department schools to start the ball rolling. Rudy Crew is trying to recentralize and get more control of the 32 districts in New York City. Rupert Murdoch's efforts to seize control of satellite communication and bypass all the wires may eventually have some effect on our cable TV agreement under which Fairfax County Public Schools has six cable TV channels.

2:45 p.m.

I do the Channel 8 interview. What do you say to parents who want their handicapped children in the neighborhood school? My heart goes out to these parents and their children, and our school system is doing an excellent job serving their needs. As in many decisions, you need to get back to core values. The welfare and the academic progress of the child are the most important things, and often these are best met at another school. Financially, we cannot afford to have every school with a program for every handicap.

2:55 p.m.

I leave for the meeting of the superintendent's advisory committee (SAC) of representative teachers, being held at Fairfax High School.

3:00 p.m.

At the SAC meeting there are concerns about the 2.5% cost of living adjustment after years of low or no increases. There are problems using the new math curriculum that focuses more on problem solving rather than calculating. The teachers are concerned that the school board will agree with me to end the practice of Monday early closing; I have promoted this change for at least ten years. Middle school grading comes up again. As usual, there are some silly questions (an actual example, "Why do elementary school teachers get only four Tater Tots in their lunches while secondary school teachers get five?"). But I have the opportunity to talk with 250 smart and articulate teachers representing all schools in the system and to listen to what they feel are their important problems. I like the give-and-take and getting to know real teachers, not just their union representatives.

4:00 p.m.

Back at the office, I meet with representatives of MGT of America, Inc., the private company that is doing a management audit of the school system for the school board. MGT is having the initial draft of the study checked for accuracy by relevant offices, and they are touching base with me. I try to get some idea of what their recommendations will be, but they are reporting to the school board.

4:30 p.m.

I return calls to school board members about confidential student expulsion cases and a personnel matter that will be discussed at tonight's executive session of the board. I also call the Area I superintendent about a parent group that wants more International Baccalaureate programs and focus schools in this area that often feels neglected by the central office. After that, I call the assistant superintendent for information technology about delays in wiring some schools for updated computer networking and then contact the assistant superintendent for general services about a report his office is doing on whether it is possible to reduce the cost of school busing by merging with the county bus system (the answer—no way, our busing operation is much too large). Lastly, I call the assistant superintendent for instructional services about problems with new state social studies standards that would ask us to rearrange our social studies sequence (it still isn't clear what the state tests will cover).

5:30 p.m.

Dinner of popcorn (thanks to the microwave) and soda with the *New York Times*. Looks like Fairfax County Public Schools will be getting some students from Zaire, too. The sexual harassment issue in the military is a long-running issue—it is everywhere. All the gun murders—guns are glorified in the United States, and there are many more in our schools than there were five years ago.

6:15 p.m.

Leave for school-board meeting.

6:30 p.m.

Executive session of the school board—expulsions and personnel issues.

7:30 p.m.

The regular meeting of the board doesn't have much on the agenda, but each board member feels he or she must have something to say on every issue that comes up. They are very concerned right now about student behavior, having enough buildings to meet the needs of increasing numbers of students, middle school grading, and the budget.

11:45 p.m.

Adjournment and home.

WHAT HAS CHANGED IN THE FIELD OF EDUCATION?

So this is what it is like to be a superintendent on a fairly typical day in a large school system toward the end of the second millennium. In my thirtieth year as superintendent, I think I can say that I have a pretty good perspective on the institution. What has changed in my 30 years? Some things not much; some things a lot. Things that have changed include the following.

The governance structure. Overall, across the nation, there is much more state involvement. Twenty years ago, there was a great deal of variation in state involvement in education. In New York State, where I spent many years of my career (three of those years as deputy commissioner for elementary, secondary, and continuing education in the New York State Education Department), there has always been substantial state involvement in education, but in New Jersey and Massachusetts, where I also worked as a superintendent, major state involvement was a more recent phenomenon. In Virginia, where I have worked most recently, substantial state involvement is a very recent development, but it has come with a vengeance. Politicians, as distinct from educators, are taking more control of education at all levels—local, state, and federal. Recent changes in New York, Chicago, and Boston are indicative of this.

Community control. Over the past 30 years, the field of education has moved back and forth between centralization and decentralization. The most significant earlier attempt at decentralization was in New York City, where the elementary and junior high schools were divided into 32 community school districts (each with its own elected school board and superintendent) in the late 1960s. The idea, of course, was that local control would mean more parent influence on what happened in schools and, thus, better education for the students. I believe that, in some cases, there were improvements, particularly in the East Harlem district where Anthony Alvarado offered parents choices of various types of schools, but the decentralization just as often led to localized corruption, domination of community school boards by special interests (voter turnouts for community school board elections were pitiful), and lack of accountability by both community and central authorities. Now the mayor of New York has sought to gain control of the school board and the chancellor has pushed decentralization. More recently Chicago has provided even more of a roller-coaster example. After radically decentralizing down to the individual school level in 1988 with parent/teacher/community councils selecting principals, Chicago has more recently received permission from the state legislature to make the mayor directly responsible for the school system, and Mayor Richard M. Daley has put his team of managers in place.

Superintendents. Superintendents morph from managers to instructional leaders. When I first became a superintendent, superintendents (and principals) were expected to leave educational decisions to the teachers in the classrooms and to curriculum experts. We were to manage the operation. Now leaders in public education are expected to be educational and instructional leaders. Also, superintendents are no longer all white males. This is one of the most positive developments. Especially in a profession such as education, where most are women, having the overwhelming majority of the leaders male does not send the right message to the rest of the profession. Equally, members of minority groups need to be more heavily represented in the leadership of a profession that so substantially affects the lives of all people, of whatever race, color, or creed.

Special education. Special education has gone from practically nonexistent, with handicapped children practically invisible in schools, to being a big budget and personnel-intensive (even for individual education program [IEP] development and monitoring—not instruction) issue with students. There are now programs in every school system. The good side of this is evident; in Fairfax County, for instance, 91% of our special-education graduates are employed or are in higher education after graduation. This is good for everyone, including being good for the economy and the economic well-being of all of us. Unfortunately, there is another side to this. To a large extent, special education has become an expensive sop to parents rather than an effort to do the best for children.

Training. Teacher training and professional development have become much more intensive, but are still under attack by the budget-cutters, in spite of the facts that many successful businesses fund and require (on company time) substantial staff development and that research on educational improvement shows that staff development is critical to the success of any instructional program.

Standards. Minimum competency testing was the accountability movement of the 1970s and 1980s, but the tests exposed the very low expectations for high school graduation and forced the current move to have much higher standards for all students. Everyone—including politicians, parents, business people, and the media—are demanding much higher standards for *all* students, in the belief, which is warranted that American students are capable of achieving at the levels of students in other developed countries *if* we expect and demand these levels.

Student populations. Our student populations are much more minority, immigrant, limited-English proficient, and low socioeconomic than they were 30 years ago. This not only reflects the general population, it *overreflects* it, as schools usually do. Unfortunately, this helps fuel increasing taxpayer reluctance to fund public education, since the population of the schools looks increasingly less like the population of taxpayers.

Incentives. Programs like teacher performance evaluation and merit pay have been used and have been successful in many school systems. For instance, in Fairfax County about 100 teachers have left the system per year because of inadequate instructional skills since performance evaluation was instituted in the mid-1980s, and Fairfax County's merit pay, although it was ultimately discontinued, spawned its own teachers' union in protest of the discontinuance. Keeping such programs going will require constant effort because there is a lot of pressure against them.

Privatization. Privatization has become something people are willing to try. To some extent, the bunker mentality of public education has led to an anti–public education movement, often led by parents who feel their children have not been able to get a good education in public schools. This has been incorporated into a more general antigovernment movement that is based on the belief that the government can do nothing well and that only the market can lead to quality goods and services. Privatized schools (along with privatization of almost everything else the government does) are the goal of this movement. At the same time, school systems (sometimes dragged kicking and screaming) have discovered that some privatization can actually improve things. But the idea of the education of all citizens as a common social interest—as distinct from the idea of the education of each child as an interest and concern only of the child's parents—has seemed almost to disappear from public discourse.

Federal education. The federal education function has gone through many permutations, from the office of education in Health, Education, and Welfare (HEW) to the National Institutes of Education to the Department of Education. Political discourse is full of warnings about the federal takeover of education, but what influence do the feds really have? A short answer is that the federal government has much influence in a few areas, such as special education, and some marginal influence in others, such as education of the poor and minorities, but hardly any influence in the mainstream curriculum and operation of schools. Certainly, federal influence and all government influence in the United States is substantially smaller than government influence in almost any other developed country, and the federal influence has probably declined over the past five years even as federal funds have declined as a percentage of total education funding.

WHAT IS CHANGING IN THE FIELD OF EDUCATION?

What is changing right now? Lots of things, such as the following.

National standards and assessments. This is pretty interesting politically. First the Republicans supported it under the Bush administration and seemed to have the support of governors from both parties, including Governor Bill Clinton, who continued his support as president, for which he received increasingly less support from the Republican Congress and, especially, from governors of both parties, who are now more likely to oppose anything federal. This all goes to show that today's bipartisan consensus can be tomorrow's partisan slugfest. This is a battle that superintendents ought to get into and stay in, trying to raise it above the partisan fray and show that some "locals" with a lot at stake (e.g., the veracity of their claims for their schools) are for strong accountability for student achievement.

The National Professional Teaching Standards Board (NPTSB). This board has spent almost ten years building consensus among stakeholders (including teacher unions) and developing and administering some assessments to a few teachers. It has produced a lot of hype and spent a fair amount of money and has yet to produce much effect or bang for the buck compared to some locally produced systems such as Fairfax County's Teacher Performance Evaluation Program (TPEP). NPTSB is too good an idea and what it has produced so far is of too high a quality not to stay on the bandwagon, at least for a few years, to see what it is able to do.

Technology. Technology is increasingly seen as a potential panacea, and public education has been asked to use it to increase the effectiveness and efficiency of instruction. To some extent this may be possible, but education will still be mostly teachers; books; and reading, writing, and figuring for a long time.

WHAT WILL CHANGE IN THE FIELD OF EDUCATION?

Following are some predictions about what will change within the next five years or so:

National assessments. National assessments are based on national standards of specific knowledge and skills in academic disciplines at graduation and other grade levels. These will be more similar to the Advanced Placement (AP) exams than any other existing testing system and will not be required of any school system or state but will be given in many schools because of pressure from parents and others in each community and because colleges and employers will want to see the results. These exams will put pressure on teachers, administrators, students, and parents to meet higher standards because nobody will be able to "cook the books" on how well students are actually doing anymore.

Much higher standards. Today's Gifted and Talented (GT) program will be tomorrow's regular program. International Baccalaureate (IB) and AP levels will be the standards for college-bound students as they strive to compete with those attending universities in the rest of the developed world. Colleges may be forced to actually develop standards for college entrance. There will also be higher standards for non–college-bound students. These standards will include both academic achievement and job skills. This will provide competition for the work forces in countries such as Germany and Korea where apprenticeship programs typically *admit* students with math at the level of trigonometry.

More privatization. Privatization and choice will develop within public schooling, as extra academic add-ons to public schooling, and as free-standing alternatives to public schools. Public schools will find themselves in competition with those who offer academic after-school programs that complement the curriculum and with schools that offer complete academic curricula outside public schools. These schools may be charter schools or they may charge tuition. There will be a strong influence on governments to provide vouchers or tax credits. More home-schooling will take place, not only for parents who have religious objections to having their children in public schools but also for parents who don't want their children in schools with children whose parents don't care about or aren't able to control their behavior. Public education itself will be at risk because of these and other nonpublic alternatives. Superintendents and those who work for them will be increasingly pushed for accountability to increase their credibility in this competition. One way to compete is to provide more choices within public schools to compete with the privatized choices. There will be many more such public schools of choice over the next five years.

Special education. Bureaucracy for special education will be much reduced and the focus will be more on helping the child than on palliating the parent, and saving money while giving the student more education.

Preparation. There will be more standards for preparing superintendents for the job rather than just moving up through the ranks. This will ensure more quality control so that school boards know they are getting high-quality superintendents. There will be real national teacher preparation standards that include both content knowledge and pedagogical knowledge and skills. Either schools of education will drastically reform, or they will be slowly forced out of business because they are not close to ready to meet such standards. University faculty from academic departments (e.g., history, physics, English, math) will be more heavily involved in teacher preparation and professional development, and nontraditional preparation of teachers (without involving schools of education) will become more common for public school teachers (as it always has been for teachers in private and parochial schools and junior colleges).

Rewards. Systems for awarding superstar teachers financially and with job portability will proliferate as schools search for the best so their students can meet higher standards. The NPTSB offers the best model so far for establishing national standards for such incentives, and many school systems already pay NPTSB-certified teachers extra. Some states and school systems, however, will establish their own incentive systems, and states will work together to provide portability.

THE UNPREDICTABLE FUTURE

But how much of the future is unpredictable? Surprising things can happen.

What happened in Clark County, Nevada (Las Vegas)? The community has grown amazingly over the past ten years. Businesses and residents have been lured by low taxes and a good business environment, but the large increases in school enrollment have arrived in schools that the community does not want to raise taxes to fund.

Fiber optics versus satellites—which do you choose? This is one of many technology issues that will arise in the next five years. Choices in these cases may create long-term financial commitments that, if you guess wrong, could put your school system in a real bind.

WHAT DO I DO?

What does a superintendent do to get ready for the future? There is no crystal ball that will help you, but there are some fundamentals.

- Make sure that you have a good, solid, traditional education and the ability to think thoroughly and quickly about complex issues so that whatever comes up you understand at least where it came from. There is no substitute for this.
- Stay on the edge, stay current in everything—*not* just with the education journals and books, but read broadly. Given the choice, read an article or book in some other area rather than in education. Also be sure not only to read articles by and listen to people whom you think agree with you. For example, reading the *New York Times* every day is recommended. This will give you a broad perspective not just on education (although its education reporting is very good) but also on science, politics, cultural trends, business, and many other areas.

One thing you can do to prepare for the future is to read this book. Some of the most knowledgeable people in the country were selected to write about the most important areas that the superintendent of the future needs to know about.

Denis P. Doyle starts us off with his comments on what we consider to be "The Main Thing." This derives from the motto, "the main thing is to keep the main thing the main thing," in which the main thing is academic learning—everything else is secondary. If a superintendent does not have a very clear idea what the main thing is, he or she is doomed, if not to failure, then to muddle. The pressures to focus on something *other* than academic learning are immense. Doyle tells us how to keep this focus.

But there are other things, as Louis Grumet tells us in the chapter titled "The Other Things." While keeping the focus on the main thing, you will need to know about and be able to deal with many other instructional issues, such as special education, English as a second language, character education, and many other things (each with its own vociferous constituency) for which someone believes school should take responsibility. If you do not have a fix on these issues, you will be pulled in too many directions and not be able to focus on the main thing.

As E.D. Hirsch said recently, speaking to the California State Board of Education, "it is almost impossible to make educational policy that is not based on research. I don't know of a single failed policy . . . that hasn't been research based, so we need to discriminate between reliable and unreliable research" (*Los Angeles Times*, June 23, 1997) because there is a great deal of the latter out there in education. J.E. Stone and Andrea D. Clements' chapter on research clarifies some of the ways that one can distinguish good research from bad, which is critical to the superintendent of the future, who will not only need to select instructional programs and methods that work but to defend those programs and methods in an atmosphere that emphasizes accountability at all levels for everything.

Still focusing on academic learning, the superintendent of the future must have a solid grasp of two particular noninstructional items—budget and personnel. Nothing will bring you down further and more quickly than these two. Rosemarie V. Rosen, who was deputy superintendent for budget and personnel when I (Spillane) was superintendent in Boston, helped me get a handle on these items under very trying circumstances. In her chapter, she explains what you need to know and how to make sure you know it about these two things, sine qua non.

And there are still other things—nuts and bolts—that the superintendent needs to manage. These are logistical issues and many affect student welfare—like buses and lunches, facilities and supplies, custodians, and stadium lighting. Gioia Caiola Forman, who has been both a principal and a central office administrator with responsibility for some of these nuts and bolts, provides guidance in these areas in her chapter.

One of the most important things to remember about being superintendent is that the vast majority of things—good and bad—that are done in your schools are done by other people. This means that getting these things done right (and getting the right things done) requires you to select the right people and motivate them to do the things you want done. Marlene C. Holayter—a "people person" of the highest and most professional level—tells us in her chapter how to ensure that things get done right and well.

Today (and tomorrow) more than ever the superintendent needs to attend to and speak to the hopes and fears of the community served by his or her school system. You do work for them, ultimately, and they do pay the bills. And "them" means more than just parents; all voters and taxpayers have a stake and should have a say in schools. Ongoing efforts to achieve and maintain community support as well as special efforts to get support for specific policies are essential. As the chapter on this subject points out, politics isn't just for politicians anymore.

Of course, your immediate bosses are the members of the school board, and working with them is a day-to-day unavoidable issue. Building and maintaining a partnership-in-policy relationship with them is critical to your success. In her chapter, Jacqueline P. Danzberger, who literally wrote the book on school boards, describes how to do this.

What your staff and community don't know can hurt you. Getting the accurate word out to both employees and the community has never been more important, and it will be even more important in the years ahead. Dolores Boylston Bohen, in her chapter on communication, tells us that, although it is not as easy as it sounds, there are many ways to get the word out. Openness, availability, creativity, and clarity are critical.

Technology is not a panacea, but it can help, and school systems cannot be too far behind the curve in this area. But how does a superintendent know what is real and what is hype? Michael S. Radlick, who has worked on all sides of this issue, answers your questions in his chapter titled "Hardware, Software, Vaporware, and Wetware."

The book concludes with some final comments from us about "Issues for the Future."

CHAPTER 2

The Main Thing—Academic Learning

Denis P. Doyle

What is the superintendent's job? Until recently, the superintendent, like his industrial counterpart, was autocrat in chief. His responsibility (and it was typically "his") was structurally similar to the captains of industry on whose jobs the superintendency was modeled. Comfortably situated at the command center, the superintendent reined supreme over all he surveyed. His dominion was the district and its employees, both certified and classified. Nominally responsible to an elected (or occasionally selected) school board, the superintendency looked like nothing so much as a medieval fiefdom. To complete the picture, the superintendent enjoyed high esteem, both within the schools and in the larger community that supported the schools.

As every student of modern schools knows, that picture is fast fading, going if not yet fully gone, but certainly not forgotten. It is no accident that the autocrat in chief is a fading memory in most modern enterprises—for-profit and not-for-profit. The reasons are not hard to discern. Successful organizations are no longer characterized by a command-control structure (just as the Soviet Union is no longer so characterized). Why? Because they do not work. Successful organizations recognize that their greatest asset is employee creativity and problem-solving capacity. These estimable traits are actively suppressed in command-control organizations. They are actively encouraged and rewarded in modern, high-performance organizations.

Employee autonomy has become the watchword of the high-performance firm, or what *Fortune* magazine has come to call *workers without bosses*. In the modern firm, as employee autonomy has slowly increased, two other major changes have occurred. First, middle management has been squeezed; in some places it has nearly disappeared. In part, this is a function of modern telecommunications and computing power—organizations are naturally flatter and leaner because of modern communications capacity. Fewer middlemen are needed when reporting relationships are shortened.

In larger part, however, the modern firm recognizes that its real wealth is its people. When firms rely on worker initiative, the lighter the hand on the administrative reins the greater the output. Put most simply, professionals respond best to rewards and incentives, not rules and regulations.

Second, as employee autonomy increased, so, too, did diversification at the top. For a century and a half the firm had been led by a single individual; today the norm is split, even fragmented, responsibility. The chief executive officer (CEO) shares duties with a chief financial officer (CFO) and a chief operating officer (COO).

Is the superintendent the CEO, or the CFO, or the COO? Unlike his or her counterpart in business or industry, he or she is at least one of the above and often all three. But the true superintendent is one more thing as well. He or she is the CAO: chief academic officer. That is what schools should be about, that is what school leadership should be about. Academics first, academics last. Everything else should contribute to the school's academic mission. Historically, among first-rate schools at least, that much was self-evident.

What are the superintendent's priorities? First is to act as CAO, then CEO, then CFO, then COO—in that order. In small districts, the superintendent, perforce, is a solo act; in larger districts, the superintendent may—nay, must—delegate much of the functional responsibility in these areas. Come what may, the buck stops with the superintendent, and the most important part of the job description is as CAO. Neglect that, and the rest of the game is not worth the candle.

Before discussing what is expected of the modern superintendent, it is worth remembering where the term comes from. The term *superintendent* is itself of modern coinage, reflecting the American passion for scientific management. The scientific management movement, spearheaded by Frederick Turner and his minions in white coats, holding stopwatches and clipboards, had its most lasting impact on the schools. Begun in factories, mines, and mills, scientific management has disappeared in the for-profit sector. But as anyone who has ever worked in or around public schools knows, it still haunts them.

Its most dramatic and pernicious legacy was the effort to "teacher proof" the schools: design the job of teachers in such a way that anyone tightly supervised could do it. Indeed, the great triumph of the industrial revolution was "dumbing down" work, making it so routinized that anyone with deft hands, a strong back, and a willing attitude could do it. Assembly-line demands were the precise opposite of the demands made by skilled trades and crafts. And just as the assembly line worked by using interchangeable parts, the workers themselves were interchangeable. The factory-model school was not metaphor but reality.

Until the twentieth century, a superintendent oversaw factories, major works—indeed, in the United Kingdom the title, superintendent of works, survives. It is a term that survives in America only in the schools and in a handful of public-sector positions, such as Superintendent of Documents in the federal government. In an American context *superintendent* became popular because it reflected the principles of scientific management that it was meant to embody. It provided *gravitas*, a source of authority, even moral rectitude. Picture an austere man in a starched white shirt with a celluloid collar; a three- or four-button black broadcloth and suit; mustachioed; and wearing or holding a black bowler. That was the superintendent of the not-too-distant past. And the "works" he (and in those days it was "he") oversaw were to be scientifically managed.

A school superintendent would see that the schools were run like a factory. The school superintendent was the literal counterpart of the factory superintendent, the school board of the corporate board, the principals of the foremen, the teachers of the workers at the assembly line, and the students of the product. This telling metaphor led the late Al Shanker to observe that if one-fourth of the "product" doesn't reach the end of the assembly line at all, and another fourth doesn't function when it gets there, you don't improve the process by running the line faster and longer (personal communication). You need a whole new metaphor.

Until the twentieth century, school heads in both the private and public sectors had been headmasters or headmistresses. They were lead teachers. This quaint nomenclature is still used in private schools and it makes an important point: The head is simply *primus inter pares*, first among equals. As the schoolmaster or schoolmistress teaches, so, too, the headmaster or headmistress oversees teaching. Academics are the central activity.

This idea is neither new nor novel in public schools, though in the modern era it is only infrequently put into practice. School districts, and the superintendents who lead them, are pulled in more directions than they can count, let alone deal with. Academics become one of many distractions—not the superintendent's central preoccupation. There is no mystery as to why this is so—the competing demands of multiple constituencies are a continuous distraction. The complexity of the modern school district is staggering. Big districts—of the nation's 15,000-plus districts there are nearly 500 with more than 15,000 students—are like city-states. (To the ancient Greeks, city-states were the ideal form of government; small enough to be governed by direct democracy, big enough to be robust. And to Aristotle, autarky—self-sufficiency—was the hallmark of the city-state. He would have been fascinated by the modern, American school district.)

A representative district of 15,000 students, spending $5,000 per student, has a budget of $75 million, a good deal of money even by Washington standards. Depending on how you count, 50 to 60% of the budget goes to direct instruction. As if the instructional budget were not complicated enough, the superintendent must oversee $30-odd million for other activities. Competing for the superintendent's attention is a wealth of programs, from varsity sports to student discipline to buildings and grounds. And just as individual programs and activities are time sinks, individuals have claims on the superintendent's time. Board members are first in line, followed closely by local, elected officials; senior staff; and faculty. So, too, community members have legitimate claims. And then there are students.

Not surprisingly, most of these claims are "negative": They reflect omissions and commissions that are "problems." (Rarely is the superintendent's time taken in personal honors or commendations.) Such is the nature of the political process, and truth be told, there are few jobs more political than the superintendency. This awkward truth should come as no surprise—the superintendent oversees not only a vast empire but presides over the distribution of important resources, both financial and immaterial.

A school district is often the biggest employer in its area and controls the biggest budget in its community. As we have seen, the financial resources that schools command are themselves significant, no matter how rich or poor the community the school serves. No school district has ever had as much money as it would like, and in the distribution of necessarily scarce resources (which is the science of economics) there are winners and losers. Equally unsurprisingly, debates about resource allocation are intense, whether the subject is vocal and instrumental music (which, in a school budget setting does not appear to calm the savage beast) or closing buildings.

And the nonfinancial resources are important as well. In the modern era, social status (and wealth or the lack of wealth it conveys) are largely the product of education. Among other things, superintendents are in the business of conferring status on staff as well as on students. Their decisions about school and program quality have real and lasting effects on real people. Think, for example, of decisions about course offerings. A college-prep sequence is essential to any student who has designs on a selective college or university. Deny students access to these courses and college may be out of the picture. A failure to offer Advanced Placement (AP) courses can handicap youngsters just as a decision to offer Scholastic Aptitude Test (SAT) preparation can significantly help others. At a more nuanced level, youngsters from working or lower class backgrounds are less likely to be tuned in to the niceties of college-prep courses. A failure to counsel them will put them on a noncollege track that they may never leave.

Even more to the point is the set of decisions about what is required for all students as a condition of graduation. Few courses have much predictive power, but two do. The sequence of algebra and plane geometry—taken successfully—is a fairly reliable predictor of college attendance. According to a college board study a decade ago, students of all races, both sexes, and all income levels are equally likely to attend college *if* they take algebra and geometry. If curriculum actually makes such a powerful difference in the lives of students, what principles should guide the superintendent in running a school district?

First, the hallmark of successful organizations—for-profit and not-for-profit, governmental and nongovernmental—is focus. As Peter Drucker (1985) observes, the effective organization *optimizes*, it does not *maximize*. Too many schools—indeed, too many organizations—fail to make this crucial distinction. By optimizing, Drucker means identifying a mission precisely, setting goals accordingly, and measuring progress regularly and accurately. Do what you're good at and do only that. Others who are good at what they do should do what they do. You can hire them when you need them, to run the cafeteria, cut checks, maintain warehouses, or teach an obscure course.

Maximizing, by way of contrast, means doing many things while trying to serve multiple constituencies. This does not work in business; it does not work in nonprofits; and it does not work for schools. In trying to serve many audiences, few, if any, are served well. No one can serve many masters. Professional life becomes a hopeless juggling act, and the enterprise as a whole falters. Everything a superintendent does must be in service to one's master: academics. The master is mastery. Academic accomplishment is what school is all about.

Schools are not custodial institutions, though they may provide custodial services; schools are not medical facilities, though they may offer limited medical services; schools are not social welfare institutions, though they are concerned with the welfare of their charges.

What is the role and what is the focus of the modern superintendent? The role in no longer that of autocrat or dictator but rather conductor or, if you prefer, choreographer. The superintendent's tasks are much like other chiefs in the for-profit and not-for-profit world: set policy, hire smart people, exhort, and get out of the way. If that is the role, the focus is threefold.

1. Set standards.
2. Establish measures.
3. Hold people accountable.

The role of the modern superintendent—as conductor—requires a democratic approach to standard setting. This is so not just because it is intrinsically wise but because it works better than the alternative. Setting standards by fiat invites complaints and obstructionism. Indeed, it is impossible to run a modern enterprise with old command-control approaches. Compliance is earned, not achieved by edict. Incentives and rewards simply work better than disincentives and penalties. In particular, schooling, to be successful, must be professional. By this I mean to revive the original meaning: professionals "profess." They are masters of a body of arcane knowledge that no one else possesses. They are the exact opposite of the assembly-line worker (indeed, sound management theory has changed even the assembly line, giving workers on it more freedom and flexibility).

The major issue in standard setting is not the hard work of identifying the standards, committing them to paper, and adopting them as policy. Dozens of sets of standards are now widely available, in hard copy and even on the Internet. The major issue is ownership. In particular, teachers must own standards; they must believe in them. So, too, the community must believe in them. Parents must be convinced that the standards make sense just as students must. The most effective way to achieve ownership is to build the standards together, as a team.

What is true of standards is true of assessments and measures. The community must have complete confidence in the reliability and utility of standards' assessment. They must believe that they are accurate, fair, and sensible. The rule is deceptively simple; if a standard is the declarative form, the assessment is the interrogative form. If the standard says that the student will be able to

> read, understand, and explain the significance of a reasonably complex international news story in a national or international news magazine

that same student will be expected to demonstrate his or her knowledge by writing a persuasive essay about the subject and making a competent oral presentation.

Another standard might be:

> Read aloud and translate by sight passages from five nineteenth-century French novelists with clarity, accuracy, and precision.

That standard, too, would be measured in the doing.

Indeed, throughout the curriculum, from a child's first day to graduation, standards must be set and standards must be met. The meaning of accountability is consequences. There must be consequences for meeting the standard just as there must be consequences for not meeting it. Low standards do no one a favor—not teachers, not students, not the community. And in the case of the poor and dispossessed, low standards are positively harmful. (Well-to-do-kids have slid through with "gentleman Cs" from time immemorial, with no old-boy network and no coupons to clip. The poor, however, cannot afford to do poor-quality academic work. Their one hope is academic success.)

Everything that the superintendent does must serve academics. Permit me to turn to a real-world example of this philosophy at work. Superintendent John Murphy (formerly of Charlotte-Mecklenburg, South Carolina) is convinced of one thing: The key issue is academic rigor. This means academic rigor at all levels among all the participants, from students to teachers to bus drivers. To ensure academic rigor, focus is essential. Focus, in turn, means that an accountability system is essential. The comprehensive focus of the organization must be the classroom. This means attending to more than teachers; hold headquarters accountable, and change the culture of the organization. Everyone must concentrate on academics. For example, the transportation department should be concerned with academics. Why? The first and last person bus riders see is the bus driver. Custodians and their work set the tone for the whole school. So, too, do cafeteria workers; clean facilities, appetizing food, and friendly service all contribute to an atmosphere that reflects high standards.

Isn't this a bit much? Is there a real example of the intersection of academics, custodial work, empowerment, and an edifying cafeteria? In Charlotte-Mecklenburg there was. Principal Pete Stone (who has since moved on) ran one of John Murphy's first site-managed schools. The principal of a brand new school—Lake Wylie Elementary—Pete decided to leave two janitorial positions unfilled. The dollar savings went to program enrichment; students performed the janitorial work. Pete used the tried-and-true-recruitment scheme developed by Tom Sawyer when he was supposed to whitewash the fence. He made working as a student janitor an honor, not a burden, and the remaining adult janitors showed them the ropes. (As a special treat for special visitors, Pete would press gang them into vacuuming the building and cleaning the blackboards in front of the assembled students and teachers. The author knows from firsthand experience.)

The secret of accountability is to not dictate. If assistant superintendents, central office staff, and principals are barking orders, they short-circuit the whole process. Every member of the organization must be accountable for themselves and their performance. Empower people in the field, and the system will run more smoothly, and processes will stay in place.

Everyone gains in this type of situation. The school has more money, it is cleaner and neater, the students learn a powerful lesson about stewardship, and the janitors become teachers. Not satisfied with this innovation (copied shamelessly from Japanese schools—the sincerest form of flattery), Pete hired as head cook a young French chef who offered a dazzling menu of French food (in the wilds of southern Mecklenburg County). Knowing he had a real draw, Pete opened the cafeteria to the community. There was one proviso, however. The adults who came to eat had to distribute themselves among the children. No cliques. In one fell swoop Pete had a happy (and well-fed) tutoring network.

Are these accomplishments the principal's or the superintendent's? The lesson is an important one: They are both. Neither could have done any of this alone. Together they could work wonders. The superintendent and the principal could both take genuine pride in the program's successes. To return to our earlier metaphor of CEO as conductor, the model is the symphony orchestra: There are no great conductors without great musicians. Or as Walt Whitman said, "there can be no great poets without great audiences."

At a more prosaic level, how is the message transmitted, how is the good news shared? In Charlotte-Mecklenburg, the nation's twenty-ninth largest district with 118 schools, the issue is not abstract. Murphy's response was characteristic. He created a leadership team made up of 11 principals. They met with him once a month to compare notes, praise the faithful, pass the ammunition, and admonish the fallen-away. Each of the 11 principals oversaw a network of 11 to 15 schools. They worked together collaboratively and met at the site level several times a month between their meetings with Murphy. Their message was clear: Focus on academics. Keep the heat on. Encourage local initiative. When something works, spread the good news. When problems appear, nip them in the bud.

What tools does the modern superintendent have to make this vision a reality? The most powerful tool is a learned borrowing from other sectors of the economy. What do other successful organizations do that have a bearing on the life of schools? In particular, do for-profit businesses or not-for-profit private organizations have anything to offer? Depending on where you stand, there are two broad views on this issue. Educators are quick to point out that schools are not businesses; their purposes are different and their cultures are different. By way of contrast, business people assert that even if schools aren't businesses, they must be run in a businesslike fashion. Who is right? Both are. There is truth in the assertion that schools are special institutions: Educating students is not like making widgets or processing documents.

Education cannot be reduced to a profit-and-loss statement. But it is also true that schools need clearly defined objectives, processes, and procedures. Schools that have sharply delineated goals, with appropriate standards and measures, are better places in which to teach and learn. The lessons from the corporate world are many and varied: goal setting, strategic planning, in-service training, and research and devlopment (R&D) are some of the more important ones. For example, no modern high-tech firm could last for long with the meager training and R&D budgets schools take for granted. Schools would do well to emulate business in these ways. But there is an even more important lesson for schools: benchmarking.

It is important to note that benchmarking is not idle theory but grounded practice. Lasting professional experience has convinced me that it has a direct and immediate application for schools.

To understand what schools have to learn from corporations, it is essential to deal at a level of specificity—and generality—that is appropriate to both. As we shall see, under benchmarking there are three broad issues and a host of lesser ones. First is standard setting, second is measurement, third are consequences. Know what your goals are and how you measure them, then hold yourself and your employees to them. In a for-profit setting this is second nature; a failure to think and operate this way invites disaster. The competition will simply eat you alive. But even in a for-profit setting it can be easy to lose sight of these objectives in certain circumstances.

Look, for example, at Xerox. One of the great corporate triumphs of all time, Xerox's rise was meteoric—once the first commercially viable machines came on line. In the beginning, Xerox developer Chester Carlson could barely secure enough capital to get his ideas into production. Few investors thought there would be a market for plain-paper copiers; fewer yet thought the market would be robust. Those few are wealthy investors today. Xerox's success was nothing short of spectacular; but spectacular success can have a price.

As the money rolled in, Xerox became careless and as copyright protections began to wane its quasi-monopoly position began to crumble. Xerox was overtaken—and nearly consumed—by the competition. Xerox saved itself by reinventing itself, by becoming lean and aggressive. As a quasi-monopoly it could keep its customers at arm's length; as a tough competitor it had to learn to meet customer requirements. The institutional secret of Xerox's success was the revival and incorporation of an idea first developed decades earlier at AT&T: benchmarking. AT&T was also a quasi-monopoly (in the beginning, a government-approved monopoly).

Now a well-run monopoly is a wonder to behold because it is the exception that proves the rule; without the stimulus of competition, the only reason to run a tight ship is because it is the right and proper thing to do. Few organizations—even the most benevolent nonprofits—can pass this test. Indeed, monopolies, both private and public (particularly public monopolies of the kind that existed behind the Iron Curtain), are not just disdainful of their workers and customers, they are contemptuous of them. Not Ma Bell.

For reasons that are not altogether clear, Ma Bell began as a well-run monopoly and actually stayed that way. At one level the reason is crystal clear: "culture." When AT&T was formed there was a widely held view that business had obligations to the community and AT&T met them. The problem with culture as the explanatory variable is that by explaining everything it explains nothing. What pieces or aspects of culture make a difference? In any case, that the money flowed in—that AT&T could do good and do well at the same time—certainly helped. Peter Drucker (1992) noted that what made the AT&T break-up all the more odd was that there was no upwelling of outraged customers or workers demanding the end of the monopoly. In any case, Ma Bell did not have conventional profits to use as either a stimulus or a measure of good performance. (Its profits were set as a proportion of its expenditures, as approved by government rate setters.) Benchmarking became a surrogate for the market, which makes its application in a school setting all the more interesting.

Benchmarking can be used by for-profit and not-for-profit concerns, by government and nongovernment entities, and by firms large and small. It is a powerful tool to improve performance because it simultaneously takes you back to the basics and forward to the details of implementation. To get at the basics, the organization must ask itself these simple questions.

- Where am I?
- Where do I want to be?
- How do I get there?

In Xerox's case the answers were straightforward.

- We're in big trouble.
- We want to regain market share.
- We restructure or fail.

The big answers to big questions lead to implementation. To implement effectively, the firm must find and carefully examine examples of best practice. Look at the competition to see both what they are doing and how they are doing it. In the case of Xerox, the competition was Kodak at home and the Japanese plain-paper copiers abroad. Ricoh and Sharp, for example, were delivering copiers to American retailers at a lower price than Xerox could make them; at issue were design and production efficiencies, not dumping or subsidies.

Going head-to-head, Xerox was not getting the same product quality for the same investment. It is worth remembering that Xerox did not beg Uncle Sam for protective tariffs or bailouts as some American producers did at the time. Xerox considered this to be their problem, and, subsequently, solved it.

To do so they did the obvious. They bought competitor's machines and took them to the engineering lab where they stripped them down to the last nut and bolt. They employed backward engineering, deducing how their competitors did it. They invited all Xerox employees to participate in the improvement process. Xerox did not compare itself to the weak part of the industry but to the best of the best. Anyone can produce a second-rate product. There's no mystery to that. What's interesting is who produces a high-quality product at low cost. That's the question Xerox asked and answered.

But Xerox's biggest insight was to go one more step, to look beyond the competition and find examples of best practice in other industries. For on-time service they identified Florida Power as the best example in the nation; for inventory control and delivery they identified L.L. Bean, the outdoor outfitter of Freeport, Maine.

The importance of benchmarking is that it provides an independent and objective reference point. It helps answer the question: How good is good enough? It also reminds you that if someone else is doing it better than you, there is a way for you to do it that well yourself. It is a moving target. Benchmarking is not one time and you're done; one time and you're ready to do it again. And again. Benchmarking is a process, not a product. It is not an end in itself. It keeps on going.

Note, too, another critically important aspect to benchmarking. It is self-imposed. It is not something "done" to the firm by a third party; it is something the firm takes on voluntarily. It is self-imposed because it is, above all, a self-improvement tool. Indeed, benchmarking cannot be imposed from on high because it must be adopted and implemented in good faith, with enthusiasm.

One of the most important aspects of benchmarking is what it does not do. It is not designed to cast suspicion or point the finger of blame. It is not pejorative, nor is it meant to hold individuals or institutions up to obloquy or ridicule. To the contrary, benchmarking is an improvement process designed to make things better; shame and embarrassment make things worse. Benchmarking reveals strengths as well as weaknesses; indeed, in the well-run firm, so-called weaknesses are simply opportunities to improve.

What are the implications for schools? Compare yours to the best schools you can find. Don't look at the weak performers; in particular, don't look at the low performers and congratulate yourself for being better. In the field of public administration, complacency is a sin, and it is the biggest single problem schools face. High-flying districts such as Montgomery County, Maryland, can look across the district line at Washington, D.C. Are the Montgomery County schools better? By a country mile. Is that any reason for self-congratulation or pleasure? None. D.C. is not the competition.

Montgomery County, Maryland, should be actively comparing itself to the best school districts it can find, within Maryland and the nation as a whole. It should also be busy comparing itself to the best schools around the world—those in Bonn, Yokohama, Taipei, Edinburgh, Paris, Christ Church, and Amsterdam. It should go beyond elementary and secondary schools and compare itself to similar organizations with similar missions: colleges and universities, both public and private. It should look at other organizations that serve children such as the Boy Scouts and Girl Scouts. And it should go beyond those to compare itself to dissimilar organizations: Xerox, IBM, and AT&T (now Lucent Technologies).

What kinds of lessons might a school district learn if it began this process in earnest? At the board level, it might find, as Peter Drucker (1990) has, that most corporate boards do too little. They do not offer enough guidance and oversight. At the same time, most honest board members would conclude that school boards almost without exception do much too much; they are consumed by an unhealthy passion for micromanagement. If they continued to look where Peter Drucker has looked, they would find the best example of an effective board known to him— one that does neither too much nor too little—the Girl Scouts of America.

At the administrative level, careful benchmarking would reveal the fact that American public schools are obsessed with credentials, not performance. They would also discover that one of the greatest strengths of the American firm is its relentless emphasis on performance and its disdain for credentials. The CEO of a Fortune 500 company does not need a "license" to do anything; he or she simply needs license to do what needs doing. (Webster defines a license—the noun—as permission to do something otherwise prohibited.)

So, too, as public schools benchmark, they will find that private schools (the competition) do not require licenses for teachers, and private school teachers are almost without exception free to choose their own books. They are professionals—white-collar workers.

Benchmarking will also reveal that other labor-intensive organizations that rely heavily on a highly trained work force invest heavily in in-service training. IBM, Xerox, Hewlett-Packard, and others expect that every single employee receives two weeks of in-service training a year; not as a prerequisite or to feel good (though it is both) but as a way to demonstrably enhance productivity. In the for-profit firm, training pays for itself in the productivity increases that it produces.

Indeed, benchmarking lessons are nearly endless: Some are so obvious as to barely warrant mentioning. In the more businesslike aspects of school operations, there are significant opportunities to improve, from cafeteria services to busing to payroll and budgeting. These opportunities should all be seized upon.

But the most important aspect of benchmarking is to understand the school's central mission and how to improve it. Academics first, academics last—that is what schooling is all about. Schooling is not child care, though schools do care for children; not child welfare and protective services, though schools may be a good venue for them; not health services, though they can be offered in schools. Neither are schools supposed to be places run for the convenience of adults, workers, or parents. They are institutions that are supposed to teach children things they would not otherwise know. The value-added of schooling is developed intellect.

The most important aspect of benchmarking is to compare yourself to yourself over time with the unswerving objective of continuous improvement. To do this requires a commitment to knowledge: Get the facts and present them. Analyze them. Act on them. Conduct an academic audit with the same rigor and care that you would conduct a financial or management audit.

As it happens, the lessons corporate America can offer schools often go begging. Business does not think to approach the schools; the schools do not think to approach business. Indeed, no two groups in America know less about each other than do business and schools. The gulf that separates them is great. More's the pity because they each have much to offer. That much of what they do is very different should not obscure the fact that much of what they do is structurally similar. That is both the challenge and the opportunity. Schools must seek out ways to improve their own performance and one of the best ways to do that is to understand what other organizations do and how they do it. The fit will never be perfect, and improvisation and adaptation will be required. But there are lessons. Let me close with three. Readers are invited to draw their own conclusions.

First is IBM's education program. With more than 7,000 teachers it is big by any measure, and it does many things well. Not least is IBM classroom policy and practice. When a certain critical mass of students—3 or 4 out of a class of 25—do not "get it," the assumption is not that there is something wrong with the students. The assumption is that there is something wrong with the teaching. It's back to the drawing board. How do we present the information in such a way that students will get it?

Second is Xerox's method for dealing with employee productivity in areas with no readily available "objective" measure (salespeople are easy to measure; what about bench scientists, speech writers, graphic artists, and so on?). The question everyone in the corporation must answer is: "Who is my customer?" Employee performance ratings are made in this context. If the CEO is your "customer" you can be sure you've got a tough customer. And to complete the metaphor, even the CEO has customers (not just the board, shareholders, and senior managers). The CEO has active accounts that he services on a monthly basis precisely as any salesperson does. That is Xerox's lifeblood, and the last person who should forget it is the CEO.

Third and last is scouting, boys and girls, and the sine qua non of scouting, the merit badge. How do scouts earn merit badges? Scouts select an area of interest—bird watching, for example—and find out what they are expected to know and do. Scouts will have to learn, among other things, how to recognize birds in the wild, on the wing (as well as out of motion), on land or water, by color, size, shape, markings, flight patterns, and song. They will need to learn about bird behavior and habitat, both as a guide as to when and where to look and as a means of identification when they finally spot one or many. He or she will do desk-bound work and do field work. They will read bird books. They will talk to other scouts about the process in anticipation of field work, while in the field, and afterward. They may visit museums. They may build or use existing "blinds." They will use binoculars, even a telescope if they have access to one. They may use still or moving cameras to document their sightings; at minimum, they will make field sketches. They will establish viewing routines and might build feeding stations.

If they know accomplished birders they will talk to them as well. They will begin and maintain a "life list" of sightings and they will gain confidence and knowledge as they advance (as well as pleasure in mastery). Finally, they will be tested, not with just true-and-false, multiple-choice tests, though the test may include some questions of this kind. They will be expected to demonstrate their mastery of the subject by a presentation to a seasoned birder. If they know their stuff, they will earn a merit badge. At the same time, they will have earned an invisible badge, of self-respect, of respect for the craft, that will lead them into a lifetime of pleasure and knowledge. They will have learned how to learn, they will have learned not just how to "read" nature but to interpret and analyze generally. They will have sharpened their observation and reporting skills. All in all, they will be the better for it.

And just as the young scout is the better for mastering a new and novel activity, the school that learns its lessons from other organizations, both similar and dissimilar, will be the better for it.

* * * * * * *

In examining what it is the modern superintendent is expected to know and be able to do, it is tempting to look to a theological model for the job description, "walks on water." But it is not as daunting as that. To be sure, the modern superintendent, committed to high academic standards, has a challenging task before him or her. And it will be especially difficult over the next decade for two reasons. First, as we have seen, the nation's schools are facing a genuine paradigm shift. No longer will schools be measured by what goes into them (though that will always be important); they will be measured by what they produce with what they have. Major changes will occur as a consequence—changes in school culture, organization, and management that cannot be fully foreseen today. In important respects, the modern superintendent confronts *terra incognita* as surely as the great sailors on voyages of discovery did. In addition to being a conductor or choreographer, then, the modern superintendent must also be part magician, part impresario.

Second, the truly successful superintendent will be measured by his or her capacity to leave a lasting legacy of reform. As Peter Drucker (1990) notes about CEOs, if they are "irreplaceable," they have not done their job. If they do their job right, the organization will run without them. That is the real promise of the standards' movement and the superintendent's concentrating on "standards set, standards met." A standards-driven system, with a flat organization chart, is measured by what it accomplishes and everyone in the system, from crossing guards to department chairs to board members, has a stake in doing well. A standards-driven system not only spares the school board the temptation (and excuse) to micromanage, it does the same for the superintendent.

Lastly, when all is said and done, the final word is President Johnson's. He was fond of saying that there were only three things worth being: a preacher, a teacher, or a politician. As he was all three, so, too, the successful superintendent must be.

REFERENCES

Drucker, P. (1985). *Innovation and entrepreneurship.* New York: Harper & Row.

Drucker, P. (1990). *Managing the non-profit organization.* New York: HarperCollins.

Drucker, P. (1992, April). The post-capitalist world. *The Public Protest,* p. 180.

CHAPTER 3

The Other Things

Louis Grumet

While it is clear that the main thing that a superintendent should be focusing on is the improvement of academic learning, there are tremendous pressures to spend his or her time on other issues, and, indeed, often superintendents focus on practically everything but the main thing. These issues usually fall into four groups. The first group includes certain intense needs of populations of students who have difficulty meeting high academic standards without a great deal of assistance. These needs range from special education and English as a second language to technology skills that are supposed to be essential to ready youngsters to better benefit from academic learning. A second group of attention-getting issues includes alternative forms of schooling, character education, the separation of church and state, and what books are allowed. These deal with widely varying perspectives on the public school's role in determining what makes the youngster a good citizen. Yet, another category of competing interest involves staff—evaluating them, trying to get a handle on in-service education and trying to get rid of staff who are not performing. A fourth category is the relationship of the school system with the not-for-profit organizations that serve children, other levels of government, and the use of school facilities by outside organizations.

STUDENT NEEDS

In many school districts, the greatest focus of public attention and angry parents and/or taxpayers and thus time of the superintendent involves not those students who are achieving at a high level but those who are not and what programs are necessary to help them achieve. The largest and most complicated of these is special education.

Special Education

If we do not get a more realistic focus on where we are heading in special education, we are going to see a massive backlash that could swallow the entire system as more and more youngsters are referred to special education in order to avoid higher standards. More and more parents of other children and taxpayers without children will deeply and more aggressively question the system until a crisis boils over that may scald everyone.

All districts in the nation are required to serve all youngsters, including those who are disabled. The theory is that with a bit of special education a youngster can make it in regular education and then in society. Shockingly, many of the youngsters once in special education never come out. It becomes a life sentence. Further, the majority of the youngsters classified as special education are mildly impaired youngsters who probably should not have been classified to start with. In some respects, the most expensive part of the education system is spending a lot of money to do the wrong thing.

Prior to the mid-1970s, youngsters who had to deal with disabilities, ranging from blindness to deafness to retardation to physical disabilities to emotional problems, were handled totally differently than other children. They seemed excluded from compulsory education requirements and were treated very differently in different parts of each district and in different parts of every state. Many of these children were not served at all. Many others were being underserved and a handful were receiving good services. This led to major litigation, a public outcry, and legislative upheaval in many states throughout the nation. Eventually it led to the congressional enactment of the Education of all Handicapped Children Act (Pub. L. No. 94-142), which is currently known as the Individuals with Disabilities Education Act (IDEA).

The legislative activities involving disabled youngsters grew out of public revulsion at the way such youngsters were being treated in development centers and psychiatric institutions across the country. This revulsion grew from a great deal of media attention involving the Willowbrook Developmental Center in New York City and court cases involving places such as the Pennhurst Developmental Center in Pennsylvania.

There was also a frank and widespread concern that the education community had turned its back on disabled children and did not want to serve them. It seemed much more professionally rewarding and popular with the taxpayers to serve children who could visibly perform. It often frightened educators to be dealing with children who could not keep their emotions under control or who looked or acted differently than the so-called normal child.

Federal and state legislation was enacted in the 1970s that required that every child with a disabling condition receive a free appropriate education in the least restrictive environment. The system for disabled children has grown to the point where the state and federal courts are spending an inordinate amount of time to define the three phrases listed above.

In short, *free* means simply that all necessary services will be provided at no cost to the student or his or her parents.[1] *Appropriate* is an ever-expanding category that appears to have no limits and even appears to include what had been thought to be medical care or assistive devices.[2] *Least restrictive environment* means that the child shall be in a program as close as possible to his or her non-disabled peers.[3]

In order to ensure that disabled children receive the services they need, a very tight system of due process was developed that includes hearing officers, appeals, and publicly funded legal costs for the youngster's parent.

The programs for disabled children have gone through several stages. The first stage was finding all the eligible disabled youngsters in the community and creating services for them or finding services that could be provided to them by outside agencies. This stage not only involved finding children who have never been in school but dealing with children who were disabled and were not being served within the school. New York City, for example, had a waiting list of almost 14,000 youngsters who had been referred for services but had not been served. One of them, a young man named Jose Perez, was 19 years old before he was identified. It had been claimed he was untestable when in reality he was deaf. The litigation that followed from his case resulted in the New York City Board of Education being held in contempt of court, a condition from which it never emerged.

The second stage was to develop and provide appropriate services. Throughout the early 1980s, the major increases in the cost of education were related to special education. Almost every school district in the country had to hire teachers who were certified in special education or who were dually certified. Classroom space had to be developed and programs had to be created.

The third stage was learning how to serve disabled youngsters in increasingly less-restrictive environments. In other words, trying to serve the youngsters in a regular classroom with support services rather than trying to serve him or her in a special class or a separate building. The development of new categories of services, such as teachers and aides, in the regular classroom to meet the needs of special-education youngsters mushroomed. Alternative testing services became a cottage industry. All these phases have resulted in an incredible expenditure of time for everyone involved. The third phase has been the most trying for superintendents.

A fourth, unanticipated, stage is the expansion of who is eligible for special education. There are large numbers of youngsters who have not traditionally been considered disabled, but who have been classified as disabled in order to get services that might not be available if he or she had not been classified. Particularly, youngsters who were having problems with reading or who had minor speech problems fell into this category as fiscal cutbacks were made during the last recession. Speech and reading teachers were excessed, and youngsters were moved into special-education programs that were mandated but that may not meet their needs. Indeed, in New York State approximately 70% of the youngsters classified as disabled fall into this last category.

The special-education program is not only a large, complicated program that requires a great deal of leadership and management time, it also arouses fears and hopes that range from the understandable to the absurd.

Parents and teachers of nondisabled youngsters often deeply resent the resources and attention being spent on the disabled. They spend a great deal of time bringing their concerns to the superintendent's attention. This resentment, too, has gone through several stages. First, it was a resistance to having such children in school. Second, it involved acceptance of the student but resentment of the priority their services had in fiscally hard times. Third, it was a deep fear that disabled students would not meet higher standards and would drag down those who did.

Parents of the disabled as well as advocates for these parents and children are rarely satisfied with the level of services being provided and are constantly demanding the superintendent's time in the form of meetings, political pressure, or litigation. The single largest amount of litigation in education today arises from these concerns. The definition of appropriate services and of the responsibility of schools to provide them is constantly expanding. Today, hearing aids, catheterization, wheelchairs, and other services previously thought of as a medical or parental responsibility are being handed to the schools as part of their responsibility.[4]

In an increasing number of cases, these demands are patently absurd. For example, some children are being classified as learning disabled in high school so that they will be eligible to have more time to take tests. Alternative testing is available for those disabled children who need it. Yet, children who previously would have gotten a little coaching so they could keep up with their classmates are now being banished to special education to be overseen by a teacher who may not be properly equipped to deal with the problem the child has manifested. Too often this is being done because special education gets extra state aid that other forms of needed assistance do not, and too many districts may be shunting youngsters off to special education in order to get that aid.

Interestingly, there is no state in the union where this state aid is sufficient to reimburse the districts for the cost involved, except in a rare case. Also for the child involved, the unanticipated cost of being in special education for the rest of the child's years in school are often inadequately considered. In New York State, most youngsters referred for special education do not return to the regular class-room.

Some youngsters, particularly ones who are large or thought to be "difficult," tend to be categorized as disabled and put into special classes merely because they are discipline problems or are thought to be discipline problems. This is par-ticularly true in areas with large concentrations of minorities, and this has led to overrepresentation of minorities in special-education programs.

In Boston, immediately following the desegregation court orders, the special-education classes rose with a heavy concentration of black males in special class-rooms instead of in segregated buildings.

We appear to have grown into the strange position of spending more money to provide the wrong programs for too many children. The laws that were enacted, for very good reason, to ensure that children would be served, have been used by special-education advocates not only to provide overly restrictive settings but also to make a youngster's transition to the real world almost impossible. At some stage soon, society is going to have to try to return the pendulum to the middle and slow down the expansion of special-education programs.

Another dimension of serving disabled children deals with discipline. Some disabled youngsters, like some nondisabled youngsters, have discipline prob-lems. Courts have indicated that these youngsters have to be treated in an entirely different fashion from the nondisabled and thus often cannot be disciplined in an efficient and effective manner. This can create extreme pressures on a superinten-dent at the same time that society is demanding zero tolerance of discipline prob-lems.

In a classroom in California, a special-education youngster who allegedly raped a teacher was returned to that teacher's classroom because he had a disabil-ity. A kindergartner, who was much larger than his classmates and who beat them regularly, was returned to the classroom because he was disabled. It is hard to believe that anyone contemplated that disabled youngsters would be treated so differently from other youngsters in discipline proceedings. Other cases have cre-ated a separate class of rights that are based on a premise that the discipline prob-lem is based on an outgrowth of the prior disability. Thus, educators are risking backlash that could swallow the entire program.

In some areas of the country, an even stranger unanticipated consequence of the discipline cases is growing because youngsters who have been accused of committing a crime are being referred for special-education placement prior to meeting the grand jury in anticipation of raising the disability issue as a motivat-ing factor.

Yet, another problem has arisen as a result of Social Security Insurance (SSI) payments where the federal government in an attempt to reimburse parents of severely disabled children with social security supplementation wound up creating an insensitivity toward disabilities to get such supplementation.

The individualized education program (IEP), which is a written document intended to ensure that the child is getting the program that he or she needs to benefit from an education, has in too many areas of the country deteriorated into a document that is used to explain why the youngster will not be forced to meet standards that he or she would otherwise get. IEPs too often do not include science or social studies and rarely recognize the need to challenge a student academically.

The pendulum that once swung in the direction of not serving disabled children has in too many instances swung too far in the other direction. Society and the education community have to stop looking at the special-education program as a way to meet many other objectives and return the program to its original concept—ensuring a free and appropriate education for every child even if they are disabled.

English as a Second Language

In many states across the nation, the second largest group of students who as a class have difficulty meeting academic standards are those who have difficulty mastering the English language and have come from a home where English is not spoken. Some of these students are new immigrants from countries around the world. Indeed, the City of New York School District serves students who speak over 133 languages.[5] This problem is not limited to large urban districts. Many rural districts have pockets of immigrant children as well. The states of California, Florida, Illinois, New Jersey, New York, and Texas have the majority of all immigrant children, but every state has large numbers of children who have difficulty with the English language.

This issue is not limited to newly immigrant youngsters, however. A growing problem faced by many districts is that there are families who are in their second or third generation of not mastering the English language.

For a superintendent, the issue of language instruction can become an all-encompassing attention grabber. It brings out basic emotions from those who resist any attempt to replace familial culture and language with English. There are also those who deeply resent any attempts to recognize and encourage a language other than English or culture other than a traditional American one.

The issues relating to language instruction are becoming hotter and more widespread. A recent example is the Oakland County School District that enacted a policy recognizing "Ebonics," or "Black English," as a separate language and authorized a program to use such a language as a tool to improve a student's ability to learn English. A nationwide controversy ensued that focused more on what kind of language was being taught than on what was being learned. Whereas the Ebonics controversy was big news, it was quite similar in many respects to the lesser-known move by the New York State Board of Regents to recognize American Sign Language as a foreign language for the purposes of accruing academic language credits. A superintendent involved in controversies such as these discovers that adult politics become more important than student learning.

The superintendent must not only deal with the politics of these different views but with their relationship to the mission of academic learning. How can we seriously contemplate passing youngsters through our school systems and graduating them into society without doing everything we can to make sure they can read, write, and communicate in the language of the society in which they will be attempting to find jobs and pursue future educational goals? The public education system is to produce an informed citizenry and to enable youngsters to obtain the skills they need to function as adults. If we don't do everything within our power to give them the language skills they will need, we will be abdicating our responsibility.

The controversy over language has risen again. The New York commissioner has recommended that the new higher standards required of all students could be met in the native language of non–English-speaking students. Chemistry, social studies, or mathematics exams would be administered in the native language. A major public outcry arose, and the debate over whether examinations have to be taken in English ensued again.

People have used language differences in attempts to segregate students by culture. In 1989, New York State established a separate district for a specific religious sect after years of struggle over how the sect's students would be taught in the public school district in which they lived. One of the major rationales for the creation of a separate school district for Hasidic school children was their parents' need to have the youngsters taught in an environment that stressed Yiddish as a predominant language.

The pressures for separate cultural-religious lines were so great that even after the Supreme Court of the United States declared that the separate district was unconstitutional, the New York State legislature enacted legislation to recreate the district.

The degree of intensity that can arise on a language issue is personified in the following situation. The Satmar Hasidim, who were involved, refused to put their children into the neighboring public schools and the legislature and two governors of different parties were willing to accommodate that refusal. Nine years of litigation have not settled the issues. The second statute has just been unanimously declared unconstitutional by the state's highest court, the New York State Court of Appeals. The governor and the legislative leaders are once again considering more legislation in an attempt to calm the parents' fears of placing their children in the regular public schools. When emotions flare on an issue such as this, the whole purpose of the public education system seems to be forgotten and sublimated to the separatistic needs of the group that does not fit into the majority culture.

The chasm between those who believe that it is best to be in an environment that reinforces the language of a non–English-speaking home and those who believe that youngsters should be taught in a predominant language that will be used in the outside work environment is widening and deepening. It is a far cry from the schools of the late nineteenth century, whose major purpose was to Americanize European immigrants as they passed through Ellis Island. Not long ago, the Smithsonian Institute had an excellent exhibit that pointed out that the purpose of the Pledge of Allegiance and the classroom American flag was to ensure that youngsters from Ireland, Italy, Russia, and Germany were all placed into the great melting pot that was thought to reconstitute these youngsters as Americans.

Today, faced with an enormous failure of our education system to use the same tactics to effectively educate African-Americans and Spanish-speaking immigrants, frustrated advocates, parents, and educators are questioning the validity of the integration principles that once underlay our public school system and are trying to test principles in our schools that would have been thought to be unconstitutional and segregationist a decade ago.

Indeed, going beyond the issue of language instruction, a number of school districts have been experimenting with creating schools for populations intended to be exclusively female, black, male, gay, or of a particular religion or ethnicity (the aforementioned Hasidic school district). These experiments all are getting involved in high-profile legal challenges that can absorb much of the time of any superintendent who is involved.

What appears to be lost in this sea of frustration, experimentation, and litigation is a recognition that what made America different from so many countries was the public school system and its ability to cut across lines of class, religion, and color. Today, that underlying principle is being challenged by those who believe that the current educational system structurally reinforces a permanent underclass.

Technology Skills

An issue that is now facing superintendents and will be doing so increasingly as we cross the bridge to the twenty-first century is that of the technology skills of their staff and their students. It was almost inconceivable just two decades ago that one of the principal determinants in a youngster's ability to succeed in his or her adult life would be his or her ability to deal with computer technology and the rapidly, ever-changing technology of the future.

Most superintendents grew up learning that to succeed in education was to produce a document by writing in legible handwriting or typing with reasonable proficiency. Today, we are awash in a sea of word-processing software replete with spelling checkers and computerized thesauri. We will soon routinely be able to speak and have our words turned into text in the computer. It is almost impossible to follow the monthly and even daily revolutions in technology. The telephone, the computer, and the broadcasting companies compete with each other to produce infinitely better systems of communication that will rival the work of the human brain.

The impact of the increasingly rapid technological changes is being felt more strongly by our students than by other adults. A student from a home whose parents are able intellectually and financially to keep up with advancing technology comes into school technologically literate. This gives this youngster a tremendous advantage over a youth who has never seen a computer, a calculator, or a cell phone. One of the most serious problems over the last several decades has been the growing gap between youngsters who come to school with preschool educational experience, who are able to read fluently and count, and students who have not had this experience. Schools must keep these youngsters challenged and moving forward while bringing the youngsters who do not have these advantages up to speed as rapidly as possible. This is a daunting, if barely possible, task, made even more challenging because the gap geometrically increases with the variation in computer skills to become an unbelievable difference in general knowledge acquisition skills.

Therefore, schools must be able to infuse and constantly upgrade technology awareness into every element of the school program for the very youngest child to the graduating senior. In order to do this, they have to face several problems that increase burdens in every area of their responsibility.

A first step toward ensuring that every child has an opportunity to maximize his or her technology skills is to make sure that every building in the district has cutting-edge wiring that will provide access to cutting-edge technology in every classroom. It means purchasing up-to-date hardware in a world where hardware is expensive and has a short lifespan. It means developing and following a major planning effort so that hardware can be upgraded and replaced as necessary. It means constantly reviewing software to make sure that the latest software is accessible throughout the school and that the software is upgraded on a constant basis. Whole areas of staffing that were unnecessary a decade ago must now be devoted to these technology efforts.

At the core of technology skills provision is the need to ensure that every adult professional who works for the district be able to use state-of-the-art technology in a state-of-the-art way. This endeavor may be more daunting than raising students' awareness, inasmuch as students tend to take more readily to technology than do professional staff.

Every major corporation that has attempted to introduce and master technology and has turned it over at a rapid pace to stay current has faced enormous resistance, fear, and anxiety from its staff. No matter how helpful the technology may eventually be, professional staff tend to fight its introduction and, once it is introduced and accepted, fight upgrading it.

An educational establishment that insufficiently trains its professionals in the latest curricular developments is even more inadequate in training them with appropriate technological skills. Every teacher today must be trained and made to feel comfortable first with technology itself and then with constantly upgrading technology and refining their skills at using it. Every teacher and teacher's aide needs to be able not only to use technology in the most effective way in instruction but also to become a role model to their students and demonstrate how technology is vital to learning. This means that every district must provide their teachers and teacher's aides access to constant training. Schools have to start putting as much emphasis on ensuring that teachers have cutting-edge skills as they do in making sure their administrative and financial staff has them. Productivity in both areas depends on this.

CONTENTIOUS ISSUES

A growing movement is sweeping the nation to open charter schools and consider vouchers to provide an environment for innovation and experimentation. This movement tends to be fairly grounded in total frustration with the system of regulated checks and balances that most states have created in response to various concerns over the years. Charter schools and vouchers are usually pushed by those outside the educational structure. It is somewhat ironic to see such strong support for totally untested programs and to treat youngsters who might be in those programs as guinea pigs for controlled testing purposes.

For example, it is fascinating to consider that the Education Commission of the States is spending so much of its resources on such unproven programs in meeting after meeting and publication after publication. It claims there is an emerging consensus for structures that have not been used. Recent studies of charter schools have begun to discern that disabled youngsters will usually be left out of such programs. Standardized test reports from experimental schools do not tend to show any sustained improvement over the public schools from which they were created. Yet, much effort is being expended on experimental schools rather than attempting to fix underlying problems with the public schools, such as the tenure system, archaic building facilities, and curriculum.

A growing concern for every superintendent has to be how to best implement his or her responsibilities for the optional learning experiences that parents are choosing for their youngsters. The media and political and business leaders talk a great deal about the value of competitive options as opposed to the traditional system of public education. There is a practical side to the issues of vouchers, charter schools, and at-home schooling. There are, of course, many constitutional issues involved, but it is the practical aspects of these issues that do not get sufficient attention outside of the superintendent's office, even though they take up a great deal of time inside.

The bottom line for any alternative educational program is that the superintendent and his or her board is still responsible for the provision of quality education to every child who resides within the district, regardless of who provides the education. It must be stressed that when that child's parents choose to use a different education mechanism than the regular public school, the superintendent and his or her board are still responsible to see that the child gets an equivalent instructional program. This involves reviewing the academic program wherever it is delivered, monitoring the youngster's progress in that program, and dealing with the rather sensitive issues that arise when either the program or the progress is insufficient. It is easy to see that every superintendent needs to have a comprehensive plan for program and student review; however, this is too rarely done before a problem arises.

At-Home Instruction

Let us start with at-home instruction. In almost every state, at-home instruction is legal; however, there is usually far too little done by the school districts to see how the children are doing. Certainly, most would agree that at-home instruction is not intended to consist of tilling the fields. However, there is a growing body of litigation on home schooling that takes an enormous amount of time to follow and that could be avoided if proper review and monitoring occur. At a minimum, the curricula of the proposed educational program should be reviewed in detail, as should the textual material or software. The youngster's relationship to public extracurricular programming and transportation services needs must be ascertained and provided.

An easily understood and objective reporting form for the parents to inform the district of the youngster's progress should be developed. The superintendent needs to establish procedures to review those forms and ensure they are accurate through on-site visits by appropriately trained staff. Also, a system of standardized testing to double-check the reports on, at least, an equal basis would be useful.

What is as necessary as the procedures described above is to have the courage to report the parents who are keeping their youngsters out of school and not providing them with educational challenges as required by law to the appropriate legal authorities. Superintendents must make their responsibilities to the child supersede their concern for controversy that a parent creates when he or she believes that a child is not receiving an appropriate education and/or is being neglected. Those who keep a youngster from education should be prosecuted for child neglect. We are failing too many of these youngsters out of concern for the political ramifications of doing the right thing.

All too many superintendents become tired and give up on their responsibility to serve these children. Once children are at home and out of sight they become out of mind. It is difficult and time consuming to send staff to check on parents who do not want you to interfere with their perception of how a child should be educated. In an attempt to avoid such antagonistic situations, too many superintendents tend to forget why we have a compulsory education law and what their responsibilities are under it.

Charter Schools

As the districts that have charter schools, particularly the larger districts, are discovering, it is very difficult to keep track of standards. In New York, the governor's charter schools proposal would eliminate the need for certified instructors and allow these schools to identify and place disabled children themselves, assuming they have any. It is somewhat perplexing that society at the same time it is pushing the education system toward higher standards is pushing it toward a number of alternative settings that can ignore those standards.

The current excitement about charter schools will develop into a lot of work for the superintendents because they will have to monitor these schools to make sure that the very independence that is their hallmark raises the degree of learning and does not diminish it. The superintendent will have to work with every charter school to plan its curriculum and to set in place a system to monitor student progress, the school's health and safety provisions, and the qualifications of the staff. Standardized testing and assessment procedures will also be necessary to ensure that the school succeeds at what it sets out to do. All of the cries against overbureaucratization will turn to attacks against the district if the schools do not succeed.

We also have to examine what we are doing in the schools that leads to the outcry for a different setting. Our first responsibility should be to fix what is broken and not to open safety valves so that some can escape the system. We must consider the great majority who will be left behind.

Almost every superintendent is in a district that has some students going to private schools. Insufficient attention has often gone into ensuring that the private school curriculum and results are equivalent to those in the public schools. One must always remember that this is the responsibility of the superintendent and his or her board. There are many excellent private schools. There are many that are only adequate and some that are mediocre. The superintendent must not abandon his or her responsibility and allow a youngster to suffer mediocrity.

Character Education

There is much made in the media today (particularly from those who wish to use vouchers in religious schools) that the public school system has failed to teach and develop good character. There are claims that schools have become neutral, and youngsters are not taught right from wrong. Interestingly, where are those who make these claims when a school district does try to discipline members of a school soccer team who have broken rules by drinking or drug abuse or indeed by planting bombs in the community? The public outcry then is to allow the youngsters to play so that the team can remain unbeaten.

One of the problems that schools increasingly face is that youngsters do not have many role models today. When the major discussion in Washington and so many of our states revolves around ethical problems with our governmental leaders, when some states, such as New York, routinely do not pass their budgets on time, do not comply with their own laws, and do end runs on the Constitution, it is somewhat difficult to instill civic responsibilities in a student body. This is particularly true when a board and/or superintendent courageously try to deal with issues regarding character, and the community turns on them. These messages have an enormously lasting impact on character development.

In New York State recently, a school district became aware that some youths were planning to disrupt the building to keep school closed after a holiday. The school district worked with the state police, who apprehended the youngsters involved. Legal action commenced. The parents of the students have now sued the school district on the grounds that the school should have had knowledge that the youngsters were doing something wrong and should have gone to the parents to prevent such action rather than trying to apprehend them while the action was in progress.

As the superintendent develops and implements his or her plan for academic education, he or she must also keep an eye on character education and his or her responsibility to ensure that each youngster becomes an outstanding citizen. A growing concern of citizenry—particularly the large percentage of the public who do not currently have children in the schools—is whether or not the schools are inculcating civic values into students.

There is a growing pressure on the public schools to teach right from wrong. The need to understand civic virtue and the principles of democracy is a matter of public attention. Many feel that the strength of the public school is its ability to turn out good citizens who can be responsible participants in a democracy. As voter rates decline and the ethics of our public and business officials come into question, the schools are faulted for their lack of emphasis in these areas.

Indeed, there appears to be less emphasis on civic virtues, public ethics, and the responsibility of a citizen in a democracy than might be warranted in the public schools. Reinvigoration of this area of instruction will be as important to the future of education as are technology skills or math or science.

The Separation of Church and State

Over the past decade, some sectors of the public seem to have lost their zeal for the separation of church and state, and there appears to be a movement to diminish the separation.

One of the toughest issues that superintendents have to deal with is the degree to which children can be exposed to various aspects of religion during their educational program. Almost no one that the superintendent deals with is neutral on this subject. All of his or her constituencies have strongly held and conflicting views.

One of the unique aspects of American public education is that it exists in an atmosphere that must, by law, be free of government endorsement of religion. Our nation was created by immigrants from other nations, many of whom fled from persecution due to their religious beliefs or lack thereof. Puritans fled from Anglican persecution, Protestants fled from Catholic countries, Catholics fled from Protestant countries, and Jews fled from all of the above.

When the United States became a nation, the separation of church and state was a major issue. At the same time, the concept of public education as it is known in the United States today did not exist. Nevertheless, the U.S. Supreme Court, in interpreting the First Amendment of the U.S. Constitution, has determined that a separation of church and state must be preserved with even greater sensitivity in the context of public education than in those public services that did exist at the time of the writing of the Constitution.

The Supreme Court has determined in numerous decisions that without a strong separation of church and state impressionable school children, who are required by state laws to attend school, would otherwise receive the impression that the government endorses and "respects" an established religion.

The religion clauses of the First Amendment have their roots in the writings of two of the nation's founding fathers who ultimately became presidents. In 1776, while he was in Philadelphia writing the Declaration of Independence, Thomas

Jefferson drafted a proposed constitution for Virginia that stated: "All persons shall have full and free liberty of religious opinion; nor shall any be compelled to frequent or maintain any religious institution."[6] Although this particular clause as written was not adopted, it nevertheless set the tone for those who subscribed to the belief that religious freedom had to exist in the new nation.

Despite Jefferson's strong opinions on this matter, in 1779, a piece of legislation was introduced in the Virginia legislature declaring, "the Christian Religion shall in all times coming be deemed and held to be the established Religion of the Commonwealth."[7] The legislation required every person to enroll his name with the county clerk and designate the society that he intended to support, whereupon the clerk would present the roll to the appropriate religious group so it could determine assessment rates. These were then collected by the sheriff and the proceeds were turned over to the church. Taxes obtained from persons failing to enroll in a religious society were to be spread across all religious groups. This piece of legislation was called up for a vote in 1784 and was entitled: A Bill Establishing a Provision for Teachers of the Christian Religion.

The bill was defeated, but its introduction caused both Thomas Jefferson and James Madison to write documents that, for the most part, became the linchpins of religious freedom upon which the First Amendment's religion clauses were established. Jefferson wrote his "Bill Establishing Religious Freedom" and Madison wrote his "Memorial and Remonstrance against Religious Assessments." Jefferson's bill was adopted into law in January 1786, seven years after it had been introduced in the Virginia assembly.

Madison's "Memorial" was of great significance and has often been referred to by the U.S. Supreme Court in support of its opinions. Together, Jefferson's and Madison's writings developed the concept of a "wall of separation of church and state" upon which the nation's church-state jurisprudence is based.

State Aid to Parochial Schools

Over the last decade or so, there has been a growing movement from parents who wished to have their children, whom they placed in a parochial school, get public reimbursement to underwrite that choice. Their perspective is that they should not be paying school taxes and tuition at the same time. Whereas, there might seem to be some rationale for this argument, it flies in the face of a long-held tradition that public education is an investment in a nation's future, not in specific children, and that every taxpayer has an obligation to share in that investment. Parents should certainly be free to pay over and above that investment for religious schools for their own children but that is not and cannot be a burden for the taxpayer on an equity basis. Those parents do not stand in any different position than do the large percentage of the population who do not have children in any school. Of equal significance, state aid to religious schools would undermine our entire form of government, which prohibits public funds from supporting any particular religious activity. The basic rule is that public funding is not available for parochial schools. However, the courts have held that in spite of the separation of church and state, public school districts may provide certain limited non-instructional services to students in parochial and private schools. In most areas of the nation, private schools expect such services, and it is common to establish regular contacts to ensure the provision of such services.

For example, it is fairly settled that a school district may provide transportation to students to and from private religious schools. Courts have the belief that the separation of church and state is not violated because the child benefits by the transportation and there is no ideological context or religious instruction involved.

The Supreme Court's conclusion in this matter was based on the theory that because every child is entitled to be transported to his or her school of choice, within certain limitations in terms of distance, the separation of church and state is not violated by expending public taxpayer dollars for this purpose. From this case, the Court developed its "child-benefit" theory that sets forth that since children benefit from the provision of transportation services and not the religious institution, then the separation of church and state is not violated.[8]

Similarly, it is permissible to lend textbooks to parochial school students free of charge. A New York law requiring schools to lend textbooks to parochial school students free of charge also has been held to not violate the Establishment of Free Exercise Clauses. This case is also based upon the child-benefit theory.[9]

However, the courts have taken a much different stand in terms of whether public funds can be used to subsidize academic programs. When dealing with instruction in religious schools, the courts have determined the constitutionality of government action under a three-part test: (1) government action must have a secular purpose; (2) government action must neither advance nor inhibit religion; and (3) government action must not result in excessive entanglement of government in religion.[10] Under this test, many types of state support for religious schools have been found to be unconstitutional.

In *Lemon v. Kurtzman*,[11] the court held unconstitutional a Rhode Island statute providing salary supplements to teachers in religious schools for secular subjects and reimbursements to such schools for salaries and instructional materials for such subjects. In *Earley v. DeCenso*,[12] the court held unconstitutional Pennsylvania's program of reimbursement to non–public schools for teachers' salaries, textbooks, and instructional material as well as the relationship of the state with the schools in auditing financial records.

A state statute providing for reimbursement to religious schools for expenses related to the administration, grading, compiling, and reporting of certain tests was held to violate the Establishment Clause because no means were provided to ensure that the internally prepared tests were free of religious instruction nor to avoid teaching students the religious tenets of the sponsoring church.[13]

A Pennsylvania statute providing for reimbursement of tuition paid by parents of students in religious schools was held to violate the Establishment Clause because it has the primary effect of advancing religion.[14]

The direct loan of instructional materials and equipment to religious schools and the provision of auxiliary services such as counseling, testing, psychological services, speech and hearing therapy, and teaching and related services for exceptional children to students enrolled in religious schools was held to violate the Establishment Clause. However, lending textbooks without charge to children attending religious schools was held to be constitutional.[15]

An Ohio statute authorizing aid to students in private religious schools in terms of the loan of secular textbooks to students, supplying of standardized tests and scoring services, speech and hearing diagnostic services provided in the religious school, and therapeutic services at a neutral site was held to be constitutional. The Court further held that the provision of instructional materials and equipment and unrestricted transportation services for field trips are unconstitutional.[16]

The cases are not always clear, however. For example, a New York statute authorizing reimbursement to sectarian schools for their expense in performing state-required record-keeping and testing services was held to violate the Establishment Clause,[17] while a New York statute that provides for cash reimbursement to religious schools to cover the cost of administering and grading state-written tests does not violate the First Amendment.[18]

The Supreme Court ruled that a New York City Board of Education program that used federal funds received under Title I of the Elementary and Secondary Education Act of 1965 to pay salaries of public school employees to teach in parochial schools in New York City violated the Establishment Clause because the scope and duration of the program would require permanent and pervasive state presence in sectarian schools receiving aid by requiring the city school board to adopt a system for monitoring religious content of publicly funded Title I classes.[19] The case provided that the provision of such services was constitutional if provided on a neutral site. This case has spawned a neutral-site industry that causes districts to spend enormous sums to provide such services in temporary sites rather than in the schools. The Court just reversed this case, and no longer sees any significant problem with sending public school teachers into a parochial school, which will mean a radical revision in the way schools do business.

A school district's shared-time and community-education programs, which provided classes to non–public school students at public expense in classrooms located in and leased from the non–public schools was held to have the "primary or principal" effect of advancing religion and therefore violated the dictates of the Establishment Clause of the First Amendment.[20]

Yet, more recently, the Supreme Court held that the Establishment Clause does not bar a school district from providing a speech interpreter to a deaf child attending a parochial school.[21] The court appears to be less rigid in honoring the call of separation when dealing with services for disabled children.

In an attempt to try to get around all of the legal and constitutional distinctions above, the New York State legislature actually created a school district, at the request of a specific religious community, to meet its needs. Whereas the village of Kiryas Joel said it was only seeking to serve its special-education students, the legislature actually created a full-service school district to act as a vehicle for services to the other several thousand students in the district as well. All of Kiryas Joel's students are in religious schools. Services for them included transportation and bilingual services that would be provided in an environment more compatible with the religious group's needs. The various courts in New York and the Supreme Court of the United States ruled that the legislature could not do this. They made it fairly clear that one religious group could not be singled out for public support. In an interesting twist, Governor Mario Cuomo, four days later, submitted legislation that would do an end run on the Supreme Court decision and reestablish the district. The tension between a school system that should be religion neutral and the increasing desire of parents to get public funding for programs that conform with their religious beliefs is going to be one of the major areas of heated controversy within the nation in 15 years.

In the original case, the Supreme Court held that in the future it might overrule prior case law that held as unconstitutional the provision of the remedial services by public school officials on the premises of religious schools.[22] It has done so.

Teaching of Controversial Items

When confronted with parents who believe that curriculum violates their religious beliefs, a superintendent is confronted with a whole range of judgmental decisions ranging from what is religious to a particular religious belief.

Curriculum matters that are thought to infringe on or enhance religious views are matters to which a superintendent should pay a great deal of attention. For example, an Arkansas statute that barred the teaching of evolution was held to be unconstitutional.[23]

An Alabama statute that required that the teaching of evolution be balanced by the teaching of creation science was ruled unconstitutional because it did not have a secular purpose.[24]

Release Time

The Supreme Court has held that a public school may not provide release time for religious instruction on public school property.[25] However, it may provide release time for students to attend religious classes off the school property.[26]

Prayer in Schools

The courts have been fairly consistent in saying that prayer may not be mandated in any public school.

A New York statute calling for nondenominational prayer in public schools prepared by the New York State Board of Regents was held unconstitutional.[27]

A Kentucky statute requiring the posting of the Ten Commandments on public classroom walls was declared unconstitutional.[28]

The issue of voluntary prayer or student-initiated prayer is currently being considered around the nation. Voluntary prayer was enjoined in school assemblies.[29]

An Alabama statute that had authorized a one-minute period of silence in public schools for "meditation or voluntary prayer" was held unconstitutional. The statute's legislative purpose was found to be solely an "effort to return voluntary prayer to the public schools."[30]

Equal Access

Another issue that has been arising all over the nation is whether or not school buildings, which are open forums for public discussion of opinions, must also be open to religious opinions.[31]

The Equal Access Act has been held not to violate the First Amendment's proscription against the establishment of religion. The act requires public high schools to allow student religious and political clubs to meet on the same basis as other non-curriculum related activities. Although the decision reinforces the constitutionality of the 1984 Equal Access Act, it expands the definition of the term non-curriculum related to refer to any student group that does not directly relate to a school's curriculum. Something is considered to relate to the curriculum if its subject matter is taught, or will soon be taught, in a regularly offered course, if that subject matter concerns the body of courses as a whole, or if participation in the group is required for a course or results in academic credit.[32]

The U.S. Court of Appeals for the Second Circuit held that a school district must permit an evangelical ministry access to its premises for the purpose of conducting an evangelical magic show because the court found that the school district had permitted its premises to be used for a "religious purpose" on a prior occasion. The court failed to answer whether New York State Education Law Section 414, which sets forth the permissible uses of school district buildings, is constitutional in excluding religious purposes from those permitted usages.[33]

The Supreme Court reversed a decision of the U.S. Court of Appeals for the Second Circuit that had ruled that a school district could prevent a religious organization, in this case a Christian evangelical church, from using a school district's facilities after school hours to show a religious film series on family issues. The Supreme Court held that since the school district would have permitted other groups to utilize its school district facilities to present their views on family issues, precluding religious groups from making similar presentations because of their religious standpoint constituted unconstitutional viewpoint discrimination.[34]

Requests by Parents To Have Textbooks Removed from the Curriculum

The U.S. Court of Appeals for the Eleventh Circuit reversed the decision of the U.S. District Court for the Southern District of Alabama that had ordered Alabama's public schools to remove 44 history, social studies, and home economics textbooks for use in Alabama's public schools because the court found such books to teach the religion of "secular humanism."

On appeal, although the court noted that some of the material in the contested books may in fact be offensive to the religion of those bringing the lawsuit, the state's purpose in instilling in Alabama's public school children such values as independent thought, tolerance of diverse views, self-respect, maturity, self-reliance, and logical decision making outweighed any possible interference with the religious rights of those involved in the lawsuit. The court noted that if school districts are precluded from including material in books that is offensive to any particular religious belief, "there would be very little that could be taught in the public schools."[35]

The allegation that the book, *The Learning Tree*, unconstitutionally advanced an antitheistic faith was rejected.[36]

A school board's decision to bar the use of a humanities text because of its objectionable selections (including Chaucer's *The Miller's Tale*) was upheld because the decision was based on pedagogical concerns.[37]

In an important decision, the U.S. Court of Appeals for the Sixth Circuit reversed the decision of the U.S. District Court for the Eastern District of Tennessee that had ordered the Hawkins County School District to allow children who had religious objections to a certain basal reading series to be excused from, or "opt-out" of, reading class whenever any of these books were taught. Under this opt-out plan, the students would go to a study hall or library during reading class and would study reading later at home with their parents.

The court of appeals held that parents and children could not successfully claim that their freedom to practice their religion had been violated by the school district's mandating that the children attend classes and be "exposed" to the basal reading series. The court reasoned, in essence, that the right to practice one's religion is not burdened simply by mandating one to be exposed to ideas with which one disagrees.[38]

Free Speech

In addition to church-state issues, superintendents have to be aware that students and faculty have constitutional free-speech rights within certain limitations.

For example, a statute requiring students to salute flags is unconstitutional. In the classic case on the subject, a West Virginia state board case was decided on free-speech grounds although the plaintiffs' refusal was for religious reasons.[39]

In another landmark case, the Supreme Court held that students "do not shed their constitutional rights at the school-house door." School policy prohibiting wearing of black arm bands in protest of the Vietnam War is unconstitutional. Schools may not restrict student's private speech absent material and substantial interference with school operation or infringement of the rights of others.[40]

A school board's motives for the removal of books from the library may be subject to federal court review, agreed a majority of the Supreme Court.[41] In this case, four justices opined that students have a First Amendment "right to receive ideas and information and a school board may not remove the books because they seek to prescribe what shall be orthodox in politics, nationalism, religion or other matters of opinion," suggesting a difference between libraries and classrooms and between acquiring and removing library books. The four justice dissent argued that boards may make content-based decisions in order to "inculcate fundamental values."

In another decision, the court ruled that a school principal did not violate the free-speech rights of a student by punishing the student for using sexual innuendo in a speech during a school-sponsored assembly. The First Amendment does not prevent school officials from determining that a student's speech "would undermine the school's basic education mission."[42]

Schools also do not violate free-speech rights of students by exercising control over style and content of school-sponsored student newspapers if the actions are reasonably related to legitimate pedagogical concerns.[43]

In another decision, the school district was upheld in denying Planned Parenthood's request to advertise in the district's newspapers, yearbooks, and programs for athletic events. The court reasoned that the district could reject advertisements inconsistent with its educational mission and that only with express intent of school authorities would a school newspaper become a public forum for expression.[44]

STAFF PERFORMANCE

So far, the focus of this chapter has been on which major academic, quasi-academic, or legal issues that concern certain students, or groups of students, take away a great deal of the superintendent's time. Each of these issues, unless they are properly dealt with will not allow pursuit of the main thing—academics—to proceed.

The next issue is that of professional staff preparation, training, and evaluation as it involves the delivery of academic learning or as it takes time away from the superintendent's focus on academic learning. A major focus of the media, the president, governors, and most legislative bodies over the last several years and the last several national elections has been on increasing the standards of performance of youngsters in our schools. Very little to nothing has been said about the performance of teachers and other professional staff who are vital to good student performance, even though education really boils down to a competent teacher motivating a student to learn.

It is clear that the superintendent must have the courage to look into the eyes of a 3rd grader or 10th grader and say: "You will learn." He or she must also have the courage to look into the eyes of that youngster's teacher and say: "You will teach according to standards. You must be a positive factor in the child's learning."

It is vital that districts develop and maintain mechanisms to promote excellence and accountability for administrators, teachers, and support staff. In most states, it is extremely difficult to develop an incentive mechanism that works, since certification and tenure laws as written do not ensure quality teaching. As a matter of fact, most such laws do not even *promote* quality teaching, and they may be responsible for the maintenance of poor teaching. Yet, if schools fail to improve the quality of classroom instruction, all other efforts and reforms are doomed to failure. The current system of education employment is more concerned with job security for adults than educational excellence for children. That must change.

Preservice Education

Every superintendent needs to develop an effective process that ensures not only that recruitment produces candidates for teaching or administrative positions who have the appropriate credentials but also that they have a proven ability to be able to teach to the standards that the state and/or district determines that the child shall meet. This not only involves careful recruiting and screening but also should involve working out relationships with institutions of higher education throughout the region. This ensures that the preservice courses that are being taught are relevant, are of a high enough quality, and have sufficient useful knowledge included. Superintendents should not have to retrain a recent college graduate upon hiring.

Supervision and Evaluation

It is also a good idea to institute a system of mentoring and appropriate supervision to help the new teacher or administrator adjust to the expectations of the district. A written set of predetermined standards should be given to the teachers, and a system of regular evaluation, which involves rigorous classroom monitoring, should be instituted and maintained. Too often, teachers are given too little direction, are asked to meet standards that are too vague or too low, and are given practically no monitoring. Administrators must be told that teacher evaluation is one of their top priorities and that it cannot be delegated. They must be encouraged to delegate other less-vital functions to make time to adequately evaluate their teachers.

Many school districts provide support for in-service education for their staff. Superintendents must sit down with their teachers and administrators and work out a very strong goal and an objective-oriented training program that is related to the improvement of classroom performance. Support should be withdrawn from in-service training that is tangential to that goal. *All* training must focus on the main thing or the main thing will never be achieved.

Having an effective work force is not a matter of chance but the end product of clearly articulated and consistently applied policies, practices, and procedures. Superintendents are responsible for ensuring that a meaningful staff evaluation process is in place, that evaluations are conducted regularly, and that supervisors conducting the evaluations are trained to do so. One of the most important responsibilities superintendents face is ensuring that our schools employ the best staff possible. A well-developed and rigorously administered staff evaluation process is key to securing and maintaining an effective district work force. The students deserve no less.

What should be the goal of any school district's staff evaluation system? Most would agree that a dynamic and efficient staff, dedicated to providing a quality education for all students, is a necessary component to an excellent educational program. Districts should strive to develop and implement an employee appraisal program that will contribute to the continuous improvement of staff capabilities and the district's educational program.

In developing and implementing an effective staff evaluation system, superintendents should ensure they are asking the right questions of administrators.

The evaluation process begins with the development of a good evaluation instrument. The instrument should be clear, objective, easily understood, and discussed with each professional employee during the recruitment process. Staff should be evaluated at least annually according to a formal evaluation procedure approved by the school board. The criteria for evaluation should include the job description and should be specifically tied to the performance of each element of the job description. Job descriptions and other evaluation instruments should be reviewed and updated annually.

Essential to the effectiveness of any evaluation process is that all individuals involved in the process understand what is expected of them. As such, the evaluation process should be disseminated to all affected personnel and included in the employee handbook. As part of a staff orientation process, all new employees should be informed of the criteria that will be used to evaluate them.

Job descriptions are critical to the evaluation process because they provide a written statement of job expectations for the employee. They also provide an ideal starting point for developing the criteria for evaluation. Job descriptions need not be lengthy, but they must adequately describe the duties required for the job. In addition, all job descriptions should be kept current and be reviewed on a regular basis by the superintendent and the board. Job descriptions should be kept in the central office, accessible to anyone who would like to see them.

It should be crystal clear which supervisor conducts the appropriate evaluations. Whoever performs evaluations should have regularly updated training, and the superintendent should make certain the necessary training is being provided. Supervisors need to be made aware that performing effective and timely evaluations is an essential function of their job and that they will be evaluated on how well they perform this job function.

Whereas one purpose of evaluation is to improve staff performance where performance is inadequate, a performance improvement plan also needs to be developed and implemented. Careful documentation of progress or lack thereof is essential. The documentation should be carefully placed in the individual's record, and those records should be the basis for any personnel activities— whether of advancement or discipline.

A major obstacle to student performance is the teacher who is not performing or who has burned out and is no longer performing. It is a disservice to the students to permit such a teacher to continue, in part because proper evaluation and/ or documentation wasn't done.

In almost every school building in the nation, poor teaching in one or two cases is the result of a combination of poor teacher performance combined with an inadequate evaluation process or inadequate documentation.

Periodic written evaluations should be based on direct observation of how a teacher is doing on the performance plan, how they are meeting agreed-on standards, and, to some degree, whether or not their classrooms are doing better at the end of the school year than they were doing at the beginning. Schools should stop ducking the issue of tying evaluation to some aspect of student performance in the classroom. When a teacher or administrator is not performing or is unable to improve, careful attention should be given to documenting the problem. The amount of time that it takes to appropriately document a problem is expanded geometrically when a case is brought against an instructor and when there is no documentation.

REACHING OUT

Back in the good old days, education was a self-contained service that dealt solely with focusing a youngster's mind on learning and helping him or her to succeed. Today, a growing portion of our population are youngsters who have other overwhelming needs that often stand in the way of their academic success. Such needs include an inability to get adequate nutrition or health care; a nonexistent or dysfunctional family life; a problem with alcohol or substance abuse; a problem of child abuse, either physical or emotional; and problems with the law. These problems often dominate the youngster's mind and distract him or her from focusing on studies.

Most of these problems have always existed and have always been a problem for the youngster, but for most of our history they were not a problem for the educational system. It was the youngster's business or his or her family's business as to how to deal with those problems. Today, society seems to look to the school to solve all of the problems youngsters bring, and people are very hard on schools when they do not meet this standard. Interestingly, they are equally hard when they think schools spend too many resources attempting to meet this standard.

We as a nation have to stop pretending that the schools can function as a multipurpose governmental safety net for every problem that a youngster faces. This does not mean schools have to go back to ignoring those problems. What superintendents need to do is to turn to their colleagues in city and county governments and open relationships that may not exist. School officials need to sit down with mayors, county executives, city councilmen, and county legislators and find out who is doing what and how they can work together. Communities need to have a regular interagency system in place so that the needy youngster has a single place to turn and does not have to agency shop. Groups need to bridge the gap in services that exist in too many areas and communities and stop the duplication of services that exist in too many other areas.

Superintendents need to be able to turn to county or city drug workers and family counselors when they are necessary. Mayors and sheriffs need to be able to turn to superintendents to educate the youngsters in their custody. The services should coordinate to ensure the youngster's success. This, of course, will require the type of cooperation and levels of understanding that require an unbelievable amount of time. In this business, as in so many others, *turf* is the worst four-letter word in the language.

In most areas of the country, it is not enough for schools to reach out only to our colleagues in counties and cities. Educators must also reach out to not-for-profit agencies and community-based organizations. Groups such as the United Way, Catholic charities, Jewish philanthropies, United Cerebral Palsy, and the Boy Scouts and Girl Scouts provide many important services that could be provided even better if they were done in coordination with the school system.

Although there are problems concerning exchanging or providing data about the educational history of students, all sides could better serve the youngster if they taught more often in some systematic way. Usually the only person who could initiate those contacts where they do not always exist is the superintendent. It is hard to delegate the establishing of good relations—it usually has to be done at the top. Working with nonprofit and community-based organizations is even more difficult than working with other governmental groups. They are less bureaucratic, which is often good, but more irregular, which is often frustrating. However, where good relationships are developed, children benefit amazingly. If as a result of that benefit youngsters can better focus on education when in a classroom, we all will benefit. The goal is to provide a seamless web between support services and the youngster's education.

ENDNOTES

1. 20 U.S.C. §602(8).
2. 20 U.S.C. §602(2).
3. 20 U.S.C. §612(a)(5)(A).
4. Irving Independent Sch. Dist. v. Tatro, 104 S. Ct. 3371 (1984), 20 U.S.C. §602(22).
5. Report on the Implementation of the Regents Policy Paper and Proposed Action Plan for Bilingual Education in New York State, April 1995, p. 11.
6. Padover, S.K. (1943). *The complete Jefferson.* New York: Duel, Sloan, and Pearce.
7. Id.
8. Everson v. Board of Educ. of Ewing, 330 U.S. 1 (1947).
9. Board of Educ. v. Allen, 392 U.S. 236 (1968).
10. 403 U.S. 602 (1971).
11. Lemon v. Kurtzman, 403 U.S. 602 (1971).
12. Earley v. DeCenso, 403 U.S. 602 (1971).
13. Levitt v. Committee for Pub. Educ. and Religious Liberty (PEARL), 413 U.S. 472 (1973).
14. Sloan v. Lemon, 413 U.S. 825 (1973).
15. Meek v. Pittenger, 421 U.S. 349 (1975).
16. Wolman v. Walter, 433 U.S. 229 (1977).

17. New York v. Cathedral Academy, 434 U.S. 125 (1977).

18. Committee for Pub. Educ. and Religious Liberty (PEARL) v. Regan, 444 U.S. 646 (1980).

19. Aguilar v. Felton, 473 U.S. 402 (1985).

20. Grand Rapids Sch. Dist. v. Ball, 473 U.S. 373 (1985).

21. Zobrest v. Catalina Foothills Sch. Dist., 509 U.S. 1 (1993).

22. Kiryas Joel Village Sch. Dist. v. Grumet 114 S. Ct. 2481 (1994).

23. Epperson v. Arkansas, 393 U.S. 97 (1968).

24. Edward v. Agullard, 482 U.S. 578 (1987).

25. McCollum v. Board of Educ., 333 U.S. 203 (1948).

26. Zorach v. Clauson, 343 U.S. 306 (1952).

27. Engle v. Vitale, 370 U.S. 421 (1962).

28. Stone v. Graham, 449 U.S. 39 (1980).

29. Collins v. Chandler Unified Sch. Dist., 644 F. 2d 759, cert. denied, 454 U.S. 863 (1981).

30. Wallace v. Jaffree, 472 U.S. 38 (1985).

31. Widmar v. Vincent, 454 U.S. 263 (1981).

32. Westside Community Bd. of Educ. v. Mergens, 496 U.S. 226 (1990).

33. Travis v. Oswego-Apalachin Sch. Dist., 927 F.2d 688 (2d Cir. 1991).

34. Lamb's Chapel v. Center Moriches Union Free Sch. Dist., 113 S. Ct. 2141 (1993).

35. Smith v. Board of Sch. Commr's of Mobile County, 655 F. Supp. 939 (S.D. Ala. 1987), rev'd 827 F.2d 684 (11th Cir. 1987).

36. Grove v. Mead Sch. Dist. No. 354, 753 F. 2d 1528 (9th Cir. 1985), cert. denied, 474 U.S. 826 (1985).

37. Virgil v. School Bd. of Columbia County, Florida, 862 F. 2d 1517 (11th Cir. 1989).

38. Mozert v. Hawkins County Bd. of Education, 647 F. Supp. 1194 (E.D. Tenn. 1986), rev'd 827 F. 2d 1058 (6th Cir. 1987).

39. West Virginia State Bd. of Educ. v. Barnette, 319 U.S. 624 (1943).

40. Tinker v. Des Moines Indep. Community Sch. Dist., 393 U.S. 503 (1969).

41. Board of Educ., Island Trees v. Pico, 457 U.S. 853 (1982).

42. Bethel Sch. Dist. No. 403 v. Fraser, 478 U.S. 675 (1986).

43. Hazelwood Sch. Dist. v. Kuhlmeier, 484 U.S. 260 (1988).

44. Planned Parenthood v. Clark County School Dist., 887 F.2d 935, affd. 941 F.2d 817 (9th Cir. 1989).

CHAPTER 4

Research and Innovation: Let the Buyer Beware

J. E. Stone and Andrea Clements

Schools are inundated with research that promises to improve achievement. Yet when programs are implemented results always seem to fall short. How can it be in school after school, year after year? The answer depends on whom you ask.

Educational researchers allege that the problem is a lack of money for research. They say that research and development has little impact simply because there isn't enough of it and they cite studies showing that funding is meager relative to the magnitude of the education enterprise. Outside observers disagree. Some 35,000 professors of education at American colleges and universities devote an average 14% of their time to research—broadly defined. Their students conduct research too. Annually, more than 7,300 doctoral students in education write dissertations. Myron Lieberman (1993) estimates the dollar value of the manpower dedicated to educational research by professors and doctoral students alone to be in excess of $700 million annually. Still other education research is authored by state departments of education, by nonprofit "think tanks," by federal agencies, and by the regional educational research laboratories. Significantly, only a small percentage of published research is undertaken by schools or school systems.

The results of this scholarly activity are readily available to schools through a variety of sources. Thousands of books, professional and academic journals, newsletters, technical bulletins, and other published sources make research available to teachers and administrators. Many recent publications are available on the Internet. A vast amount of material is indexed in the federally sponsored Education Resources Information Center (ERIC). ERIC includes a Current Index to Journals in Education and a microfiche library of mostly unpublished research called Research in Education. Research in Education is available in education libraries throughout the United States. The amount of research available through these several sources is staggering, and most of it is directly or indirectly related to the problem of improving school achievement.

The idea of improving teaching through the application of science has been around since the earliest days of organized teacher training. John Dewey, for example, believed that the scientific study of child development would improve classroom instruction by suggesting ways in which teaching might be fitted to the learner (Dewey, 1916/1963). However, it was not until the 1960s that governmentally funded research began expanding to present-day levels. The Johnson administration's "war on poverty" infused federal dollars into university research institutes and education laboratories on an unprecedented scale. Head Start (U.S. Department of Health and Human Services, 1985) and Follow Through (Proper & St. Pierre, 1980) are prime examples. Both were designed to improve the school success of disadvantaged children and they are among the largest educational research projects ever mounted. The Follow Through project alone cost nearly $1 billion.

Has the money and manpower spent on research been justified by improvements in schooling? If the findings reported in *Education Week's* "Quality Counts" (Wolk, 1997) are any indication, the answer would have to be no. Despite the pressures for improvement created by reports such as the National Commission on Excellence in Education's *A Nation at Risk* (1983), measured achievement has stayed essentially flat. The National Assessment of Educational Progress scores in math and science have risen only a few points on a 500-point scale since 1973 (U.S. Department of Education, 1996). Of course there are isolated examples of significant improvement, but the broad picture is that the schools are (in the words of "Quality Counts") "treading water."

WHY SO LITTLE IMPACT?

If there is a significant amount of research—although arguably not enough—and the findings are widely available, why is there not at least a trend toward improved achievement? Again, researchers have an answer: Good research is available but schools fail to implement it. In other words, schools talk as though they adopt research-based innovations but at the classroom level they keep doing the same old thing (Cuban, 1993). There is more than a little truth to this claim. The innovative programs publicized by school administrators are not always translated into classroom practice. Teachers have a great deal of independence in the classroom and they are taught to fit their teaching style to students' needs. Remaining with accustomed approaches is, indeed, the tendency if only for reasons of comfort and familiarity.

Another explanation offered by researchers is that schools don't know good research when they see it. They are easily drawn to familiar practices supported by weak evidence. Unfamiliar practices supported by very credible evidence are often ignored. As discussed below, there is merit to this view. From the standpoint of science, experimental studies are far more convincing than descriptive and correlational ones, yet school personnel often ignore the stronger and adopt innovations suggested by the weaker. For example, during the 1960s and 1970s correlational studies suggesting self-esteem enhancement as a means to improved achievement led to sweeping changes in teacher training and schooling. Experimental findings to the contrary were ignored (Scheirer & Kraut, 1979). They showed that self-esteem and achievement are correlated mainly because achievement enhances self-esteem, not because self-esteem enhances achievement.

One other explanation popular with researchers is the institutional inertia warps and retards progress. Plainly this view also has merit. All organizations encourage some possibilities and restrict others. All are comfortable with certain ways of conducting themselves and uncomfortable with others. Teacher unions, for example, may resist changes that make teachers' jobs more laborious. Administrative customs may resist change that make jobs look too easy. Of course, community expectations, regulatory policy, and public oversight can all exert resistance to change.

In marked contrast to the views of researchers, schoolhouse "insiders" (i.e., teachers and administrators) say that research has little impact because much of it does not work in the real world. As they see it, schools are doing everything they can to implement the latest findings, but social and economic realities impose limits. Implementing research is like rebuilding a ship in the midst of a voyage. Staying afloat has to be the first consideration. Rebuilding during a storm is even more problematic. Schools can and do make the changes suggested by research, but circumstances can trump even the best-laid plans. Even with successful implementations, effects are obscured or nullified by factors such as limited resources, two-earner families, increased crime, teen pregnancy, drug abuse, gangs, television, and a host of other hindrances and adversities (Olson, 1997).

Despite the often limited benefit of research-based innovations, schools continue to adopt them—if only to keep up with the latest trends. Which research and which innovations, however, often depends less on the quality of the findings than on the channel through which the research comes to the school's attention. School personnel are frequently exposed to "the latest" research at workshops, professional meetings, and in-service training. Typically, the teachers, administrators, and board members who attend these meetings have a limited understanding of research and/or of the findings pertaining to the innovation in question. More often than not, presenters and programs for such meetings are selected not because their ideas are well grounded but because they have a stimulating presentation. In addition, audience interest is often spurred by a regulatory mandate or incentive funding, not a burning desire for improved student achievement.

Other pragmatic considerations play a role as well. For example, attractiveness to students, teachers, parents, and other school system stakeholders can weigh heavily in research selections. So can public relations. For example, the desire of school leaders and board members to demonstrate "progressive leadership" often plays a contributory role. In short, the selection of research-based programs and innovations brought back from workshops and meetings may be substantially influenced by considerations other than evidence of effectiveness.

The Restrictions Imposed by Doctrine

Another factor that influences decisions about research is educational philosophy. The practice of injecting popular psychological theory into schooling—often without regard to effectiveness or applicability—has been a chronic problem in American education (Davis, 1943; Hilgard, 1939). Currently, a poorly recognized but longstanding educational doctrine called "developmentalism" (Hirsch, 1996; Stone, 1996) permeates the public schooling community. Developmentalism frames teaching and learning issues in a way that favors certain types of research and disregards others.

Developmentalism is a derivation of eighteenth-century romantic naturalism. The French philosopher Jean Jacques Rousseau (1712–1778) is the most influential of its early proponents. The works of John Dewey (1859–1952) and Jean Piaget (1896–1980), however, are more directly responsible for its present-day acceptance. Developmentalism is a view of age-related social, emotional, and cognitive change that presumes a child's native tendencies to be a fragile expression of the individual's natural and therefore optimal developmental trajectory (Stone, 1996). It conceives of education as a set of experiences that serves to facilitate and preserve that trajectory by fitting the educational experience to the individual.

Developmentalism contrasts sharply with the classic tradition in education and with the American tradition founded by the Puritans. Both sought to civilize and better the individual, not merely accommodate his or her emerging tendencies. Both classic tradition and the common school aimed to discipline natural impulses in service of a higher good. The significance of this philosophic issue as an impediment to effective schooling would be difficult to overstate. Most public schools seek achievement to the extent permitted by students' natural inclinations. They are "learner centered." Most parents and policy makers want schooling that impels achievement beyond that to which most students are inclined by their youthful proclivities (Steinburg, 1996). They are "learning centered."

The dominance of learner-centered pedagogy is in no small part an accident of history. Progressivism—a social and philosophical offshoot of romantic naturalism—predominated in American intellectual circles in the late nineteenth century and early twentieth century. These were the years during which universal public education came to be public policy as well as the formative years of many teacher-training institutions. Accepted teaching practices of that day were often harsh and punitive; thus progressive methods were a welcome alternative. The premier teacher-training institution of the early twentieth century was Teacher's College, Columbia University (Cremin, 1964). Its graduates led the development of other such programs around the country. Even today, the educational methodologies that prevail in the public education community are those that agree with the philosophic leanings of the Teacher's College faculty of the early 1900s (Hirsch, 1996).

Developmentally informed pedagogy has come to dominate public schooling but without clear public recognition of its nature and its role. Over the past 75 years it has emerged and reemerged under a variety of names. In the 1920s it was called "progressive" and "child centered." Today it is termed "reflective" and "learner centered" (Darling-Hammond, Griffin, & Wise, 1992). However termed, it has consistently maintained that teachers should seek to instruct only through activities that students find engaging and enjoyable. Thus, instead of employing the most enjoyable of teaching methods that are known to result in learning, teachers have been trained first to seek activities that are enjoyable and engaging and to use them in ways that will produce learning. Thus good teaching has come to be thought of as teaching that is well received and that incidentally produces some degree of learning.

Uncertainty about learning outcomes was not considered a pedagogic weakness by progressive education's founders. Neither John Dewey nor progressive education's great popularizer, William Heard Kilpatrick, considered conventionally prescribed educational objectives to be the proper aim of schooling. Instead, both argued that schooling should seek the emergence of an individually defined and broadly conceived intellectual development. Dewey, in particular, wrote at length about the harm done by teacher insistence on externally defined aims (Dewey, 1916/1963). Viewed from the progressive/learner-centered perspective, research that seeks to demonstrate a teaching methodology's ability to produce a preconceived learning outcome is inherently faulty and inconsistent with the proper aims of schooling.

Despite public repudiation in the 1950s, Dewey's view remains the foundation of today's cutting-edge innovations. It has spawned a remarkable array of educational terms and concepts, and they have been widely propagated by agencies and organizations such as the U.S. Office of Education, the state departments of education, teacher-training programs, accrediting agencies, professional and academic societies, and the like.

The education community seeks to improve schooling through the use of research, but learner-centered strictures guide the adoption process. The impression created by the vast assortment of current educational terms and concepts is one of abundant variety. In truth, however, most conform to the same progressive vision of education. As noted by E. D. Hirsch (1996), "within the educational community, there is currently no *thinkable* alternative" (italics in the original, p. 69). Recent permutations and derivatives include the following:

- lifelong learning
- developmentally appropriate instruction
- brain-based learning
- situated learning
- cooperative learning
- multiple intelligences
- multiaged instruction
- discovery learning
- portfolio assessment
- constructivism
- hands-on learning
- project method
- thematic learning
- integrated curriculum
- higher-order learning
- authentic assessment
- whole-language reading

How Learner-Centered Thinking Restricts Choices: The Case of the Follow Through Project

Learner-centered doctrine discourages the use of results-oriented research (Stone, 1996). Studies concerned with improving achievement typically test an intervention or treatment (i.e., an action taken by the researcher that is intended to produce change in the student). The success of the intervention is judged in reference to some predetermined expectation. In contrast to the goal of inducing results, the goal of developmentally informed research is to accommodate schooling to the individual and to do so in a way that achieves the ends to which the individual is inclined by nature, not those prescribed by the curriculum.

One of the clearest instances of results-oriented research rejected on learner-centered grounds comes from the Follow Through project (Proper & St. Pierre, 1980). Follow Through was a huge federally funded research project of the late 1960s and early 1970s. It was launched in 1967 by the Ninetieth Congress in response to President Johnson's request to "follow through" on project Head Start. Improved achievement in the basic skills of disadvantaged students was its prime objective. It remains the largest educational experiment ever.

Nine educational models were compared in 51 school districts over a six-year period. Of the nine, all but two were learner centered; and contrary to the prevailing educational wisdom, the two exceptions significantly outperformed the field. Of greater significance, five of the seven learner-centered models produced *worse* results than the traditional school programs (i.e., the nontreated control groups) to which each Follow Through approach was compared. What makes the contrast especially striking is that the outcome measures included not only basic skills but "higher-order" cognitive skills and a measure of self esteem—the very sort of outcomes that learner-centered methods are intended to enhance.

The most successful of the nine models was Direct Instruction (Engelmann, Becker, Carnine, & Gersten, 1988)—a structured and so-called teacher-centered approach. Despite its overwhelming success, Direct Instruction was disparaged and largely ignored by the education community (Watkins, 1988). A lengthy critique of Follow Through was published in *Harvard Educational Review* (House, Glass, McLean, & Walker, 1978), and the U.S. Department of Education's National Diffusion Network—a bureaucratic agency responsible for disseminating only the "best" research—concluded that all nine programs were valid and all were recommended for further funding. In fact, added funding was given to the failed models on the grounds that they needed strengthening.

The Follow Through Direct Instruction findings are by no means the only research that has been ignored because it disagreed with the learner-centered view. Herbert Walberg (1990, 1992) summarized some 8,000 reports of demonstrably effective teaching methods. Like Direct Instruction, most were structured, teacher-directed, and designed to produce measurable gains in achievement. Most could be described as learning-centered instead of learner-centered. Many employed drill, recitation, and incentives for student effort. A review of research literature by Ellson (1986) found 75 studies of teaching methods that produced achievement gains at least twice as great as those of comparison groups. Many of them were popular at one time but none are learner-centered and none are in widespread use today.

The reception accorded Direct Instruction and other learning-centered research is important because it highlights a critical difference between the public's educational objectives and those of the learner-centered schooling establishment. Public Agenda (Johnson & Immerwahr, 1994) and other public polling organizations have found that the public wants schools that produce conventionally measured academic achievement. The public is not opposed to the goals of learner-centered schooling, but it considers them secondary to conventional academic achievement. To the public, outcomes such as improved self-esteem are attractive, but schools that fail with respect to academic achievement are nonsense no matter what else they may produce. The same priorities are embodied in state-level school accountability policies. They focus primarily on academic gains operationally defined by achievement tests. By contrast, learner-centered research gives equal priority to "intellectual growth," enhanced self-esteem, and gains in knowledge and skills. If one or more of the three are produced, the research is taken to be informative and potentially valuable for school implementation.

Why Researchers Remain Learner-Centered

Despite the ever-growing demand for improved achievement, neither researchers nor schools are able to break away from learner-centered thinking, and for several reasons. Both researchers and most school personnel are indoctrinated in learner-centered thinking, and powerful incentives encourage them to remain loyal to that point of view.

For researchers, funding is a prime incentive. Fund allocations are almost inevitably influenced by other educators, and most of them subscribe to learner-centered orthodoxy. Funding affords a researcher time to work, and to have a reasonable chance at funding, one's proposal must appeal to the views of other educators.

For most researchers, funding is tied to institutional support. Most researchers are college faculty, and their primary responsibility is teaching. If a faculty member needs time to conduct a study, the institution must at a minimum relieve the individual from teaching. Ordinarily it will hire someone to teach in his or her place. Research grants provide the funding for the substitute instructor. If the researcher's employer does not like a proposal, it may decide against released time. A proposal that appeals to the views of learner-centered administrators and colleagues is more likely to find support.

Grants also pay what are called "indirect costs" for the use of the institution's facilities and other forms of overhead. These are additional funds that may amount to 50% or more of a research project's direct costs for a substitute instructor, equipment, supplies, and so forth. The funds an institution receives for such costs are typically added to various administrative budgets, thus enabling substantial discretionary spending. College administrators consider faculty who generate big indirect cost contributions to be their most productive and deserving faculty. Grants are key to a faculty member's career advancement at major institutions. Grants that are readily funded for big amounts (e.g., grants from state education agencies) are thus extremely attractive.

Second, there is the matter of publication. In order to advance their academic reputations, researchers must publish. Research that is not published is assumed to be of lesser quality, and rightly so. Research that is published in the most respected journals is stringently peer reviewed. Reviewers and editors do not rule out findings that are inconsistent with orthodoxy, but such reports inevitably receive much closer scrutiny and are thus less likely to be accepted. A record of successful publication also contributes mightily to a researcher's chance of acquiring more funding.

Third, there is the matter of acceptance in the schools. The learner-centered view is more attractive to researchers because it is more easily marketed to the schools. Public school administrators typically have been trained in learner-centered thinking, thus such research has an intuitive appeal. That it may not produce intended results is a downside, but one that is frequently overlooked. School administrators are never fired or penalized because an innovative program fails. After all, how could an administrator be blamed for accepting the recommendations of scholar-experts who are supported by prestigious institutions. Because success is defined more in terms of funding than outcomes, appeal to decision makers is more important than demonstrated effectiveness. One need only observe the indicators of organizational advancement that are trumpeted in the media to verify the truth of this conclusion. Media releases talk about money and organizational expansion, not increased student learning.

The learner-centered view is comfortable to other stakeholders as well. Its convenience and vague expectations are significant considerations to teachers. In the learner-centered view, teachers are responsible for affording a quality educational experience, not the production of measurable academic outcomes. Learner-centered teachers consider outcomes to be governed by factors outside teacher control, thus the quality of teaching cannot be judged by results. Also, teachers find that learner-centered approaches are flexible and can be blended with existing practice without inconvenience and disruption. Factors of this sort make the task of adopting learner-centered practices simpler than, for example, implementing Direct Instruction—a methodology requiring more than the usual day or two of in-service training.

Learner-centered instruction also appeals to students. It seeks to accommodate them, not to shape them. By contrast, schooling that produces results typically requires a concerted student effort, and the time devoted to such an effort can infringe on more attractive pursuits (Steinberg, 1996). It should be noted, however, that students' short-term satisfactions come at the cost of very substantial longer-term cost. Lost educational opportunity may result in permanently impaired career prospects—a delayed cost that students are unable to anticipate. Lost opportunities also cost taxpayers both in failed human resource development and the cost of remediation. Schooling that permits students to waste their own time and taxpayer-funded educational opportunity is an enormous but largely overlooked public disservice.

RECOGNIZING USEFUL RESEARCH

Research that can add to the efficiency and effectiveness of public schooling is available, but school personnel must be able to recognize it. Otherwise, there is a very substantial chance that they will be drawn into adopting one of the many

fads that dominate the educational landscape. Recognizing credible, useful studies requires an understanding of certain basics of research.

Both medicine and education rely on a scientific knowledge base. Medicine,
however, relies on relatively mature and exact sciences such as physics, chemistry, and biology, whereas education relies on the far less mature social and behavioral sciences. These differences in quality of research and precision of
measurement are reflected in the certainty and internal coherence of the knowledge base on which the two professions rely. Competing and contradictory findings are not uncommon in the behavioral sciences; thus the matter of determining
which findings are credible, important, and applicable is a formidable challenge
to the educational practitioner.

Given facts open to selective use and interpretation, educators frequently rely
on knowledge that is equivocal or that may be contradicted by other evidence.
Recognizing this condition, Anderson, Reder, and Simon (1995) offer the following caution:

> [N]ew "theories" of education are introduced into schools every day
> (without labeling them as experiments) on the basis of their philosoph-
> ical or common sense plausibility but without genuine empirical sup-
> port. [Instead] we should make a larger place for responsible
> experimentation that draws on the available knowledge—it deserves at
> least as large a place as we now provide for faddish, unsystematic and
> unassessed informal "experiments" or educational "reforms." We
> would advocate the creation of a "FEA" an analogy to the FDA which
> would require well designed clinical trials for every educational
> "drug" that is introduced into the market place. (p. 24)

Another limit on sound educational research is the inherent variability in
human behavior. People think, feel, act, cooperate or don't cooperate, and so
forth. Unlike inanimate objects, their actions are influenced by a range of extra-
neous variables that limit the applicability of findings. Behavioral sciences such
as psychology have evolved standards that enable meaningful research despite
these uncertainties. Unfortunately, many studies ignore them and consumers frequently fail to recognize the inevitable deficiencies and limitations. Thus it is not
uncommon for educational administrators, grant writers, and program developers
to stretch findings beyond their intended meaning or inadvertently to misrepresent results.

Quantitative versus Qualitative Research

Quantitative research includes both descriptive and explanatory studies.
Descriptive studies are concerned only with establishing the existence of a phe-

nomenon of interest—student achievement, for example. How much of it exists, where it exists, and what kinds of it exist are typical descriptive hypotheses. Explanatory studies are concerned with the causes of a phenomenon of interest. For example, does the use of Direct Instruction improve achievement? Technically stated, explanatory studies are concerned with the discovery of functional relationships (i.e., relationships in which the state of a given phenomenon is said to be a function of a preceding event or condition). Less technically said, explanatory studies are concerned with whether a given effect is the result of a particular cause. Causal relationships are examined in experiments and experimentlike studies called quasi-experiments. More is said about experiments below.

Descriptive studies address a wide range of topics. For example, a report of average test scores for students at different schools would be descriptive. So would a study of the number of words comprising recognition vocabulary of children at succeeding ages. Descriptive studies include a number of subtypes. For example, studies of characteristics such as preferred types of play or ability to perform certain intellectual tasks may entail observation of fresh samples of children at successive chronological age levels. Such studies are called "cross-sectional" descriptive research. Studies that examine the same characteristics but observe the same individual children over a period of years are called "longitudinal."

Quantitative descriptive studies also include reports of correlational relationships between variables. An example of a correlational study would be one that describes the degree of relationship between family socioeconomic status and school achievement. Another example is hyperactivity's relationship to junk food consumption. Correlational studies are among those most frequently misinterpreted by users of educational research.

Despite its current unpopularity among educators, there is a great deal of high-quality quantitative research in education. It includes disquieting descriptive findings such as falling SAT scores and reports of low math and science achievement and similarly disquieting experimental results such as those of the Follow Through project. In the opinion of the authors, quantitative research's unpopularity may well be related to its disagreeable results. Findings that affirm orthodoxy are clearly more popular.

Qualitative research in education is a growth industry. It is a type of research long used in fields such as cultural anthropology. Qualitative research relies on written description instead of objective measurement, and its findings are subject to all the vagaries associated with written descriptions of any kind. Rather than attempting to affirm hypotheses and make generalizations that are grounded in an agreed-upon objective framework, qualitative research is more concerned with description as subjectively perceived by an observer in context. Such descriptions are thought to be more honest and realistic than descriptions that purport to be objective and at arm's length. It is a form of research premised on a postmodern, multiculturalist view of science. It argues that the objective understanding to which traditional science aspires is nothing more than an arbitrary Western convention—one educators should be free to reject.

By avoiding a focus on particular variables of interest, qualitative research presumably avoids the imposition of cultural bias. Of course such a process ignores the very information typically sought by the consumer. For example, a teacher's question about whether one teaching method produces greater achievement than another would not be answered by a qualitative study. Qualitative studies do not "prove" or "disprove" anything. They can only describe. The validity of such studies is simply an open question (Krathwohl, 1993).

The vagueness of the methods used in qualitative studies invites observer bias. Observers are necessarily selective in their observations. For example, an observer who dislikes the punishment seen in a classroom may tend to note the negative emotional reactions of students more than would a disinterested observer. By contrast, a more impartial observer might give greater attention to the increased on-task behavior that may be effected by the use of punishment. Although there are ways to make such observations more reliable, they are far more subject to researcher bias than most quantitative reports.

Action Research

Like qualitative research, action research has gained in popularity among educators. Wiersma (1995) describes it as research "conducted by teachers, administrators, or other educational professionals for solving a specific problem or for providing information for decision making at the local level" (p. 11). Action research is typically quantitative but less rigorous in design and methodology than conventional quantitative research. The following is a classroom level example: A teacher is having discipline problems during her fifth-period class. She arranges the desks differently and assesses whether the discipline problems are reduced. A written report of her investigation, including data, analysis, and a brief discussion, would be considered action research. Would such a finding be a sufficient basis for recommending that teachers employ rearranged desks as a means of treating discipline problems? In theory it would not. Practice, however, is another matter. Despite methodological weaknesses—in the present example, a single class sample and no control group—such findings are sometimes used to bolster proposals for new and innovative programs.

Pseudoresearch

Pseudoresearch is a form of scholarly writing that appears to make factual claims based on evidence but, in fact, consists only of opinion founded on opinion. Previous studies are cited, but they contain only theory and opinion. Legitimate empirical reports traditionally present a review of literature that enables the reader to put new findings in context and to strengthen factual generalizations (Stanovich,1996). However, previous studies containing only opinion do nothing to strengthen the report that cites them.

Commonsense educational claims are often supported by such "research." For example, if an expert opines that schooling is improved by greater funding and if other experts cite and endorse that original claim, subsequent reports will contain what appears to be substantiation. If the claim seems plausible and thus goes unquestioned, it appears to gain acceptance as a fact without ever being tested. Such claims are said to be supported by "research" but it is "research" in the sense of a systematic review of relevant literature, not in the sense of studies that offer an empirical foundation for factual assertions.

Educational innovations that are consistent with popular educational doctrines are often supported by such research. The controversial but widely used whole-language reading instruction (discussed below), for example, goes unquestioned by most educators because it fits hand-in-glove with learner-centered pedagogy. It is supported primarily by favorable opinion among like-minded educators, not demonstrated experimental results.

A type of research that seems to produce empirical facts from opinion is a group-interaction process called the Delphi method (Eason, 1992; Strauss & Zeigler, 1975). However, instead of creating the appearance of empirically grounded fact from multiple reports of opinion (as does pseudoresearch), the Delphi method creates facts *about* opinion.

In Delphi research, the opinions of experts are collected and synthesized in a multistage, iterative process. For example, if a researcher sought to determine the future occupations open to high school graduates, he or she might consult a panel consisting of career counselors, former high school students, employers, and economists. The panelists would be asked to compose a list of prospective jobs, and they would each share their list with the other panelists. After viewing the lists of other panelists some members might choose to change their estimations, and their changes would then be shared with the other panelists in a second round of mutual review. Ideally, three or so rounds of sharing and realignment would produce a consensus. The "fact" resulting from such a study is that experts agree about the future availability of certain jobs, not that certain jobs have a high probability of being available.

A recent attempt to find effective institution-to-home "transition strategies" for disabled juvenile delinquents illustrates how a Delphi consensus can be confused with an empirically grounded conclusion. Following three rounds of surveys, Pollard, Pollard, and Meers (1994) concluded that the priorities identified by the panelists provided a "blueprint for successful transition" when, in fact, the surveys produced only a consensus about what may or may not prove to be a successful blueprint.

Rand corporation is credited with developing the Delphi technique as a means of distilling a consensus of expert opinion. Sackman (1974) has summarized its primary shortcomings. The expert status of panelists is not scientifically verifiable and neither is the assumption that group opinion is superior to individual opinion.

One other confusion about the Delphi technique pertains to its use by the leader of a deliberative body. Delphi methodology can create the appearance of consensus where none exists—a problematic outcome of a deliberative process. Technically, the Delphi technique does not force a consensus; but as a practical matter, it is designed to produce a consensus and it puts substantial pressure on dissenters for conformity to the group. When employed by the leadership of a deliberative group, it can turn what should be an open and fair-minded exchange of views into a power struggle. Minority viewpoints can be isolated and marginalized. The result is more mindless conformity than reasoned agreement. The conclusions reached by committees and policy-making bodies can easily be distorted by Delphi methodology.

Experimental and Quasi-Experimental Research

Experiments are quantitative studies in which cause-effect relationships are tested (Campbell and Stanley, 1966). Quasi-experiments attempt the same but with certain limitations. Other studies may suggest or imply causal relationships, but their findings are far more ambiguous and subject to misinterpretation. Experiments are not foolproof, but they afford the best evidence science has to offer.

From a purely scientific standpoint experiments are important because they attempt to answer the primary question with which science is concerned: "What explains or accounts for the phenomenon under investigation?" All sciences aspire to this kind of understanding. They are valuable from a practical standpoint, too, because they address the question of whether a given program, teaching method, treatment, intervention, curriculum, and the like produces expected effects. Because schooling is intended as means of making a difference in the lives of students, the armamentarium of professional educators should contain tools that are well tested and demonstrably effective. Ideally, they should also be convenient, cost-effective, and well received by the student; but at a minimum, they must be effective. The critical importance of experimental evidence in establishing effectiveness is not well understood by educators, but it is just such an understanding that is at the heart of knowing which research is valuable and why.

The aim of science is said to be the explanation of natural phenomena. However, the term *explanation* itself requires a bit of explanation. As the term is used by scientists, *explanation* refers to cause-and-effect explanation. For example, a phenomenon such as achievement in school is said to be explained (or at least partially explained) if it can be shown that the presence or absence of achievement is functionally (i.e., causally) related to a preceding event or set of events termed a *cause*. A functional or causal relationship is initially stated in a tentative form called a hypothesis and is not considered a valid explanation until affirmed by evidence.

Experimental research is the business of collecting evidence that might support or disconfirm causal hypotheses. It entails the manipulation of a hypothesized cause for the purpose of inducing an expected effect. If a given effect (technically, a change in the "dependent variable") follows alteration of the purported cause (technically, a change in the "independent variable"), the causal hypothesis is said to be supported. Other types of quantitative research and even qualitative research may be valuable in suggesting cause-effect hypotheses, but only experimental research can provide a direct test.

Internal and External Validity of Studies

Whether an empirical study is capable of demonstrating a causal relationship is one issue, but whether a given experiment was properly conducted is another. Moreover, even a properly conducted experiment may have limited applicability and usefulness in the "real world." Whether the procedures used in an experiment permit valid findings is the matter of internal validity. Whether the findings of an experiment are generally applicable to the "real world" (i.e., applicable under conditions beyond those under which the study was conducted) is the matter of external validity.

A wide variety of technical considerations can adversely influence the internal validity of an experiment. For example, the manner in which subjects were assigned to treatment and comparison groups can profoundly affect the outcome of an otherwise well-designed experiment. Technical issues with respect to type of sampling and type of population sampled, for example, can greatly influence the external validity of a study. Accurate assessment of these and other technical details requires considerable expertise. Even well-informed investigators may overlook significant threats to the validity of an experiment. Cook and Campbell (1979) provide an authoritative discussion of the myriad considerations that should be considered. Happily there are at least three considerations that a nonexpert can examine to assess the internal validity of a study: source, convergence, and replication.

Source. If a study is reported in a peer-reviewed scholarly journal, chances are good that it meets acceptable standards of internal and external validity. Peer review typically entails blind review of a manuscript by a panel of experts selected by an editor. Panelists are not given the author's name and the author is not given the reviewers' names. All criticisms and replies are exchanged through the editor. The most reputable and selective journals use this process. Reports reviewed only by an editor may be valid, but peer-reviewed scholarship is generally conceded to be the most credible. Again, the process is not foolproof, but it is the best science has to offer. Unpublished reports and reports that are not subject to editorial review—grant proposals and reports of funded research such as those included in the ERIC's Research in Education, for example—are of uncertain quality and should be treated as such.

Convergence. If a study's findings are generally consistent with (i.e., they converge with) the findings of other investigations in an area of research, they are generally assumed credible (Stanovich, 1996). Any competent research report will include a review of relevant literature. Consistencies and discrepancies within the existing literature and between the report at hand and previous studies are analyzed and discussed. Articles called "reviews of literature" and "meta-analyses" are dedicated to citing and summarizing all of the findings relevant to a given topic or area of study. Although new and revolutionary findings are sometimes uncovered by a single study, competent observations of the same or similar phenomena usually result in similar findings. Most scientific advancements come as incremental additions to understanding, not breakthroughs.

Replication. Replications are repeats of an original study by another investigator using a fresh set of subjects. The credibility of a study that has been replicated is greatly enhanced. Findings that have been replicated are considered valid even if they do not converge with other reports in the same general area of investigation. Only a small percentage of studies in the behavioral sciences are replicated, however.

The Need for Both Experiments and Field Testing

Few experimental investigations are able to fully satisfy requirements for both internal and external validity in a single study. The controls, artificial conditions, and other constraints necessary to ensure internal validity tend to interfere with external validity. Conversely, unanticipated and uncontrolled events can confound or invalidate an otherwise well-conceived study that is conducted in a natural environment such as a school. Because of this inherent conflict, programs or interventions derived from experimental investigations should be field tested prior to implementation.

Field tests are trials of an experimentally supported finding in the classroom or clinic or other setting for which it is intended. Not infrequently they result in the discovery of limitations, cautions, and restrictions on the applicability of experimentally validated findings. Even findings that have been field tested elsewhere may lack local applicability because of peculiar local conditions. Thus, large-scale programs, in particular, should also be locally tested on a small scale in what is called a pilot study. Pilot studies are especially important when the implementation of research findings entail significant time and energy costs for school personnel or learning opportunity costs for students.

RESEARCH AND EDUCATIONAL FADS

The failure of schools to employ reasonable precautions in adopting research-based innovations has been directly responsible for much wasted time, money, and educational opportunity (Carnine, 1993, 1995). Fads are marketed like snake oil, and schools often adopt them with little credible evidence that they will work as promised. With taxpayers footing the bill and school personnel tracking the results, accountability is often minimal and adverse consequences rare. Typically once an investment is made, school personnel will either say good things about a program or say nothing at all. In the absence of a competitive marketplace, only students and taxpayers lose.

Despite the minimal risk entailed in adopting new programs, schools do seek to adopt those that seem most likely to succeed, yet they are often saddled with lemons. Naiveté about research is part of the problem, but so is ignorance of history. Today's fads are often nothing more than the latest incarnation of a philosophy or movement that has emerged and reemerged over many years. The learner-centered or child-centered or student-centered education concept noted below is the best example of an idea that has failed historically yet seems to have at least nine lives.

Still, one must ask why professional educators would be so gullible. Many are aware of history and most have the experience necessary to recognize what might work or not work. In a recent copy of *Principal*, a school administrator of 20 years offered the following reasons as to why educators are quick to jump on bandwagons:

- We believe and hear out of ignorance.
- Most education programs for teachers and administrators do a pitiful job of teaching students to differentiate viable research from poor research.
- We like doing whatever is in vogue.
- We tend to move from one fad to another in order to demonstrate that we are "state of the art"—even though most of the activities have little impact.
- We seek a quick fix that will help all children succeed. If it doesn't work, we scrap it and try something else. But there are no quick fixes.

- There is big money in selling educational programs. Consultants use "research says" to sell programs that purportedly can fix just about anything (Walker, 1996, p. 41).

In the following section we discuss selected fads and innovations from the standpoint of their foundations in research. Clearly, considerations other than research play a role in their adoption, but our aim is to show how that in most instances a review and critical analysis of research would reveal weaknesses and raise questions about making a large-scale commitment of resources.

Current Fads

A prime illustration of how innovations with a weak or nonexistent research base can snowball into a movement is the current brain-based learning movement. The brain-based learning bandwagon has gained so much momentum that it has been cited as grounds for federal legislative proposals. Briefer analyses of other recent fashions including constructivism, developmentally appropriate practice, situated learning, authentic assessment, learning styles, and whole-language follow.

Brain-Based Learning

Any educational proposition gains an aura of credibility if it can be tied to research in the hard sciences, and that is indeed the way in which brain-based learning makes use of neuroscience. The neuroscience on which brain-based learning is based is the product of legitimate research in the medical and biological sciences. Brain-based learning principles, however, are dubious interpretations of neuroscience, and their educational application is wholly untested (Bruer, 1997).

Making Connections: Teaching and the Human Brain, by Renate and Geoffrey Caine (1991), was published by the Association for Supervision and Curriculum Development (ASCD) and has been widely disseminated within the education community. Its recommendations regarding instruction are loosely based on "information from the neurosciences" (Regnier, 1996). The authors concede that direct translations of neuroscience findings to educational practice are risky and speculative, but they forge ahead with a list of suggestions.

For example, relying on Epstein's (1978) view that "spurts" in brain weight are related to increases in mental ability, Caine and Caine (1991) suggest that greater amounts of material can be taught during spurts and lesser amounts during suspected "slow growth" periods. Not only is their idea untested, it may have a more fundamental flaw: Epstein's idea is itself not well accepted by biological scientists; to the contrary, it has "long been known that there is little or no relationship between brain weight and brain functioning . . ." (Good & Brophy, 1986, p. 35). In other words, the educational effectiveness of their suggestion is not only unknown, it appears to be founded on questionable neuroscience.

Another claim made by both Caine and Caine (1991) and Healy (1990) is that neuroscience has demonstrated "brain plasticity" or an ability to adapt to new conditions throughout the life span. The notion of brain plasticity appeals to educators because it agrees with the popular educational concept of lifelong learning. Two problems are evident, however. First of all these authors use the concept differently from its use in neuroscience, and furthermore their idea is inconsistent with the evidence. *Plasticity* as the term is used in neuroscience refers to the ability of undamaged parts of the brain to take over the function of damaged areas, not an ability to learn at any age. Second, neuroscientists have shown that true brain plasticity is greatest in young children, less in adolescence, and still less in adulthood (Pascual-Castroviejo, 1996). As do other proponents of brain-based learning, Caine and Caine appear to interpret and redefine neuroscience terms to suit their pedagogic purposes.

A third example of neuroscience interpreted in service of educational theory is Edelman's (1987) concept of "neural Darwinism." Edelman's view is founded on two analogies: that the brain can be thought of as a multilayered jungle and that it grows, changes, and adapts in much the same way as the immune system. Although Edelman's theory is only now undergoing study by neuroscientists, educational implications of neural Darwinism have been given cover-story treatment in widely circulated education periodicals. For example, in a 1994 *Educational Leadership* article, Sylwester asserts "Edelman's model suggests that a jungle-like brain might thrive best in a jungle-like classroom that includes many sensory, cultural, and problem layers that are closely related to the real-world environment" (1994, p. 50). Such a view fits nicely with Sylwester's apparent preference for unstructured, discovery-oriented pedagogy. What Sylwester fails to mention is that his interpretation is unsupported and his recommendation for classroom practice is in disagreement with a substantial body of evidence supporting the educational value of a well-ordered classroom.

Similar freewheeling interpretations of neuroscience are common. Cohen (1995) cites other proponents of brain-based learning as a basis for the assertion that educators need to throw out curriculum, textbooks, worksheets, and separate disciplines on the grounds that such curricular structure is inconsistent with our knowledge of how the brain works. Notably, he presents no evidence as to what happens with student achievement when such changes are implemented. Cohen goes on to say that many current "best practices" (i.e., portfolios, cooperative learning, and thematic curricula) are supported by brain research yet cites no research to vindicate these claims. Plainly, Cohen's references to neuroscience are nothing more than rhetorical props for his beliefs about "best practices" in education.

The value of assessing research-based claims on the basis of their source is well illustrated in the case of Sylwester's "What the Biology of the Brain Tells Us about Learning" (1994). The majority of Sylwester's references were published by one source—Basic Books. Basic Books, a commercial publisher, is also the publisher of Edelman's popular account, *Neural Darwinism* (1987). Not only were they mostly from one commercial publisher, Sylwester's scientific references were drawn from one source—a special issue of *Scientific American*. Well-founded claims typically have a much broader base in research, especially claims that are sufficiently well confirmed to serve as a guide to classroom practice.

Jane Healy is another widely known proponent of brain-based learning. Her *Endangered Minds: Why Children Don't Think and What We Can Do About It* (1990) suggests that societal changes have caused changes in brain structure that are responsible for deficient student achievement. She brings together many recent neuroscience findings, but like other proponents of brain-based learning she selectively draws implications that serve to support "pedagogically correct" views of teaching. For example, Healy says that "research has shown that good readers actively pursue meaning . . ." (p. 298), but offers no research in support of her claim. Her view is really nothing more than an attempt to lend credibility to the widely accepted "constructivist" view of reading.

Like Caine and Caine's *Making Connections* (1991), Healy's book is published by a nonacademic publishing house. It was intended primarily as an explanation for why kids today seem so different from those of previous generations. Many of Healy's ideas are intuitively appealing (e.g., we need good teachers; tailoring the school day and school year to families' schedules will help students and parents; children should be taught to listen effectively) but they are not supported by research. This is not to say that they are demonstrably wrong; rather, they are speculative and unsupported by credible evidence. The same can be said about her hypothesis that society's fast pace and electronic complexity have caused fundamental changes in children's brains. At best, the evidence is merely suggestive and subject to other interpretations. Deficient evidence notwithstanding, Healy draws conclusions and pronounces learner-centered educational orthodoxy vindicated. Her recommendation: If brains have been adversely affected by the environment, schools must change to accommodate them—whatever impact such changes might have on the outcomes of schooling. The idea that schools might act to shape student thinking processes in a way that is conducive to the intellectual characteristics commonly associated with a good education is not considered.

Much more can be said about educational claims that derive from neuroscience, but all suffer from the same general flaw. Bruer states it simply: "Currently, we do not know enough about brain development and neural function to link that understanding directly, in any meaningful and defensible way to instruction and educational practice. [Furthermore] we may never know enough to be able to do that" (1997, p. 4). In truth, brain-based learning appears to be little more than one more attempt to justify the learner-centered educational doctrines that have dominated the education community for decades.

Constructivism and Developmentally Appropriate Practice

Constructivism is an educational doctrine founded on the idea that each individual constructs his or her own understanding and knowledge from personal experience. It implies that schooling should concern itself not with the acquisition of an accepted body of knowledge but with the process of helping students discover and create their own understandings. It is consistent with the poststructuralist and deconstructionist perspectives in literary theory. In education, it is consistent with the progressive/learner-centered view of learning articulated by John Dewey. Dewey held that education should result in an intellectual "growth," not the achievement of preconceived educational outcomes.

Present-day educational constructivism is primarily tied to the concept of intellectual development formulated by the Swiss theorist Jean Piaget. Like Dewey, Piaget viewed intellectual growth as the prime outcome of education and experience the best teacher. Piaget's concept of "adaptation" argues that children construct a personalized grasp of the world by alternately "assimilating" various understandings of the world (called schemata) and refining those understandings through "accommodation." The aim of schooling from the Piagetian perspective is to optimize the "growth" or "adaptation" of the individual by fitting educational experience to the characteristics and proclivities of the individual student. Attainment of conventionally measured student achievement is a secondary and incidental outcome (Stone, 1996).

Piagetian constructivism is the theoretical foundation for what the National Association for the Education of Young Children (NAEYC, 1991) calls "developmentally appropriate practice" (DAP). DAP seeks to facilitate the construction of understanding (i.e., intellectual development) in ways that are compatible with level and pace of the individual's developmental trajectory. It is thoroughly child centered in the sense that children are not prodded or induced to undergo experiences that might be incompatible with what Piagetians suppose is a naturally shaped and therefore optimal developmental progression. DAP avoids subjecting the child to any sort of normative expectations for effort or accomplishment because even these subtle pressures might put a child's longer-term intellectual development at risk.

The practical problem of knowing a student's current level of intellectual development places an additional restriction on developmentally appropriate teaching. Because intellectual development can only be known through overt performance and overt performance is influenced by both learning and maturation, a child sufficiently mature to engage in intellectual tasks beyond his or her present level of performance may not appear ready for instruction. In effect, DAP encourages teachers to await the appearance of intellectual readiness even if a child's apparent lack of readiness is due to deficient motivation—a waiting period that may place the individual far behind peers (Johnson & Johnson, 1992).

DAP reduces a hypothetical risk to intellectual development, but it does so at the expense of teachers' taking a very passive role in fostering academic attainment. However, from the standpoint of DAP's proponents and that of other constructivists, the delayed academic progress of some students is not any legitimate grounds for criticism. In their view, DAP is intended to produce a pattern of intellectual growth unique to the individual, not a pattern of achievement that compares favorably to norms. Thus, exponents would reject the view that DAP is ineffective merely because students fail to learn as defined by conventional measures. Rather they believe that DAP protects children from overly ambitious expectations—a questionable tradeoff in the view of the few parents and other consumers who understand DAP's aims.

Despite DAP's rejection of age-referenced academic expectations, the effectiveness of teaching practices very similar to DAP—"open education" and "discovery learning"—were investigated in the 1960s and 1970s. Open classrooms sought to take away the desks in rows and teacher-directed classroom activities and replace them with rooms containing learning centers and student-directed exploration and discovery. In truth, these innovations of the 1960s were reincarnations of the child-centered classrooms of the 1930s. Student freedom afforded in a facilitative school environment was expected to incite "intrinsic motivation." Learning that had formerly required orderly didactic instruction was expected to emerge as a result of a spontaneous engagement with interesting activities and materials.

The experiment failed. Discovery learning and other experiential methods were found to be more expensive and more time consuming, and they left behind many students who just did not seem to blossom despite facilitating conditions (Good & Brophy, 1986; Rosenshine, 1978). With regard to discovery learning, "the larger, better controlled studies tend[ed] to favor traditional education—especially on achievement measures" (Good & Brophy, 1986, p. 212). Open education was a particularly visible "bust." In a meta-analysis of 153 studies, Giacomia and Hedges (1982) found small negative effects in all areas of achievement and a substantially greater deficit in achievement motivation. In other words, students experiencing the DAP style of teaching not only failed to learn but failed to acquire the motivation necessary to subsequent school success.

John Anderson, Lynne Reder, and Herbert Simon at Carnegie Mellon are among the foremost cognitive psychologists in the United States. Their take on both constructivism and situated learning (discussed below) is that the claims are unproven and, in several respects, at odds with well-known scientific findings (Anderson, Reder, & Simon, 1995). Moreover, their practical worth in the classroom is suspect at best. As with so many other widely known innovations, they flourish within the education community not because they are supported by sound research but because they are well accommodated to the prevailing learner-centered orthodoxy and unchallenged by demands for accountability.

Situated Learning

Situated learning is another example of an idea about teaching that has gained acceptance within the education community not because of its demonstrated effectiveness but because of its compatibility with the learner-centered perspective. Again, educational concepts that are very like what is now called situated learning can be found in writings of John Dewey and William Heard Kilpatrick. Both called for a curriculum built around student projects and both believed that experience is the best teacher. In Dewey's view, human evolution had selected intellectual abilities that made learning from experience the most natural and most effective form of education (Stone, 1996). Dewey argued that challenging students with true-to-life problems would eliminate the rigors and artificialities of traditional classroom instruction while making schooling both more effective and more attractive to the learner.

The core principle of situated learning similarly argues that anything learned in the context of the situation to which it will be applied is learned more thoroughly and in a more useable form. Situated learning is thought to provide not only context for learning but an incentive that is missing from classroom exercises. Situated learning is consistent with the idea of "hands-on" educational experiences and it argues for the use of "authentic assessment" (discussed below) rather than conventional tests and classroom exercises. For example, the situated-learning approach to teaching math might entail student participation in a construction project. Otherwise boring math skills could be practiced by estimating the quantity of needed materials. Presumably the project would make the learning activity more attractive (i.e., intrinsically interesting and socially engaging) and the circumstance would ensure that the acquired math skills would be integrated with other skills such as measurement and thus made useful in the real world. Isolated and decontextualized "book learning" would be avoided. Too, failure or success in completing the project would give students real-world feedback about the quality of their skills as well as provide the teacher a visible indication of how much and how well they had learned.

Despite its motivational appeal and the merits of learning in context, enthusiasts give little attention to situated learning's prospective shortcomings. Its primary weaknesses are inefficiency, cost, and uncertainty of outcome. Traditional schooling attempts to teach by breaking the learner's task into a series of simpler, more manageable tasks and building on these basics. Situated learning starts learners at the application level and attempts to teach the basics later. It appeals to students, but its effectiveness has not been demonstrated. Individuals who do learn via such experiences may be highly motivated at the outset, but reality can quickly take its toll. For example, novice tennis players who begin by attempting to play competitively quickly discover that stroking the ball is not as easy as it looks on television. Frustration and discouragement theoretically are overcome by mentoring, but whether they do so in fact has yet to be empirically validated.

In the judgment of Anderson, Reder, and Simon (1996), the claims made for situated learning are not only excessive, they ignore or reject much that is known about the value of abstract and decontextualized learning. Situated learning is recommended when time-tested practices might be simpler and more effective. "It is a well documented fact of human cognition that large tasks decompose into nearly independent subtasks" thus enabling simplification of the learner's task (Anderson, Reder, and Simon, 1995, p. 3). For example, the acquisition of useful computation skills does not require one to learn addition and substraction in the context of doing one's income tax. Moreover, in at least some areas of instruction, abstract and generalized learning is more efficient than contextualized methods because it only requires the learner to apply known concepts to new circumstances. By contrast, learning closely tied to a specific task and context may require the learner to retrain completely for each new application.

Other researchers argue that situated learning can be detrimental. Shiffrin and Schneider (1977) and Winn (1994) suggest that specific skills learned in context may actually work to the learner's disadvantage. They conclude that the automaticity associated with expert performance of a given task may encourage the development of inflexible and difficult-to-generalize skills. In other words, at least some skills are more useful if they are taught as abstractions rather than in context.

Anderson, Reder, and Simon (1996) object to other situated learning's claims as well. Citing a body of psychological research that has accumulated since the mid-1800s, they argue that situated learning's proponents ignore a large number of studies that show that training in one context can be transferred to a novel situation or task. For example, skill in using one word-processing editor can make the acquisition of proficiency in the use of a second editor far quicker and easier. Thus contrary to the studies that have been highlighted by situated-learning proponents—ones in which transfer did not take place (Glick & Holyoak, 1980, 1983)—Anderson, Reder, and Simon find successful transfer a common occurrence. Not only is transfer common, it can often be prompted by something as simple as a suggestion that a previous task and a new task have certain features in common. Again, their conclusion is that classroom exercises and "book learning" do not somehow disadvantage the learner (Hunter & Hunter, 1984) but, in fact, are often enabling.

Situated learning and the many other variants of contextualized learning have a huge intuitive appeal. Everyone can think of personal examples in which they learned well through experience and mentoring. The problem is that much of what students are expected to learn in schools requires understanding of the decontextualized symbols and abstractions that represent the distilled experiences of previous generations. Unassisted access to this wealth of experience requires proficiency in accurately decoding and making use of information represented in this form.

The primary adaptive value of education is that it equips the learner for future conduct. Learning in a naturally occurring context may be a richer and more meaningful experience, but the advantage of the educated over those familiar only with immediate experience is that the educated have much greater knowledge of and access to the experience of others. In the face of uncertainty, the educated are better equipped to anticipate which paths of action lead to which ends. Thus possession of a fund of abstract and symbolic information and demonstrated proficiency in decoding the enormous body of written and spoken knowledge is a significant adaptive advantage that seems slighted by situated learning.

Dewey may have been correct in arguing that the human species is better equipped to learn from experience than from exposure to symbols and abstractions. In fact, his view is consistent with the observation that the human ability to compress past experience into symbolic information and to store it outside the body is a relatively recent development in human history. Yet it is precisely because the benefits of widespread access to such information are so enormous that all modern societies have some system of formal education; and in an information age, proficiency with symbols and abstractions are of unprecedented importance.

Even if decontextualized, learning is more challenging and less immediately satisfying than hands-on, contextualized experience, and competence with symbols and abstractions must be education's chief priority. Situated learning and other forms of learning in context may be attractive to the learner, but their cost effectiveness in producing adequate levels of literacy and numeracy are unproven at best. An individual's opportunity to learn is not unlimited. Students have only so many unencumbered years. Adults have only so many years during which they can make use of that which they have learned. Socioeconomic communities compete with each other, and investment in education pays off only to the point that it remains an economic advantage. Schooling that places student satisfaction ahead of these economic realities is disadvantageous and in the longer term unsustainable.

Authentic Assessment

Authentic assessment is a means of measuring student learning in which life-like tasks or their products are observed. For example, the ability to use nouns and verbs correctly might be assessed by observation of students writing a letter rather than by counting correct responses to exam items. The ability to read might be assessed by observation of students using a recipe to bake a cake rather than by listening to them reading. Other names for this kind of assessment are direct assessment and performance assessment. The term *portfolio assessment* refers to the practice of collecting "best" authentic products over a period of time as a measure of overall achievement.

As is the case with so many educational innovations, authentic assessment is well regarded less because of its value in precisely appraising academic progress than its compatibility with a learner-centered vision of schooling. It fits Dewey's view that the outcomes of schooling should reflect the aims of the learner, not the aims of some external agent such as a school board. It is compatible with constructivism and situated learning and for the same reason. Each viewpoint reaches the learner-centered conclusion that standards for learning should consider that which is important to the learner rather than merely that which is important from the standpoint of an imposed standard.

There are shades of opinion among authentic assessment proponents as to the precise role of external standards in judging quality. At the extreme are constructivists who argue against the application of any standards. In the opinion of Anderson, Reder, and Simon (1995, p. 20), "The denial of the possibility of objective evaluation could be the most radical and far-reaching of the constructivist claims." For example, Madaus (1994) argues against tests on the grounds that they construct, control, and dominate social persons and thus are instruments of social and political control.

The primary argument on behalf of authentic assessment is that it avoids student learning intended merely to pass tests rather than gain integrated knowledge and useful skills. It does so by requiring application-level educational outcomes in which the individual learner presumably has a stake. Its weakness, however, is that application-level performances can be superficial and misleading, and assessments based on them can overlook important aspects of learning (Baker, O'Neil, & Linn, 1993).

Application-level competence is clearly a desirable schooling outcome, but it is assumed that such demonstrations are an expression of more generalized understanding and ability. In fact, successful performance under authentic conditions may or may not represent a grasp of critically important knowledge and skills. For example, if students working in a cooperative group successfully repair an automobile, their performance may seem to demonstrate that they are able to read a repair manual and order parts correctly. In truth, it may indicate only that they are able to follow the advice of a knowledgeable friend or parts store clerk.

The key difference between authentic assessment and conventional educational measurement lies in the purposes they are best suited to serve. Conventional assessments measure whether students are able to decode accurately and interpret information presented in symbolic and abstract form. Can they accurately interpret a communication? Do they get the message? Do they understand the question and know the relevant information? Authentic assessment is best suited to determining whether students are able to carry out a task or activity successfully. Can they solve the problem? Can they complete the task however they go about it?

Performance founded only on previous experience in doing an activity or task may tell the observer nothing about the learners' knowledge and understanding or their ability to make use of knowledge and understanding. Exclusive use of authentic assessment not only makes possible schooling that ignores learner capability with the use of symbols and abstractions, it encourages the exclusive use of the hands-on, experience-oriented teaching methods that may avoid reading and writing entirely.

Assessment of student ability to engage in real-world tasks and activities has traditionally been a part of classroom instruction. What is new with the current emphasis on "authentic assessment" is the notion that such assessments should be used exclusively (i.e., in place of conventional tests, even where the assessment is a basis for educational accountability). If schools are to be accountable for both conventional and application-level outcomes, both types of assessment are needed.

Authentic assessment is plagued with other difficulties as well. From a technical standpoint, there are problems with reliability, validity, and cost (Willson, 1991). Reliability is the matter of consistency in measurement. For example, if the readings of a bathroom scale vary only slightly when an individual steps off and on again, its readings would be termed reliable. Of course, it could be consistently wrong by 50 pounds. If, in addition, the scale's readings correctly showed the weight of a 100-pound object to be 100 pounds, the scale would also be called valid.

Because reliability is a prerequisite to validity, authentic assessment has problems in both areas. Authentic assessment typically requires observations of products and performances made by multiple observers. Often the observers disagree by unacceptably large amounts. If observers cannot agree as to the quality of a product or performance, their reports—individually or collectively—cannot be treated as valid.

Despite strenuous efforts to improve consistency through the use of trained raters, detailed scoring guidelines, and other means, inter-rater reliability remains an expensive problem and major limitation. Hoover (as cited by Willson, 1991) estimates the extra expense entailed by authentic assessment to be 10 to 100 times that associated with traditional methods of testing. In contrast, less expensive traditional tests "(a) are actually effective; (b) are free of unwanted negative consequences; (c) meet established and reasonable psychometric criteria for validity, reliability and freedom from bias" (Hambleton & Murphy, 1992, p. 10). Hambleton and Murphy modestly suggest that much more research needs to be done before authentic assessment is used exclusively.

Authentic assessment's popularity is not founded on a body of findings that show it to be a vast improvement over conventional testing. If anything, it is less reliable, less valid, and more expensive (Baker, O'Neill, & Linn, 1993). Rather, it has gained the attention of educators because it sets real-life performance as the defining measure of school achievement. From the standpoint of learner-centered pedagogy, such indicators are an enormous advancement over the narrow, fragmented, and decontextualized knowledge and skills required by traditional objective tests. However, as a means of assessing student understanding and proficiency in the use of symbols and abstractions—the core of what it means to be an educated person—authentic assessment is uncertain at best.

Cooperative Learning

Cooperative learning is another "hot" educational methodology. Woolfolk (1998) defines it as an "arrangement in which students work in mixed-ability groups and are responsible for each other's learning" (p. 350). The presumed advantage of cooperative learning is that students will gain in cooperative social skills while achieving academically at levels equal to or greater than those associated with traditional instruction. Instead of encouraging students to compete, cooperative learning encourages them to assist each other. Instead of encouraging students to rely on teacher direction, cooperative learning encourages them to rely on each other.

Cooperative learning is only the most recent incarnation of an idea that has emerged repeatedly in American educational history: instruction through small-group interaction (Lorge, Fox, Davitz, & Brenner, 1958). Eighty years ago, William Heard Kilpatrick's *The Project Method* urged schooling centered around group projects. Very similar methodology is today called "project-based learning" (Stern, 1996) and is thought to be the cutting edge of educational innovation. Another version of learning via group interaction is the discussion-group methodology that was popular in the 1950s and 1960s (Hare, 1962). Both project groups and discussion groups were attempts to harness group-interaction processes to the task of teaching. Both methods improved student motivation and student satisfaction, but neither succeeded in significantly improving conventionally measured achievement. Again, as with so many teaching practices, project-oriented groups and discussion-group methods have gained popularity not because of their demonstrated effectiveness but because of their fit with the learner-centered view of teaching. From the learner-centered perspective, if man is by nature social and knowledge is a social and cultural construct, then an interactive social context must be more naturally conducive to learning than the traditional isolated learning activities.

Does cooperative learning work as advertised? The answer depends on which of its many versions is considered and for which students. There is a rather large body of research on cooperative learning, and overall it shows that cooperative learning does produce modest achievement effects (Slavin, 1995). A possible weakness, however, is that not all members of cooperative groups benefit, and it may be that cooperative learning benefits lower-achieving students at the expense of those who are more talented (Druckman & Bjork, 1994). Cooperative learning groups are typically heterogeneous, meaning they are comprised of students with varying ability levels. Stevens and Slavin (1995) found effective benefits and achievement gains for all students as a result of cooperative practices in an elementary school. Special education students, however, made the greatest gains. A study reported by Bramlett (1994) similarly found achievement gains only for the lowest one-third of students. No studies of cooperative learning have found exceptional benefits for high ability students.

Cooperative learning has gained a reputation as an innovative teaching methodology that is more than a mere fad. It works. Robert Slavin (1995)—the creator of cooperative learning—identifies two crucial elements to the successful use of cooperative methods: There must be some type of reward or recognition for the group and there must be individual accountability for members of the group. When these two conditions are met, cooperative learning usually succeeds. However, should cooperative learning be considered a primary tool for teaching in the public schools? The answer is a matter of educational priorities.

Clearly, cooperative learning does produce achievement and it is an improvement over various other forms of instruction, but should schools settle for modest achievement gains or limited gains with more talented students as a price of achieving social and emotional ones? In other words, should social and motivational outcomes be put on an equal plane with academic outcomes? The teaching profession may say yes, but the public would probably disagree. On balance, parents and policy makers want achievement to be an unrivaled priority. Most parents, especially parents of intellectually talented students, want their child's abilities maximized, not constrained by socially oriented pedagogy.

Learning Styles, Individual Differences, Diversity, and Attribute–Treatment Interaction Research

The idea of fitting instruction to the unique characteristics of the student is one of the most intuitively appealing notions in pedagogic theory and one of the oldest modes of learner-centered education. It originated with the child study movement of the early 1900s (Spaulding, 1903) and has been researched repeatedly since (e.g., Davis, 1948; Caplan & Ruble, 1964). In the view of proponents, if learners have unique social, emotional, and intellectual characteristics, it should be possible to optimize learning by fitting schooling to them. Not only has learning style research been dedicated to this idea, many studies that are technically concerned with aptitude, personality, and developmental assessment have been enlisted in the effort. These areas of investigation are not all recognized as such but, in principle, all might be included under the broad heading of attribute-treatment interaction research (Snow & Swanson, 1992).

The general problem with regard to studies of student attributes and their relationship to achievement is that numerous differences in personality, intelligence, learning styles, and other characteristics have been described, but appropriate intervention has been only suggested or left to the imagination of the teacher. In other words, they are long on diagnosis but short on treatment. The many studies identifying learning styles illustrate the problem (Entwistle, 1981; Snow, 1992). As Slavin puts it: "What has never been studied, to my knowledge, is the question of whether teachers who adapt to students' styles get better results than those who don't" (cited in Ellis & Fouts, 1993, p. 69). Studies of multicultural diversity are broad attempts to identify race, gender, language, and other group differences that correlate with educational outcomes—again, for the purpose of better fitting schooling to the student. They too are long on diagnosis and short on proven interventions. Many differences are identified, but the matter of how to fit schooling to those differences in some advantageous way is left unanswered. In truth, the attention given studies of individual differences and diversity bears little relationship to their usefulness in improving academic achievement. Rather, they are a product of Dewey's learner-centered view buttressed by social and political considerations.

The core problem in interpreting research on student differences is knowing whether the relationships that have been discovered are functional relationships (i.e., causal relationships) or merely incidental correlations. In other words, do the correlations between race or gender or learning style and school success mean that schools can take some action that would improve outcomes? Despite any clear indication of what, if anything, about the school environment may be responsible for some groups performing less well than others, schools are frequently stampeded into making changes and accommodations that generally presume that diversity has been insufficiently accommodated or welcomed. Changes in teaching, organization, funding, hiring practices, curricular content, faculty training, pupil assignments, and leadership are only some of the responses that have been undertaken and, in general, they have shown little systematic relationship to achievement.

A case can be made that accommodations to race and gender differences, for example, have at least resulted in gains such as lessened stereotyping and greater racial tolerance, but even these nonacademic gains are not an unmixed blessing. Interventions based on a premise that differences are related to deficiencies suggest the condescending notion that differences are disadvantages—a view that contains the seeds of self-fulfilling prophecy and a ready-made excuse for failure.

Whole-Language

Whole-language reading instruction is premised on the idea that children can and should learn to read "naturally" (i.e., through the same socialization processes that teach them to speak). It calls for reading instruction to be indirect, unsystematic, and nonintensive and it assumes that structured, sequenced, skill-building approaches to reading are likely to be harmful. Again, the influence of learner-centered education is evident.

Everyday observations seem to contradict whole-language's assumptions. As the Canadian Organization for Quality Education has observed, virtually every toddler learns to speak and communicate, but there is a large number of adults who never learn to read (Dare, 1997). In a world in which the printed word is ubiquitous and literacy is common, how could so many not learn? Plainly, even if there is some natural socialization process that will produce competence in reading, the necessary conditions are not as widely available as those that engender speech. Repeated studies of whole-language versus phonics-based reading instruction have found the structured phonics-based methods to be more effective—especially with at-risk students (Chall, 1967/1983). Yet, disagreement persists about the quality of the underlying research and even which outcomes are most important (Carbo, 1988; Turner, 1989). A recent summary of experimental findings, however, makes it clear that if schools are to reduce the growing number of poor readers—40% of third grade students lack proficiency—they need to think of phonics, not whole language (Grossen, 1997): "Treatment intervention research has shown that appropriate early direct instruction seems to be the best medicine for reading problems. Reading is not developmental or natural, but is learned. Reading difficulties reflect a persistent deficit, rather than a developmental lag in linguistic (phonological) skills and basic reading skills. Children who fall behind at an early age (K and grade 1) fall further and further behind over time."

Previous comparisons have found little support for whole language. Stahl and Miller's (1989) comprehensive review found no evidence that whole language produced stronger effects than basal programs, and in a number of investigations, poorer results were reported. Examining the conceptual basis for whole-language, Vellutino (1991) states, "I think it is fair to say that the major theoretical assumptions on which whole-language approach to instruction are based have simply not been verified in relevant research testing those assumptions" (p. 442).

By contrast, there is a wealth of experimental research demonstrating the value of reading instruction using artificially taught decoding skills (i.e., phonics). Foorman (1994) compared phonics-based reading instruction with whole-language and found phonics clearly superior. Her findings are consistent with those of Paulu (1988), Adams (1990), Brown and Felton (1990), Engelmann (1992), Groff (1994), and Sears and Keogh (1993), among others. The accumulated evidence seems clear as to which methodology is best suited to producing the educational outcomes wanted by parents and policy makers.

Current Fads and Innovations: A Common Impediment

The learner-centered vision of schooling is a thread to which all of the above innovations are linked, and it contains a concept that is responsible for both their marginal effectiveness and their lack of experimental support: It is the idea that true learning can come only from an inner or intrinsic motivation. Learner-centered schooling presumes that a well-fitted learning environment will produce a spontaneous and "intrinsically motivated" student effort—one commensurate with optimal learning outcomes for the student (Stone, 1996). If the student fails to experience such an urge, the deficiency is presumed due to some lack of environmental accommodation, not a shortcoming on the part of the student. In other words, the student is expected to act only out of a genuine sense of interest and enthusiasm, not one of responsibility or dedication, and certainly not in response to any extrinsic pressures or inducements.

Such a perspective presents a formidable if not insurmountable challenge to the teacher. Extensive empirical evidence demonstrates that learning requires time, attention, and action on the part of the student (Pirolli & Anderson, 1985; Steinberg, 1996), yet the learner-centered teacher is permitted only to accommodate the student's needs and to otherwise await the student's cooperation. Whether a teacher views his or her task as one of accommodating to spurts in brain growth or engaging students in cooperative activities, student effort is needed. Teacher-directed intervention, however, is considered an intrusion into naturally occurring learning and development processes and is presumed capable of causing harm.

In the end, the learner-centered vision leaves teachers and schools with the responsibility of getting students to undertake the activities that are essential to educational success, but they are sharply restricted in the kind of steps they can take. They are expected to energize and excite but prohibited from directing, inducing, impelling, or otherwise taking action that might not be well received by the student. In other words, from the student's standpoint, effort in the learner-centered school is optional and expected only if the individual "feels" so inclined.

The practical teaching and learning problems that flow from the learner-centered view are obvious to experienced educators, yet the learner-centered orthodoxy is so powerful that more directive teaching practices are considered beyond the realm of competent and ethical discussion. Many who administer America's public schools believe that students are harmed if teachers insist that they pay attention, study, and behave themselves. In the absence of adult insistence on appropriate constructive activity, students are drawn to the activities encouraged by peer groups, commercial interests, and other noneducational influences.

A second shortcoming of the above-discussed innovations stems from the way in which the learner-centered vision frames the question of teaching effectiveness. Again, the root difficulty is the idea that true learning is a function of intrinsic or endogenous factors, not some external agent. School and classroom conditions are thought to influence outcomes only to the extent that they accommodate the unique proclivities of the individual learner. These external or exogenous conditions are considered relevant not as agents of change but merely as conditions that facilitate the working of endogenous agents. In other words, the actions of teachers and schools are not intended as independent variables that stand in some causal relationship to schooling outcomes. Rather, they are ad hoc adjustments made in anticipation of or in response to student idiosyncrasies that presumably permit the successful working of the endogenous causes of learning.

As an example, the developmentally appropriate practice viewpoint holds that learning occurs when development has advanced sufficiently and appropriate facilitating conditions are in place. The factor primarily responsible for learning is the student's endogenous development, and the teacher's contribution is a secondary one of affording proper accommodations. Conceptually, the teacher's actions do not produce the outcome. Rather, the teacher facilitates an outcome that is some unique product that issues from the confluence of developmental processes and exogenous conditions comprising school, home, and all other influences. Constructivists, for example, say that the resulting student understanding is "constructed" by the student. Thus, experiments in which teacher actions and school conditions are treated as causes of learning are conceptually questionable.

Given such a framework, it is not surprising that most learner-centered educational practices have only been the subject of descriptive studies, not experiments. The actions of the endogenous developmental agents can only be inferred from secondary indicators such as age or student success in performing certain tasks. Measurement of these indicators permits researchers to conduct studies in which academic achievement is forecasted (i.e., descriptive or correlational studies), but the less ambiguous experimental studies are largely precluded. Experiments require systematic manipulation of "independent variables" (i.e., hypothesized causal influences) for the purpose of affirming or disconfirming their impact on outcomes.

Effective, Research-Based Educational Methods

There are studies that demonstrate effective teaching methods, but they are not well accepted by a teaching community that has been indoctrinated in the learner-centered thinking. By and large, the effective methods conceive of teachers as causal agents rather than facilitators of learning induced by other agents. References to many of these reports can be found in the articles noted above by Ellson (1986) and Walberg (1990, 1992). Other reviews of literature and meta-analyses of research add to the conclusion that effective methodologies are available but little used (Ellis & Fouts, 1993; Lipsey & Wilson, 1993). In most cases, the effective interventions are structured, teacher-directed, and designed to produce preordained academic and intellectual outcomes. In contrast to the interventions such as brain-based learning, developmentally appropriate practice, and others, most are *learning-centered*, not learner-centered (i.e., they are intended to induce or impel certain activities and outcomes, not merely energize and excite).

Broadly speaking, these are studies of methodologies intended to produce what the public wants from its schools: measurable academic achievement. The mainstream education community ignores or rejects them as antiquated, too artificial and mechanical, overly reliant on extrinsic motivation, and generally unenlightened. The evidence, however, generally illustrates that they are more effective and efficient than the prevailing learner-centered approaches.

WHICH RESEARCH, WHICH AIMS?

This chapter began with the question of how there could be so much research yet so little improvement in the achievement of students, and it has attempted to show that much of popular educational research is not intended to serve the public's educational aims. Choosing credible research is to a very great extent a matter of understanding the educational aims that a particular piece of research is intended to serve. There is a body of educational research that in a reasonably impartial way demonstrates the effectiveness of various educational methodologies and the ineffectiveness of others. Examples of such research have been cited throughout this chapter. They include the Follow Through findings (Proper & St. Pierre, 1980; Engelmann, Becker, Carnine, & Gersten,1988) and the many studies cited by Ellson (1986), Walberg (1990, 1992), Lipsey and Wilson (1993), and others. Such reports are plentiful and found in journals such as *Review of Educational Research, Journal of Applied Behavior Analysis*, the *American Psychologist*, and numerous other peer-reviewed scholarly journals.

There is also a substantial body of educational research that is said to represent the best and most up-to-date findings, but it is dedicated to conceptions of education that do not consider academic achievement to be the highest priority (see Heffernan, 1958, for an excellent illustration of turn-of-the-century concepts introduced as the cutting edge of educational thinking). Many of these studies have also been cited above. It is research that places objectives such as student satisfaction, enhanced self-esteem, equity, social justice, and other nonacademic outcomes as equal or superior to academic achievement. It is very often nonexperimental or even nonempirical, and its objectives, however laudable, are not advantageous from the standpoint of optimized academic achievement. Frequently it is this type of research that is cited in support of popular educational innovations. Educational innovations based on such research are adopted not because they afford the kind of education most parents want for their children but because they constitute what many educators believe to be a superior view of schooling (i.e., a learner-centered view). Thus there is much research and relatively little improvement because the kind of research that best suits the public's aims is only infrequently implemented by the schools.

REFERENCES

Adams, M.J. (1990). *Beginning to read: Thinking and learning about print*. Cambridge, MA: MIT Press.

Anderson, J.R., Reder, L.M., & Simon, H.A. (1995). *Applications and misapplications of cognitive psychology to mathematics education*. Unpublished manuscript. Department of Psychology, Carnegie Mellon University (accessible at http://www.psy.cmu.edu/~mm4b/misapplied.html).

Anderson, J.R., Reder, L.M., & Simon, H.A. (1996). Situated learning and education. *Educational Researcher, 25*(4), 5–11.

Baker, E.L., O'Neil, H.F., & Linn, R.L. (1993). Policy and validity prospects for performance-based assessment. *American Psychologist, 48*(12), 1210–1218.

Bramlett, R.K. (1994). Scientific practitioner: Implementing cooperative learning: A field study evaluating issues for school-based consultants. *Journal of School Psychology, 32*, 67–84.

Brown, I.S., & Felton, R.H. (1990). Effects of instruction on beginning reading skills in children at risk for reading disability. *Reading and Writing: An Interdisciplinary Journal, 2*, 223–241.

Bruer, J.T. (1997). Education and the brain: A bridge too far. *Educational Researcher, 26*(8), 4–16.

Caine, R.N., & Caine, G. (1991). *Making connections: Teaching and the human brain.* Alexandria, VA: Association for Supervision and Curriculum Development.

Campbell, D., & Stanley, J. (1966). *Experimental and quasi-experimental designs for research.* Skokie, IL: Rand McNally.

Caplan, S.W., & Ruble, R. (1964). A study of culturally imposed factors on school achievement in a metropolitan area. *Journal of Educational Research, 58,* 16–21.

Carbo, M. (1988). Debunking the great phonics myth. *Phi Delta Kappan, 70,* 226–240.

Chall, J. (1967/1983). Learning to read: The great debate. New York: McGraw-Hill.

Carnine, D. (1993, December 8). Facts over fads. *Education Week,* p. 40.

Carnine, D. (1995, May 3). Is innovation always good? *Education Week,* p. 40.

Clay, M.M. (1988). *Studying developmental change with a successful intervention.* Unpublished paper. (ERIC Document Reproduction Service ED 299 556).

Cohen, P. (1995). Understanding the brain: Educators seek to apply brain based research. *Education Update, 37* [Online Document]. Available at http ://www.ascd.org/pubs/eu/septu95.html.

Cook, T.D, & Campbell, D.T. (1979). *Quasi-experimentation, design & analysis issues for field settings.* Boston: Houghton Mifflin.

Cremin, L.A. (1964). *The transformation of the school: Progressivism in American education 1876–1957.* New York: Vintage Books.

Cuban, L. (1993). *How teachers taught: Constancy and change in American classrooms, 1890–1990.* New York: Teachers College Press.

Dare, M. (1997). *Backgrounder #1: Learning to read.* Organization for Quality Education. [Online Document]. Available at http://www.interlog.co.

Darling-Hammond, L., Griffin, G., Wise, A. (1992). *Excellence in teacher education: Helping teachers develop learner-centered schools.* Washington, DC: National Education Association.

Davis, R.A. (1943). Applicability of applications of psychology with particular reference to schoolroom learning. *Journal of Educational Research, 37,* 19–30.

Davis, W.A. (1948). *Social class influences upon learning.* Cambridge: MA: Harvard University Press.

Dewey, J. (1916/1963). *Democracy and education.* New York: Macmillan Publishing USA.

Druckman, D., & Bjork, R.A. (Eds.). (1994). *Learning, remembering, believing: Enhancing team and individual performance.* Washington, DC: National Academy Press.

Eason, S. (1992, January). *Power assessment and the Delphi process.* Unpublished paper presented at the annual meeting of the Southwest Educational Research Association, Houston, TX.

Edelman, G. (1987). *Neural Darwinism: The theory of neuronal group selection.* New York: Basic Books.

Ellis, A.K., & Fouts, J.T. (1993). *Research on educational innovations.* Princeton Junction, NJ: Eye on Education, Inc.

Ellson, D. (1986, October). Improving teaching productivity. *Phi Delta Kappan,* 111–124.

Engelmann, S. (1992). *War against the schools' academic child abuse.* Portland, OR: Halcyon House.

Engelmann, S., Becker. W.C. Carnine, D., & Gersten, R. (1988). The Direct Instruction Follow Through model: Design and outcomes. *Education and the Treatment of Children, 11,* 303–317.

Entwistle, N. (1981). *Styles of learning and teaching.* New York: Wiley.

Epstein, H. (1978). Growth spurts during brain development: Implications for educational policy and practice. In J. Chall and A. Mirsky (Eds.), *Education and the brain: The 77th yearbook of the national society for the study of education, part II.* Chicago: University of Chicago Press.

Foorman, B.R. (1994). Exploring connections among reading, spelling, and phonemic segmentation during first grade. *Reading and Writing: An Interdisciplinary Journal, 6,* 65–91.

Giacomia, R.M., & Hedges, L.V. (1982). Identifying features of effective open education. *Review of Educational Research, 52,* 579–602.

Glick, M.L., & Holyoak, K.J. (1980). Analogical problem solving. *Cognitive Psychology, 12,* 306–355.

Glick, M.L., & Holyoak, K.J. (1983). Schema induction and analogical transfer. *Cognitive Psychology, 15,* 1–38.

Good, T.L., & Brophy, J.E. (1986). *Educational psychology* (3rd ed). New York: Longman.

Groff, P. (1994, January). Rethinking whole language. *Executive Educator, 16*(1), 33–35.

Grossen, B. (1997). 30 years of research: What we now know about how children learn to read. A synthesis of research on reading from the National Institute of Child Health and Human Development commissioned by the Center for the Future of Teaching and Learning with funding support from the Pacific Bell Foundation.
http://www.cftl.org/30years/30years.html

Hambleton, R.K., & Murphy, E. (1992). A psychometric perspective on authentic measurement. *Applied Measurement in Education, 5,* 1–16.

Hare, A.P. (1962). *Handbook of small group research.* New York: Free Press.

Healy, J.M. (1990). *Endangered minds: Why children don't think and what we can do about it.* New York: Simon & Schuster.

Heffernan, H. (1958). Evaluation—more than testing. *National Education Association Journal, 47,* 227–229.

Hilgard, E.R. (1939). The relation of schools of psychology to educational practices. *California Journal of Elementary Education, 8,* 17–26.

Hirsch, E.D. (1996). *The schools we need and why we don't have them.* New York: Doubleday.

House, E., Glass, G., McLean, L., & Walker, D. (1978). No simple answer: Critique of the Follow Through evaluation. *Harvard Educational Review, 48,* 128–160.

Hunter, J.E., & Hunter, R.F. (1984). Validity and utility of alternative predictors of job performance. *Psychological Bulletin, 96,* 72–98.

Johnson, J., & Immerwahr, J. (1994). *First things first: What Americans expect from the public schools (a report from Public Agenda).* New York: Public Agenda.

Johnson, J.E., & Johnson, K.M. (1992). Clarifying the developmental perspective in response to Carta, Schwartz, Atwater, and McConnell. *Topics in Early Childhood Special Education, 12*(4), 439–457.

Krathwohl, D.R. (1993). *Methods of educational and social science research: An integrated approach.* New York: Longman.

Lieberman, M. (1993). *Public education, an autopsy.* Cambridge, MA: Harvard University Press.

Lipsey, M.W., & Wilson, D.B. (1993). The efficacy of psychological, educational, and behavioral treatment: Confirmation from meta-analysis. *American Psychologist, 48,* 1181–1209.

Lorge, I., Fox, D., Davitz, J., & Brenner, M.A. (1958). A survey of studies contrasting the quality of group performance and individual performance, 1920–1957. *Psychological Bulletin, 53,* 337–372.

Madaus, G.F. (1994). Testing's place in society: An essay review of "Testing testing: Social consequences of the examined life" by F. Allen Hanson. *American Journal of Education, 102*, 222–234.

NAEYC [National Association for the Education of Young Children]. (1991 March). Guidelines for appropriate curriculum content and assessment in programs serving children ages 3 through 8: A position statement of the National Association for the Education of Young Children and the National Association for the Education of Early Childhood Specialists in State Departments of Education. *Young Children*, 21–38.

National Commission on Excellence in Education. (1983). *A nation at risk: The imperative for educational reform*. Washington, DC: U.S. Department of Education.

Olson, L. (1997, January 22). Keeping tabs on quality. In Quality counts, an Education Week/Pew Charitable Trusts special report on the condition of education in the 50 states. *Education Week, 16* (Suppl.), 7–11, 14–17.

Pascual-Castroviejo, I. (1996). Neuronal plasticity. *Review of Neurology, 24*, 1361–1366.

Paulu, N. (1988). *What we know about phonics: Research in brief*. Office for Educational Research and Improvement. (ERIC Document 297–298).

Pirolli, P.L., & Anderson, J.R. (1985). The role of practice in fact retrieval. *Journal of Experimental Psychology: Learning, Memory, & Cognition, 11*, 136–153.

Pollard, R.R., Pollard, C.J., & Meers, G. (1994). Determining effective transition strategies for adjudicated youth with disabilities: A national Delphi study. *Journal of Correctional Education, 45*, 190–196.

Proper, E.C., & St. Pierre, R.G. (1980). *A search for potential new Follow Through approaches: Executive summary*. Cambridge, MA: Abt Associates.

Regnier, P. (1996). *Research, reason, truth, and education: Policy decisions and the intellectual life of schools*. Unpublished manuscript.

Rosenshine, B. (1978). Review of teaching styles and pupil progress. *American Educational Research Journal, 15*, 163–169.

Sackman, H. (1974, April). *Delphi assessment: Expert opinion, forecasting, and group process*. (R-1283-PR). Santa Monica, CA: RAND Corporation.

Scheirer, M.A., & Kraut, R.E. (1979). Increasing educational achievement via self-concept change. *Review of Educational Research, 49*, 131–150.

Sears, S., & Keogh, B. (1993). Predicting reading performance using the Slingerland procedures. *Annals of Dyslexia, 43*, 78–89.

Shiffrin, R.M., & Schneider, W. (1977). Control and automatic human information processing, I: Detection, search and attention. *Psychological Review, 84*, 1–66.

Slavin, R.E. (1995). *Cooperative learning: Theory, research, and practice* (2nd ed.). Needham Heights, MA: Allyn & Bacon.

Snow, R.E. (1992). Aptitude theory: Yesterday, today, and tomorrow. *Educational Psychologist, 27*(1), 5–32.

Snow, R.E., & Swanson, J. (1992). Instructional psychology: Aptitude, adaptation, and assessment. *Annual Review of Psychology, 43*, 583–626.

Spaulding, F.E. (1903). The teacher's practical application of the results of child study. *Journal of Pedagogy, 16*, 34–42.

Stahl, S.A., & Miller, P.D. (1989). Whole language and language experience approaches for beginning reading: A quantitative research synthesis. *Review of Educational Research, 59*, 87–116.

Stanovich, K.E. (1996). *How to think straight about psychology* (4th ed.). New York: HarperCollins.

Steinberg, L. (1996). *Beyond the classroom: Why school reform has failed and what parents need to do.* New York: Simon & Schuster.

Stern, D. (1996). *Active learning in students and teachers.* Paris: Organization for Economic Cooperation and Development.

Stevens, R.J., & Slavin, R.E. (1995). The cooperative elementary school: Effects on students' achievement, attitudes, and social reactions. *American Educational Research Journal, 32*, 321–351.

Stone, J.E. (1996). Developmentalism: An obscure but pervasive restriction on educational improvement. *Education Policy Analysis Archives, 4*(8).

Strauss, H.J., & Ziegler, L.H. (1975). The Delphi method and its uses in social science research. *Journal of Creative Behavior, 9*, 253–259.

Sylwester, R. (1994). What the biology of the brain tells about learning. *Educational Leadership, 51*, 46–51.

Turner, R.L. (1989). The "great" debate: Can both Carbo and Chall be right? *Phi Delta Kappan, 71*, 276–283.

U.S. Department of Education. (1996). *NAEP Facts* (National Assessment of Educational Progress). Washington, DC: Author.

U.S. Department of Health and Human Services. (1985). *The impact of Head Start on children, families, and communities: Final report of the Head Start evaluation, synthesis, and utilization project, executive summary.* Washington DC: Author.

Vellutino, F.R. (1991). Introduction to three studies on reading acquisition: Convergent findings on theoretical foundations of code-oriented versus whole-language approaches to reading instruction. *Journal of Education Psychology, 83*(4), 437–443.

Walberg, H.J. (1990, February). Productive teaching and instruction: Assessing the knowledge base. *Phi Delta Kappan*, 470–478.

Walberg, H.J. (1992). The knowledge base for educational productivity. *International Journal of Educational Reform, 1*, 1–10.

Walker, M.H. (1996). What research really says. *Principal, 75*(4), 41, 43.

Watkins, C.L. (1988, July). Project follow through: A story of the identification and neglect of effective instruction. *Youth Policy*, 7–11.

Wiersma, W. (1995). *Research methods in education* (6th ed.). Needham Heights, MA: Allyn & Bacon.

Willson, V.L. (1991). Performance assessment, psychometric theory and cognitive learning theory: Ships crossing in the night. *Contemporary Education, 62*, 250–254.

Winn, W. (1994, October). Why I don't want to be an expert sitar player. *Educational Technology*, 11–14.

Wolk, R.A. (1997, January 22). Quality counts, an Education Week/Pew Charitable Trusts special report on the condition of education in the 50 states. *Education Week, 16* (Suppl.).

Woolfolk, A. (1998). *Educational Psychology* (7th ed.). Needham Heights, MA: Allyn & Bacon.

CHAPTER 5

The Sine Qua Non—
Budgeting and Personnel

Rosemarie V. Rosen

While it is very difficult to reach real educational leadership, a superintendent can actually survive without it, for many others are ready to fill that need. You can function well by adopting the ideas of others if you are an effective facilitator and people manager. In this way, you can have a long if not distinguished career as a superintendent. There are, however, two areas without mastery of which you cannot survive and they are the subjects of this chapter: budget and personnel. These can be career killers if you are not comfortably in control of them in all their manifestations. No superintendent will survive long who allows deficits, failing budgets, protracted contract negotiations, and inappropriate hiring. Equally important, you cannot accomplish what you want to do educationally if these two areas are not in hand—your hands, not the business manager's, the board president's, teacher union's, or assistant superintendent's.

This chapter discusses that which budgeting and personnel encompass both today and just ahead and offers some suggestions for how to gain and stay in control of them. They are only important as systems that help you achieve your real, educational agenda, and they take on disproportionate importance only when not under control. That is a simple truth that underlies everything here. It is a good notion to always keep in mind.

YOU EAT THE BEAR OR THE BEAR EATS YOU

First, you must be honest and confront hardheadedly the strengths and weaknesses you have in the areas of budget and personnel. Warren Bennis (1985) called this management of self—knowing one's skills and deploying them effectively. It is especially important to be prepared for how much of your time management will really take. Some philosopher-educators will tell you to readjust your management style and change the proportions to focus more on building staff, planning, developing ideas, and leading. This is just not the real world. It would be much better to have someone else write the district's long-range plan around your outline of ideas than to have someone else develop your collective-bargaining package.

Second, match your strengths and weaknesses with staff. If you do not have a strong background in the technical administrative areas, look for people who do, either on staff or newly hired if you have that opportunity. Be clear about the fact that you value effective administrative management and that you want to stay close to, and informed about, these areas. Whether or not you have a grounding in budget and personnel, you will be relying on others to carry out the day-to-day tasks. Get to know these staff well. The goal in terms of their characteristics is twofold: solid technical reliability and loyal commitment to you. If you can't get the latter, settle for the former, build in some checks with people you can trust, and watch your back. Creativity is certainly highly valuable in administrative staff, also. It is difficult to find and is something more likely to come from you, especially if you ask the right questions and don't easily take no for an answer. This is, of course, second nature to you by now in any terrain.

In terms of the demands on your time that these areas will take, it will always be more than you would think or wish. In 1995, the university at Albany, State University of New York, convened a symposium, the Future of the Superintendency. Thirty-five superintendents were invited from diverse districts around the state to share a day of conversation about their experiences and what they saw for the future. The districts represented ranged from student populations of over 10,000 to under 1,000, encompassing small city, suburban, and rural. The largest number were rural or blue-collar in the 1,000 to 3,000 range. No large, urban district was represented. The group of superintendents reflected the statewide profile, as compiled by the New York State Council of School Superintendents (NYSCOSS), consisting of about 11% women and having a mean age of early fifties. All of these superintendents had doctorates, although statewide only 43% did. The discussion group was required to cover one question on the New York State Compact, not relevant here, and the following three questions:

1. What were the major issues you faced last year?
2. What was your experience with collective bargaining, and what do you see for the future?
3. How much time do you spend "promoting" yourself and your programs?

In response to question one, the overwhelming answer, often offered apologetically or with barely restrained frustration, was budgets and negotiations. In answer to question two, the area of greatest and most intense frustration was clearly collective bargaining. In answer to question three, all concluded that superintendents are always "on," selling themselves, their districts, and their programs. These answers are consistent with the last NYSCOSS survey of superintendents across the state (Barretta, Davis, Volp, & Whitehill, 1995). The areas on which most respondents spent the most time were budget and contract negotiations. The area most often cited as the one respondents wanted to change was this proportion of time usage. Most felt they should be spending less time on administrative matters and more on education or programs. Throughout the symposium discussion, there was a sense that the superintendents were waiting for some time when they could just get past the budget battles or bonding campaigns or contract negotiations. Then at this future time, dearly sought after, they could really work on developing and installing their educational goals. The point here is that administration and programs are not separable. There will never be a time when administrative issues go away and programs emerge exclusively. You must regard them as integrated and work at them simultaneously, achieving programs through budget and personnel.

BUDGET

Budget, budgeting, or fiscal management should be thought of as providing the means to get done what you are striving for educationally. Whatever your educational and program goals—newer technology, new texts, more math and science, more reading and writing, staff development in alternative assessment, or just holding the line on what you've got—budgeting will get you there.

There are three aspects of budgeting:

1. fiscal management or the controls on how (for example, procurement procedures) and when (cash flow) you spend your money
2. program budgeting that here means the real financial translation of each year's activities within the limits of what you actually have available to spend
3. the budget development process (The public budget is one of the primary ways in which you communicate with your various constituencies.)

In this era of antigovernment sentiment and consumerism, the budget development process can be extremely prickly.

Fiscal Management

All three aspects of budgeting are, of course, interrelated. For example, the more confidence your board and community have in your fiscal-control mechanisms, the better your chances of reaching the budget you need. For this reason and others, a fiscal management system is indispensable.

The purpose of a fiscal management system is both control and information. You must have at your fingertips information about expenditures and cash flow. You must also be confident that your spending activity is consistent with all the pertinent laws, rules, and requirements of good practice. Most of the regulatory requirements serve you well in terms of good management, the board's and the public's protection, and personal interest. However, laws and regulations are designed to achieve the greatest good for the greatest number. You need to be sure your staff uses their own common sense and you yours even when applying local restrictions where none exist or when using the rules creatively to get done, rather than impede, what you need.

Several years ago in New York, many school districts got caught up in investing in a certain mutual fund. There were no regulatory restraints at that time. The fund showed very high yields but was heavily engaged in buying derivatives, a practice that very few people, even savvy business officers, knew much about. The market dipped unexpectedly and districts all over the state lost big investments. The more conservative fiscal officers had not participated. This was the same kind of investment that bankrupted Orange County in California, and much more is known about it now. The experience gave rise to more controls and certainly more caution. It is a good example of the need to look out for your own interests.

Most districts will have time-honored fiscal management systems already in place. Take advantage of these and of the veteran staff who run them. The Boston Public Schools (BPS) had a business manager who had survived corrupt school committees, regular deficits in the millions, and four superintendents in three years. I was brought on board in a new position of deputy superintendent for administration, and my job was to turn bad practice around. Here was this business manager who had control of everything. This man not only had close ties to the school committee and the community, but his tenure was ironclad and he had all the books. The superintendent spoke of him publicly with honor and respect and from that I took my cue. I set up a meeting early on, and when it came, I walked very visibly down a long corridor flanked by the desks of the accounting and clerical staff. I walked into his office and sat down in front of his desk, which had on it not one piece of paper. I looked at his wise, old, and unmistakably amused face, and I said, "Leo, I have enormous respect for all you've done here to keep things moving despite unsettling changes. The system needs you and I need your help." Without saying a word, he pulled out a thick printout and showed me a major portion of what I needed to begin. He was not always an ally, but when he could have been an insurmountable obstacle he helped instead.

Many systems that are already in place will be strong on control but will not be as good at the kind of information you need at your level of management. Many systems are also designed for central office control and serve as barriers to building or on-site management flexibility. A basically adequate fiscal management system should do the following:

- process transactions quickly and accurately, for example, supplies are ordered in a timely manner and requisitions are filled quickly
- maintain accurate records that are relatively easily understood and that would withstand any scrutiny
- produce regular, timely, and comprehensible reports for regulatory agencies and management at a variety of levels

Bidding is a good example of a basic procedure that is needed. The details will vary with the nature of the purchase—a personal service contract for review of your psychometrics capacity or buses, for example. The amounts will vary accordingly. In any case, the basic bidding procedures should include the same elements, such as,

- specifications and evaluation criteria that are public, clear, and effective at articulating what you need
- a standardized review process that every bidder undergoes
- representative participants and thorough documentation of all steps

The front-end time on a bidding process is worth the investment in terms of public scrutiny as well as ensuring that you get the best quality, price, and suitability of product.

The superintendent will need reports that serve various audiences, for example, the expenditures for instructional supplies back three years and projected forward or the costs of transportation by school building or catchment area. Especially, you need to know at any time how much you have to spend and that expenditures are occurring as planned. If you commit to having a new text in place by September, or a new assessment tool with training in place by May, you should be able to rely on the fact that the mechanics of procurement aren't allowed to undermine you.

Program Budgeting

Program budgeting is an ongoing process from which you and your administrative staff can build whatever public budget is required. This is your spending plan or operating budget—a component of your program plan. It helps implement your program plan and helps hold accountable those charged with its execution. This is generally the actual budget that keeps things moving day-to-day. It includes the number of teachers and other staff by cost center (that could be by building or subject area or both, for example) as well as non–personal service needs, from instructional supplies to sports equipment to food supplies.

The three largest segments of a typical budget are staff, transportation, and capital costs. The largest, capital costs—building expansions, new laboratories, and enhanced technological capacities—are often obtained through bonding. Capital funds are spent and monitored differently over multiple years. While the debt service is part of the annual budget, these costs are usually not included in the per-capita operating expenditures that are so often used publicly to measure a school system's (and your) performance. Debt service should not be allowed to become an overburdensome portion of the budget. Further, it must be kept in mind that transportation and capital expenditures are usually the largest and most visible expenditures. Bidding for construction projects, for example, must be done with care and scrutiny. These projects should include the involvement of outside experts such as state education department advisors, if these are available, or experienced citizens. If funds are available, your hiring consultants—also through a bidding process—is worthwhile. For these large projects, the more thorough planning, review, and documentation the better.

Budget Development

Budget development is a budget process that varies from state to state but is a key element in the superintendent's and district's public relationship. The aim is to achieve solid support of a budget that funds the district's program goals without any rancorous aftermath that often lingers and can undo the board–superintendent relationship. Where you have a budget that goes to a public vote and is defeated, you cannot recover if the board feels you sent them out into a community with a higher spending package than the community can tolerate. It is also difficult to recover, except through a new board election, if the budget wins but you have had board members campaign against it. The budget is something on which you and the board must be in partnership. It is an understatement to say that this is sometimes very difficult to achieve. This is where the demands on your time and selling ability come in most heavily.

Paul Nutt's (1989) book on decision making has very good and practical models on how to involve stakeholders. It is axiomatic that information and participation be part of your process. How much and in what forms depend a great deal on the individual district and community. One of the superintendents at the Albany conference mentioned above had spent his entire first year in full-bore lobbying to seek passage of a budget that would support what he called his strategic educational vision. He met regularly with the local newspapers, and attended and spoke at all the Kiwanis, Rotary, Elks, or whatever other community group meetings would have him. There were parents on several budget development committees and the process took from October through March. The superintendent felt as if he had done little else, but he believed it was an essential first move. The budget failed, although his relationship with the board remained fairly solid. In talking quietly with some community members afterward, he learned that he had been perceived as too aggressive, and the budget was simply more than people felt they could afford or wanted to spend on a school program that was thought to be adequate. A more modest and less exciting budget passed on a second vote. The point here is that loads of communication and involvement may not be called for, and they aren't a guarantee. Find out what your community values are and what the recent economic experiences have been. Tailor your approach to your community. You can usually take cues from the board in this regard.

There are at least two different approaches to the budget development process (and combinations of these two in between), depending on how much energy and time you have to spend and how risk oriented you are. The first approach involves full-blown participation—coffee hours, press conferences, community committees wrapped around the board, and lots of public appearances. Passage of the budget is still a flip of the coin in this model if the percentage of tax-rate growth is too high.

In the second approach, you have only a few public meetings. There is the appearance of information made available, but the public documents are only vague overviews. Any controversial or fringe items (in some communities, these include field trips) are pushed out to PTA bake sales or individual item referenda. Administrative costs are kept very low; per-capita expenditures compare well to regional and statewide averages, and you make this well known. Make your principals accountable for getting out the budget vote (only pro budget if possible) building by building. Keep the process short and sweet. This scenario works best if your teacher salaries are already regionally high and you're not forced to make structural adjustments. It also helps if the community will support a bond for big-ticket changes such as technology. There is a caveat with this approach. Be sure that the board and key parents are well informed of any sensitive changes.

In a local district, one that hasn't had a budget defeat in a dozen years, the budget was almost torpedoed two years ago and the process got very messy because the superintendent buried what he thought was a constructive change in the budget materials. He planned to eliminate the jobs of the special-education aides and replace them at a substantial savings with graduate-student interns. He had already worked the program out with local universities. The aides, however, were parents and community people who wanted to keep their jobs. The superintendent thought he could count on the support of the board because the parents of the affected children would certainly want specially trained graduate students rather than noncertified, nonprofessional staff working with their children, right? Wrong. The aides made the budget process a very public fight all about their positions. The board and the specific parents felt loyal to these people, and the rest of the district became very split. The final compromise was very costly, but was what it took to move the budget. The original aides' positions were restored and the commitment to the interns was honored as well.

In terms of the content of the budget, most items grow incrementally and many cover fixed costs. The largest segment is for staff, usually 80 to 90%. You do not need to develop a zero-based or elaborate program-based budget for your own or public purposes. You do need to be able to identify clearly the budget components and show a relationship between your key program goals and proposed spending. If you've emphasized staff development or strengthening the science curriculum, for example, there need to be dollars in the budget to support activities that will implement these programs. That does not necessarily mean increased dollars.

While you don't have to develop the budget on a zero-based approach, that is, examining every dollar anew, you should be sure that base expenditures really are necessary. You may be able to find ways to reinvest funds, for example. Doing more with less is today's rhetoric. Doing more without an increase is highly desirable (not, of course, with salaries).

Separate fixed costs and the increases they drive from discretionary spending. The latter should be a small portion of the total budget and be clearly program driven. It should be made apparent to the board and community that votes to reduce the fixed-cost increases are really votes to cut back on existing services—educational program services. You should never seem to simply be arguing for the status quo. If, for example, you have a line item for text replacement, keep it but acquire a text in a new area each year or two.

Trade a vacant administrative position for a science teacher and a lab technician. A caution: This is especially popular these days and is gaining completely unfounded credibility as part of political, educational quick fixes. New York is going so far as to aim a premium in state school aid at districts that keep their administrative costs below a certain level, such as 3%. There are two fallacies here. First and foremost, except for big-city district bureaucracies, schools are already shakily low on administrative costs. The administrative hierarchies and support staff were delayered in education long before Jack Welch, chief executive officer (CEO) of General Electric, set the standard for eliminating middle management in business. I have never seen an analysis of how much it costs to have superintendents or principals make copies, type up their own newsletters, or bring cookies and coffee for building council meetings. Second, there is no uniformity in the way schools account for expenditures in categories such as instructional versus noninstructional. There will perhaps not ever be a correction for the first problem. We are now going in the opposite direction. There is no choice but to use the second situation wisely. This is to say, it is important to keep administrative budgets down, but be sure to credit, wherever appropriate, the costs that are a part of instruction. The salary of the assistant director for curriculum is an instructional, not an administrative, cost.

The relationship of the board to budget development bears emphasis. Even if you don't go to a public vote with your budget, the costs of the schools are what board members feel they must answer to their publics about. They must feel informed and be committed to speaking on behalf of the costs if called upon. It is best if you can be sure the board will speak positively about their support for the budget. This is now harder than ever. While you and the board are striving to work in partnership on fiscal matters, there is an inherent conflict working against you. You, as the educational leader, are by definition an advocate for programs and children and whatever costs you think appropriate and necessary to support them. It is correct and required that you play the advocacy role. At the same time, while boards should also have an advocacy role, they are increasingly elected on antitax, antigovernment platforms. This perspective is not one that is interested in programs. It is only interested in shrinking costs. There are no easy answers to this dilemma. It is a trend that public education is confronting everywhere, and at the very same time political rhetoric is again stirred up over standards. The only way to handle this at the individual district level is to take it into account. Be sure to emphasize and include in your budget proposals, cost-containment approaches, and especially outcome measures. Try to balance program growth with savings or solid evidence of accomplishment. It is important never to underestimate how political the budget is. This becomes very apparent if you must resort to layoffs. These are often difficult and divisive, so be absolutely certain they are necessary. You may achieve enough savings through an incremental freeze rather than through losing bodies.

A final word on budget development has to do with where your district's money comes from. Take a good look at the state aid share and whether you are at 40% or 70%; be sure to stay in touch with the state aid legislative process. You can do this best through the professional organizations, but you may also want to maintain a relationship with the legislators from your district. There are many opportunities to involve legislators and other appropriate officials in the schools—introductions at district assemblies, opportunities to present student awards, recognition by students of the good workings of government. Once you make a connection, legislators will provide you with current information on the state budget process and how your share of state aid is doing. You usually cannot influence, as a result of the impact on your one district (unless you're a big city), the outcomes of state aid formulas that are being shaped by statewide political agendas (such as the weightings for special-education students in New York). You may, however, be able to avoid being a loser district in all the general formula tinkering that goes on if you pay attention.

PERSONNEL

There are myriad aspects to personnel or human resource management. There are all the statutory requirements, such as the Occupational Safety and Health Act, the Civil Rights Act, whatever your state requires in terms of affirmative action, and so on. There are, at the more discretionary end of the spectrum, components such as staff development, evaluation, and labor–management relations. The superintendent will not be involved in all of these, but it is important that you make your philosophy clear, both to your board and your staff. Be clear that you expect personnel systems practices that ensure statutory compliance. Staff must understand that you always expect them to do the right thing. The tricky part is that they must understand how to function in a way that is institutionally protective while at the same time pro employee. The best way to ensure that staff will act in this way is to model this behavior whenever you have the opportunity. Fairness, consistency (but not at the expense of compassion), and openness are important. Whether you are disciplining an employee or rewarding them, the employee and others who are observing must be able to discern a caring evenhandedness in your actions whether they agree with the specific action or not. Typically that means open information and a sensible amount of due process. Sensible means limited.

Personnel decisions and actions do not improve through committee. Most often these actions are best taken quickly, though never precipitously. Personnel situations do not improve or go away with time. It is best to confront and deal with them as openly as possible. There is one clear area where standards of expected behavior cannot be compromised and that is in terms of impact on students. Saying all that, it must be noted that board habit and policy concerning personnel will affect the superintendent's ability to exert his or her own style of managerial control and practice. It is a very important area to discuss and on which to get clear ground rules from the board. In any case, try to be sure the board has whatever information it needs on personnel transactions on a regular basis. They should have an opportunity to let you know in advance of board meetings if there are concerns. Personnel matters should not be sources of contentious discussion at open board meetings. It's up to the superintendent to develop whatever procedures and relationships help avoid that. An area of personnel that it is extremely important for you to control directly is the relationship between you and administrative staff. If board members insist that principals report to them or be hired and evaluated by them, not you, that's a major problem and probably is indicative of other problems.

Like budget and fiscal management, the two faces of personnel management are control and service. Both of these convey messages about the adequacy of your managerial skills.

Given that you have made your philosophy clear, you only need to be personally involved in the few areas of personnel management that are the most political and the closest to your desired educational outcomes. For the technical areas, even if you have expertise in them, stay away. You cannot do everything and this is a good area in which to develop strong staff. Able and reliable technical staff can run the day-to-day personnel matters—payroll and transactions that move people and items. This will work if you and your key staff agree on two things: (1) personnel is a fiscal function, in fact one of the most important because it drives the largest part of the budget, and (2) there must be good access to information about positions (as well as personnel records but only under special conditions that protect confidentiality).

A position is a unit of budget. Controls on how and when positions get filled, as well as ready and reliable information about positions and what they cost, are essential elements in a well-run system. Although a surprisingly large amount of savings can accrue while positions remain unfilled, this should only happen by design. Underspending, especially if services are being denied as a result, can be as troublesome as overspending.

Employees of a district regard personnel as a service function that ensures their paycheck as well as their health benefits and many other protections. This service provides information, if they need it, on promotion, retention, tenure, loss of job, bumping rights, and so on. The personnel office is also the place that implements all of these transactions. Personnel staff must understand that prompt, courteous, and reliable responses to employee needs are expected and valued. This contributes to good morale and smooth operations, both inside and outside the classroom. It is also a very good way to convey to the community what kind of shop you run. Many employees live, vote, and have lots of friends in the community.

Evaluation and Staff Development

The two areas of personnel that require the direct involvement of the superintendent are the performance evaluation system and labor relations.

The approach to evaluation described by Sergiovanni (1991) in his book on the principalship is very useful as well for superintendents, although you cannot be quite as personally involved as suggested. Key elements are clear standards of performance designed for growth not discipline—opportunities for self-goal development and self-evaluation along with real opportunities to enlarge experience (leadership of district-wide special projects, committees, public speaking).

The same notions of fairness and consistency in dealing with all staff are required for effective leadership with your key managers, that is for the most part, your principals. You are looking for more among this group, however. The best situation is a sense of mutual commitment and respect. The short tenure of superintendencies makes this difficult. Also, chances are that principals are more tied by education, family, and so forth to the district than is the superintendent. In any case, you are still building professional growth and respect. Too many managers in various settings rely on fear to lead. While that can work for you if you are close to the board, it does nothing to build capacity. If you never look back, fine. There is a very important, but delicate aspect to evaluation (and the supervision that is implicit in this). In most districts, everyone knows who the weak administrators are. People have a pretty good idea, also, of who is salvageable and who is not. How the superintendent handles these administrators is another way messages are sent. There should be systems of support available to strengthen the skills of deficient administrators, with adequate monitoring and progress points.

Truly problem administrators must be dealt with as quickly and firmly as possible. The due process can be time consuming and expensive but must be pursued intensely. This is another area where working closely with the board is essential. Transferring principals among schools in a district is a conditional answer. It is usually simply a way of avoiding the tougher problems of development and accountability, however. Transferring without a thorough evaluation system in place is a sham. Transferring with support can work. Not every administrator is well matched with his or her school. If there is talent, potential, and a good attitude, a transfer for a better match and as part of a sensitive process can be the best solution.

I put evaluation and staff development together because, aside from some specific, formal requirements, they ought not be thought of separately. Staff, especially teachers, but really all staff who work under difficult conditions in many schools, must be given opportunities to grow. They must also be encouraged to develop a strong identification with, and a sense of having a stake in, the whole organization. Only then, not through an annual evaluation process, will overall organizational growth be enhanced.

In studying leaders across the country, Warren Bennis (1985) found that effective leadership created an organization in which employees had certain characteristics: They felt comfortable trying things even if they made mistakes, and they felt part of a team or community. While superintendents may not feel they have time for long-term building of this kind of organization, they can model these values for even short-term gain.

Labor Relations

The final and perhaps most difficult area of personnel is collective bargaining or, more broadly, labor relations. The difference is that collective bargaining happens periodically while labor relations is the condition under which employees and often their organizations and management, represented by the superintendent, function with each other day-to-day. Some states do not have collective bargaining in the formal sense. Work relationships, however, are still vital. Where it does exist, collective bargaining is one of those areas of administration made much easier when there is money to spend. Many a contract contains all kinds of language that was bought or traded with financial incentives that are gone forever. Nonetheless, the contract language remains.

Depending on your outlook, the current tight economic condition in which schools find themselves makes bargaining easier and harder—easier in the sense that there is little to talk about except benefits and wages, and the talk is within much narrower parameters; harder, because there may be structural changes you want to achieve and that is very difficult with empty hands. As mentioned earlier, this can be one of the most frustrating things with which a superintendent must deal. Make no mistake, this is not something that can be delegated. It is not the board's responsibility. This is one of those areas that is critical for a superintendent to handle successfully. It is also one of the most uncharted territories right now.

There are no formulas or simple ways to avoid the difficult context within which collective bargaining must now play out. The course of action chosen by the superintendent very much depends on the circumstances of the individual district and community. Factors like bargaining history, comparable salaries in neighboring communities, and state aid elements that may hurt or help (whether there is money for staff development, for example) are important. Again, there are basic elements to consider. Extremely important is how to put together your bargaining package. Preparation is essential. Understand where your compensation terms (and any other aspects that are important to you) are and where you need to go. Anticipate what is important to the employees and their organizations. Have staff you trust do research on comparability using a variety of factors. Especially important is spending time with the board to develop a mutual understanding of goals and boundaries. You absolutely do not want to get to bargaining without a close relationship with the board regarding your positions.

Bargaining is about compromise, not about winning and losing. You have to work with the people on the other side of the table. They have to teach or drive or feed students for whom you are responsible. They should feel good about their work and the terms and conditions of their employment. If the board has sent you into bargaining to slay a dragon and beat up the other guys, you have a problem. Try to help everyone understand what is really important and what is doable. Sometimes there can be incremental change. Sometimes change happens best through side letters or study committees. A bargain that supports and enables an ongoing relationship is best. If you are in a system that does not have collective bargaining, there are still principles of respect and mutual support that are critical. The superintendent's relationship with staff, largely teachers, is a defining element of what can really be accomplished. Whether you are dealing with a union, a professional organization, or informal leadership, communication between you and staff is essential. When I ran for school board, I met with the leadership of the school bus drivers, the food service workers, and the teachers. I did not ask for their support, I asked what was important to them and how they saw the district. I found out that these workers could, if given the opportunity, bring forth tremendous insights and practical ideas about things such as how to plan better and cheaper cafeteria menus and how to improve the bus routes. No one had ever had quite these same conversations with them before. I believe they helped get me elected and, more important, I passed the good ideas on to the administration.

In summary, there are some general observations to follow about maintaining effective working relationships with employees, especially those with instructional responsibilities.

- Keep talking and looking for common ground; always keep a professional tone, no matter how hard.
- Treat employees with respect.
- Misconduct or short-changing students cannot be tolerated. Use, to the absolute ends of your resources, every process open to you to eliminate inappropriate behaviors. It sends a good message.
- Always take the positive approach. Constantly look for ways to recognize and reward employees, and remember that teachers make the schools and you look good. They are where the rubber hits the road and where students and parents connect with the schools. They must know you value their work.
- Know that there are lots of other employees, too, who make the schools work. Even when you are confronted with entrenched attitudes that may seem to you to interfere with your ability to reach teachers as professionals, don't make them the enemy. This only draws battle lines, and most superintendents don't have the time these days to fight long, protracted battles.
- Engage teachers, administrators, and other employees in marketing the schools. It usually convinces everybody, including them.

These approaches will not get you all that you want nor allow you to reach all of your educational goals. They will contribute to labor harmony and permit you to focus on what's most important—those educational outcomes. Remember, that's why you came.

WHAT DOES THE FUTURE HOLD?

Conventional wisdom says there is nothing new under the sun, especially in education. Much that is happening today in education, and as far ahead as we can foresee, is familiar. But, like any trends, those that are reappearing are slightly but significantly changed by the current context in which they now appear. It is difficult to separate what is confronting education into the budget and personnel areas, but, if anything, both these areas have become even more sensitive.

There are four trends that are developing now and just ahead.

1. There is a demand for more and more accountability. This is manifest in the press for uniform standards at every level of government. This is not new. It is a residual from the national reports of the early 1980s and even before. It is the simplest way for the political process, especially at the national level where there is no direct role in education, to become involved. While this is a familiar strain, it has broad support this time around in a better-informed taxpayer base. Who can deny that there should be outcomes for tax dollars?

2. More information about costs, student needs, and outcomes is critical to the well-being of public education. Vouchers, charter schools, and other forms of competition will continue to proliferate. This is not going away because anyone insists on the sanctity of public education. Like any sophisticated corporate entity, public education must invest in practical research to prove its worth. Any experienced educator knows with certainty that school programs for urban student populations cost more. Yet, over and over, we hear statements of public policy such as: If students are doing so badly in those schools even though we are spending so much more per capita, money can't be the answer. Where is the resounding educational response to such flawed thinking? In budgeting and personnel, information systems tied to inputs and outcomes are no longer frills. They are essential. When I went to work as an administrator for the BPS, the first question the community wanted answered was, how many employees worked for the BPS? When we gave them the answer reliably and pretty quickly, we had their attention and a small window of confidence.

3. The corporate voices that equated their ability to compete internationally with quality public education have gone silent and education has lost their attention. The most successful corporate entities have eliminated national barriers and automated their work forces or farmed out to cheap foreign labor the least technical of their jobs. They are no longer looking to invest in a work force. A large dependent work force is no longer an asset but a liability against the need to anticipate and constantly reinvent market direc-

tion. Corporate interests do not want to pay for public services, not even schools.

4. At the same time, the demands on public education will grow, not diminish. The real value of salaries is in decline. The delayering of the corporate workplace has eliminated thousands of high-salary, middle-manager jobs that will not return. More and more people will be forced to rely on public education but without the ability to support adequate budgets.

What we have learned about organizational behavior and success is also changing. It may be discouraging for superintendents or aspiring superintendents to contemplate all that is expected of them and how little time they are given in which to accomplish it all. As Peter Senge (1990) advises in his writings about organizational change it takes time. Organizational behavior is driven by structure and interrelationships. These are not always easy to see, let alone change. The job of the leader, according to Senge, is not to dictate his or her vision, but to find and nurture a shared set of values and vision for the future. This view is encouraging in the sense that you can't expect yourself to turn a whole school system around. Unfortunately, you will still have to show some successes to retain the support necessary for long-term change. In other words, pick doable short-term victories while you are continuing to build something more lasting. You may find that budget and fiscal management issues are better candidates for short-term improvements than is academic achievement.

Whatever you are able to tackle, given the circumstances of the system in which you find yourself, keep trying to build organizational capacities. Drucker (1993) reminds us of the value of the process the Japanese call kaizen. You must help the organization work toward continuous self-improvement. This is especially true in today's competitive world. Drucker (1993) has reminded us that in the next 50 years schools will change more drastically than they have over the last 300 years. A superintendent must help build the management of change by preparing principals and other managers to develop their own knowledge and capacity. One of the most valuable things the administration I was a part of in Boston accomplished was its intense work with 12 schools to build a school-based management capacity. Twelve principals had the support and opportunity to grow and prove they could lead their schools to success. They and the schools were never the same. They built shared values and decision-making structures that had a long-term, residual strength even after we had all left.

Finally, like any chief executive officer (CEO) position, the superintendency is an isolated and independent job. It reminds me of the marshalls of the wild west, at least as they were portrayed in old TV westerns. They were expected to do impossible jobs that no one else had the courage to do while they led personal lives beyond reproach, took little pay, and stood up to the bad guys all alone. If they got shot, the town would just look for the next one, although a few lived on in legend and folk tale, becoming larger than they were in life. This too can change. Superintendents can support each other more. Their organizations must become stronger and more vocal about what is going on in schools and what is needed. We all know school improvement is going to cost more, not less. There needs to be a voice that says that. Groups that are now separate, such as the organizations for superintendents, school boards, principals, and even teachers should be speaking and working in greater harmony because they share many common goals that only they have the credibility to pursue.

In terms of the administrative areas of budget and personnel, the future means more scrutiny and more demand for accountability. Better information systems are an indispensable tool and the strategies described under each of the various components above should apply in the future. They will help, but they will not change a basic truth—it is better, and usually easier, to have money than not. Effective administrative management and political skill will continue with increased intensity to be important. Remember that and work discreetly to get, and keep, good people on your boards.

REFERENCES

Barretta, A., Davis, G.H., Volp, F.D., & Whitehill, W.E. (Eds.). (1995). *Snapshot of the superintendency II: A study of school superintendents in New York State, 1994–1995.* Albany, NY: New York State Council of School Superintendents and the Membership Committee.

Bennis, W. (1985). *Leaders: The strategies of taking charge.* New York: Harper.

Drucker, P.F. (1993). *Post-capitalist society.* New York: HarperCollins.

Nutt, P.C. (1989). *Making tough decisions: Tactics for improving managerial decision making.* San Francisco: Jossey-Bass, Publishers.

Senge, P.M. (1990). *The fifth discipline: The art and practice of the learning organization.* New York: Doubleday Currency.

Sergiovanni, T.J. (1991). *The principalship: A reflective practice perspective.* 2nd Ed. Needham Heights, MA: Simon and Schuster.

CHAPTER 6

Nuts and Bolts

Gioia Caiola Forman

In the nineteenth century, the Quincy School in Boston, Massachusetts, had the students place their toes on a chalk line and recite the lesson. The students had to "toe the line." Times have changed, and now it is the superintendent who must toe the line. The responsibilities of the superintendent have increased with more behind-the-scenes emphasis on liability issues and support programs. You no longer just worry about the cost of transportation and routes, but you worry about who's driving the buses. Who's fixing and serving breakfast and lunch and keeping the schools clean? Have background checks been done on these individuals? Do they understand and respect diversity among the students and work force? Is the security of students and facilities a priority? Are students safe while performing in musical productions, participating in sports, playing outdoors, or drinking the water? Have you gotten the best price on toilet paper or did you pay top dollar while someone got a free jacket? The superintendent must have these nuts-and-bolts issues under control as he focuses on the instructional program. He must "sweat the small stuff" so they don't become issues. When the teachers run out of red construction paper for their Valentine art project in February, some will complain they have been denied essential instructional materials. This can lead to complaints about procurement of supplies and use of appropriated monies. They will forget they had reams of red in December for their holiday projects and that pink could now be substituted. It's the little things that can cause headaches and can jump up and bite you.

SWEAT THE SMALL STUFF

For a superintendent, paying attention to the nuts-and-bolts issues in a school system, or sweating the small stuff, will yield large dividends in terms of avoiding potentially big problems.

SAFETY AND SECURITY—WHAT DOES IT ALL MEAN?

Dear Parents:

On February 11, we will hold the annual Sweetheart Dance. The attendees will be required to submit to a breathalyzer test upon arrival to ensure that they have not indulged in any alcoholic beverages. In addition, a urine sample will be taken to test for any illegal substances. The students will walk through a metal detector before entering the dance. In addition, every student attending must be accompanied by a parent or guardian to help maintain safety and security.

The staff, students, and I are excited about this annual event. The seniors have established the theme, and the junior class is already busy decorating the gym. The staff and I look forward to seeing many of you next week with your dancing shoes.

Sincerely,

Principal

The fictitious letter, unrealistic, but certainly comforting for the superintendent, illustrates the issues districts now face. A safety and security plan will help the superintendent be aware and plan for potentially dangerous situations, such as those suggested in the letter.

Bad days in schools used to be when rude students talked back to the teacher and made too much noise changing classes. These days superintendents are confronted with student disruptions, serious disciplinary problems, and even criminal behavior. When establishing district rules for security and safety, remember that the vast majority of students do exactly what you want them to do.

The issues dealing with the safety of students is a shared concern. You, as the superintendent, should involve staff, the community, businesses, parents, and students to work together to develop a disciplined environment where learning can and will take place. *Creating Safe and Drug-Free Schools—Action Guide* (1996), which was developed by the Office of Juvenile Justice and Delinquency Prevention, U.S. Department of Justice and Office of Elementary and Secondary Education, U.S. Department of Education, outlines essential ingredients for creating safe, orderly, drug-free schools.[*]

- Place school safety high on the educational agenda. Such a priority involves making a personal and community commitment toward creating a safe, welcoming, respectful, gun-free, and drug-free school. Districts are sponsoring antiviolence days in elementary schools. Children turn in their toy weapons for certificates and other rewards. In Irvine, California, the toy guns and water pistols they traded were then used to create a collage and sculpture with an antiviolence theme.
- Involve parents and citizens. No plan can succeed without the participation of parents and citizens from the community. Planners must make certain to bring these participants to the table often to shape strategies and programs together. Most people dislike having things "done to them." However, they enjoy being a part of planning, carrying out, and evaluating programs in which they have invested concern and time. Those affected by safe school plans should be involved throughout the entire process.
- Build and develop the team. Making schools safe is a joint responsibility requiring a broad-based team and a working attitude emphasizing collaboration and cooperation. Team members should include educators, parents, students, law enforcers, community and business leaders, probation and court representatives, social service and health care providers, and other youth-serving professionals.
- Conduct the school site assessment. Team members should determine the specific issues and concerns that the local community believes are most important. This step begins the process of developing a meaningful safe school plan that will foster an increased level of community commitment.
- Review the law. The law is at the heart of every major school-safety issue today. Laws are intended to articulate the reasonable standards that define the delicate balance between student rights and student responsibilities. The law proclaims what must be done, implies what should be done, and establishes limits for what may be done. The law constitutes a code of professional expectations for school administrators and youth-serving professionals. As planning begins, school and community leaders should consult with the school district's attorneys to ensure that legal issues are appropriately addressed. Constitutional issues, as well as other concerns ranging from ade-

---

[*]*Source:* This list is reprinted from the partnership Between the Office of Juvenile Justice and Delinquency Prevention, U.S. Department of Justice and Office of Elementary and Secondary Education, U.S. Department of Education, *Creating Safe and Drug-Free Schools—Action Guide*, September 1996, pp. 3–4.

quate liability insurance to the effective screening of volunteers, may arise with the implementation of a comprehensive violence prevention program. The federal Occupational Safety and Health Act (OSHA) requires that an employer takes steps to ensure a safe and healthful workplace for its employees. OSHA will issue citations under Section 5(a)(1) of the act. This section, commonly known as the general duty clause, requires employers to seek to reduce or eliminate recognized hazards that may cause death or serious injury. This is of special importance to support staff.

- Create a safe school plan. This is an action plan that not only includes the substance of what is necessary to accomplish, but also identifies the processes by which those goals will be achieved, including short-term objectives and long-term systemic changes. It is most important for team members to understand that they can make a positive difference in the quality of life for themselves, their community, and all the children they serve. Suggestions on developing a safe school plan follow in the section, "Safety and Security Plans," of this chapter.
- Formulate a contingency plan. Having a backup plan for handling emergencies and crises simply makes good sense. Such foresight can prevent a crisis and preclude successive crises while creating an effective mechanism for managing school problems.
- Create an educational climate. Team members should evaluate the current educational atmosphere and propose modifications that will transform it into a safe, vibrant learning environment in which students and teachers respect each other.
- Search for ways to serve students and ways students can serve. Young people should always be included as part of the solution to the problems associated with juvenile delinquency. Actively engaging students in school and community projects and activities creates a level of ownership that supports the success of every child. The state of Maryland now requires all students to participate in community service as a requirement for graduation. The superintendent of the future will work with traditional classrooms and correctional classrooms, and will spend time engaging community-based organizations to provide services for students and their families.
- Get the message out—communicate. Working with the media may be one of the most successful strategies for building awareness of both the issues involved and the progress being made. With simple newsletters, schools can share success stories and break down barriers with other districts and schools. Districts may also have an opportunity to develop their own cable television programs, using both paid employees and student-run programs.

- Evaluate progress. It is important to monitor activities, measure impact, and evaluate how the plan is working. A safe school plan should be modified and improved whenever necessary. The superintendent can rest assured that there will be an unlimited number of "suggestions" from parents and the media who are more than happy to sweat the small stuff, if there is any perception that the plan is not working.

SAFETY AND SECURITY PLANS

All staff and parents have a joint responsibility to provide a safe and secure environment at school and to ensure that all students learn how to protect themselves. In addition, superintendents should periodically remind students, staff, and parents of the importance of school safety and security through training activities and through the use of announcements, newsletter items, and other types of communication. Every school should develop a safety plan in cooperation with staff and parents and submit it to you. Most importantly, the plan should specify which doors will be locked. You need to make sure that the plan is balanced between safety and security. Too often in the past, schools have violated fire codes by chaining their exit doors closed in the name of security. A plan that causes serious injury or death is a plan that needs to be reevaluated. In some schools, all doors, except the main doors, are to be locked during the school day. In some districts, even the front doors are locked and a buzzer system is used to let people in. Visitors identify themselves by either an intercom system or a camera. Signs should be posted on all doors directing visitors to report to the main office. Elementary and middle school students shall not be left alone or unsupervised anywhere in the building or on school grounds during the school day.

As superintendent, you should involve the school board, community, and staff in developing and updating a cohesive and comprehensive safety and security plan for the district. The plan should incorporate some of the issues addressed below. The district should have a security and fire alarm system. Most districts have an electronic alarm system that uses various types of sensors to detect fire and intrusion. The fire alarm component of the system functions 24 hours a day, year round. The intrusion function is operated by designated personnel and is activated whenever the building is unoccupied or only partially in use. Some districts have alarms that go directly into the fire department and/or police department and some monitor their own from a central station. Fire drills must be scheduled on a regular basis, not just when disgruntled students want a break from class and pull the alarm.

It is not uncommon to read about intruders in schools who have terrorized or even killed students and staff. Some superintendents require personnel to wear photo-identification badges and use a visitor-pass system. An increasing number also require photo identification for students. The security industry now offers a variety of high-tech badges for visitors and substitutes that are void after a ten-hour period. Although surveillance cameras have been used on school buses for some time, there are districts installing them inside buildings and at locked front doors. Parent security volunteers also walk the schools' hallways and are present at school events. School systems are using volunteers in this way and are providing them with training, walkie-talkies, and T-shirts or jackets for identification. Obviously, the human error factor is of great importance. Identification badges will only work if they are checked: The face in the photograph should match the person wearing the badge—not their pet.

The security hardware of cameras, metal detectors, and walkie-talkies are being installed across the country. Even in districts where weapons have not been a problem, metal detectors are used to take a proactive stance. Districts have been removing students' lockers for years. While superintendents are adopting this policy and claim it reduces crime, vandalism, graffiti, and tardiness to class, they report it also saves on maintenance, and teachers say that it has even made the school quieter. Schools without lockers tend to smell better, having lost the strange mix of smells from wet shoes and long forgotten lunches. However, superintendents are being criticized that security measures such as these lend the school a prisonlike atmosphere. If you are planning to adopt hardware policies, be certain to include staff and community members to help communicate the reasons.

School districts are entering into cooperative efforts with other agencies to promote safety. In Fort Wayne, Indiana, city firefighters patrol the school neighborhoods in the morning and at the end of the school day. The firefighters patrol the streets to deter crime in neighborhoods and give assistance to students walking to school. They drive their firetrucks while on patrol and wear uniforms, so their presence is felt.

There are current issues that are particularly troublesome to superintendents. Increasing cooperation with other agencies and appropriate legislation may ameliorate some concerns in the future. These issues include firearms, bombs, water activities, and information highway dangers.

Firearms

Since the mid-1970s, the number of juveniles involved in homicides involving firearms has increased. The U.S. Department of Education reports that juvenile arrests for weapons violations increased 117% during this period. A number of studies have been done, including one by the Centers for Disease Control and Prevention, confirming an increased propensity among young people to carry guns. As you deal with guns, sweat the small stuff. Do you have requirements for the necessary starter pistols for sports? Who has authority to use them? How are the pistols and blanks stored at the school? Who issues pistols, keeps an inventory, and enforces guidelines for transporting pistols to athletic meets. Sweat the small stuff.

Bombs—A Growing Phenomenon

When we hear, "Oklahoma City," "TWA Flight 800," or "Atlanta's Olympic Centennial Park," who doesn't think of bombing, terrorism, and the loss of life? School superintendents' attention is now being given to real bombs, not the bomb threats of the past. In the past, bomb threats occurred around exam time. Schools have become targets because of the propaganda value and media visibility surrounding bomb threats. A district should have in place procedures for handling bomb threats, and it begins with the person receiving the call. Have another person listen to the call if possible. Take notes for police investigation, and record the caller's exact words. Attempt to determine the caller's gender, age, accent, or other distinguishing speech characteristics and demeanor. Listen for background noises that may help in identifying the location of the caller. Ask the caller the time of detonation, location, type, physical appearance, and the reason the device was placed at the school. Even ask the caller's name. If your phone system is direct service, attempt to identify the number from which the person is calling. All phones that can receive incoming calls should have a bomb checklist available. Procedures and evacuation plans will help keep everyone calm and prevent injuries. The evacuation plan should include a predetermined area that gets students at least 350 feet from the building.

My one and only bomb threat provided me firsthand experience about how people deal with crises and how to establish an emergency plan that keeps everyone informed. The original plan was developed solely by the administration, with no input from staff. The emphasis was on getting students and staff out of the building. After evacuating and waiting for the bomb squad, it was clear that staff had never been given clear instructions on what to do once they were evacuated. This was not a fire drill, where they took attendance, accounted for all students, kept them orderly, and then returned to the classroom. This was true-life drama— fire engines, police cars, bomb-sniffing dogs, TV cameras, and lots of activity. Individual staff reacted to stress differently. The custodian would not jeopardize his safety and walk the building with the bomb squad, high-strung teachers needed reassurance that everything was under control and were reminded that the students were looking to them for guidance. It was the small, seemingly unimportant things that caused the most stress. Concerns that handbags and car keys were left in the building were monumental, the beloved secretary who left her daughter's wedding photo proofs in the office was in tears, and the first grade's rabbit had not been evacuated. These sorts of concerns become big issues. When everything was back to normal, it was the small stuff that caused the most criticism. The postcrisis committee drew up guidelines that included the two items most important to staff. They needed to be kept informed throughout the crisis regarding the findings of the authorities, and they wanted an administrator assigned to handle their personal concerns during any future crisis.

Sweat the small stuff on your security plans. Remember that during a crisis, some people will be competent, noble, sensitive, and problem solvers, while others will show disgusting behavior. Technology and the media make communication with the general public instantaneous, without regard for accuracy. Parents, citizens, and gawkers will come to the scene and watch. This will build more pressure and anxiety. When you have a crisis, it calls for high-level leadership, and everyone will look to you for direction.

As the adrenaline flows prior to opening schools, sweat the small stuff the weeks and days immediately preceding school opening. This time period often brings an increase in vandalism and arson to school buildings. Make sure you have plans for protecting the buildings so they can open in a timely fashion. In the spring, sweat some more and have a security check-up around the outside of the buildings. As shrubs and trees begin to grow, identify those that may need to be trimmed to prevent their blocking windows and to eliminate potential hiding places around the school.

Water Activities

When an event is planned that will include water-related activities, and knowing that going into or onto water can be dangerous under certain conditions, a superintendent should ask questions to assess the level of risks and develop a plan to deal with them. The superintendent may decide that the planned activities (or some of them) are too dangerous and should be eliminated (e.g., jet skis, surfing, cliff diving, shark feeding); or, they are only moderately dangerous, but certain precautions must be implemented prior to the activities (e.g., the purchase of an insurance policy, verification that a lifeguard will be on hand, Coast Guard certification of a boat, publication of safety rules).

Even under the best of situations, tragedies can occur. On a recent overnight retreat at a Virginia campsite, one of our high school bands had a student drown. A group was out canoeing on the lake. All students had on life vests; there were parent and teacher chaperones supervising. A boat overturned and a 16 year old drowned when his untied life vest came off. There is nothing worse then losing a young life in an accident. This will haunt the district for years while the courts decide the liability, the parents deal with the tragedy, and the superintendent reevaluates what activities he will allow. Bans on white-water rafting, proms on boats, pool parties, and water skiing are happening nationally. Superintendents are sweating the "wet stuff."

The Information Highway

Who would have imagined that the superintendent would be worrying about students' and employees' safety on the information highway? As more technology is put into schools, more teachers and students are on-line. Students are logging onto commercial services, private bulletin boards, and the Internet; the district must monitor the systems and exercise reasonable supervision when the students are using on-line services.

Students should be instructed not to give out identifying information (school name, home address, telephone number, or picture). Students should be instructed never to arrange a face-to-face meeting with another computer user without parental permission. Superintendents must now sweat who will be their "crossing guards" and "safety patrols" along this busy highway.

DISTRICT-SPONSORED SPORTS: ONE STRIKE AND YOU'RE OUT

Overview*

It's sometimes suggested that the best way to prevent accidents, injuries, and any resultant claims and suits is to stay in bed in the morning. In other words, avoid any exposure to risks, and you avoid all of the above. Avoidance is, in fact, a recognized method for managing risks.

It isn't possible, however, for schools to completely avoid exposing students to the risks of accidents. School employees have a duty to exercise reasonable care for the safety and health of students. In a school setting, a reasonable person acting responsibly would make plans and carry out procedures designed to provide a reasonably safe environment. Ensuring that playground equipment is safe and supervising students' activities are the actions of a responsible person. Remember, not even parents can guarantee the safety of their own children, although they sometimes forget this fact when accidents occur at school or at school-sponsored activities.

With a proactive approach, your school system can champion safety for its student-athletes and save you the agony of litigation.

Source: Adapted with permission from G.C. Forman and R.L. Webb, One Strike You're Out, *Public Risk,* Vol. 9, No. 8, pp. 9–11, Copyright © 1995, Public Risk Management Association.

Sports are such an integral part of today's high school and middle school programs that it's hard to imagine a time when they weren't around. Yet, the combination of schools and sports has left its mark on American education since the late nineteenth century, when high school boys modeled their games after college athletic clubs. At first, the games were purely recreational, with no record of there being coaches. Because there were few rule books and knowledge of rules was limited, the players learned the games by participating and by watching others. Although schools didn't sponsor these fledgling competitions, the teams often took their schools' name. This worried some administrators and teachers who thought the frequent fights between rival teams reflected poorly on the schools and their academic mission.

School sports have evolved since their formative years. From the types and numbers of games to the involvement of coaches and parents, a tremendous change has occurred. Basketball alone has more than one million student-athletes in this country, with millions of fans witnessing their games. (It's a far cry from the sport's humble beginning in 1891 when the city of Denver formed the first known high school basketball league.) To basketball add football, tennis, track, cheerleading, volleyball, wrestling, swimming, lacrosse, rugby, and fencing—just to name a few—and on an annual basis you have millions of young people involved in school-sponsored sports.

Most significantly, nearly all American schools now recognize sports as official extracurricular activities. In the process, they've acquired official responsibility for the safety of participating students. Of course, all of these sports expose students to potential injuries and school systems to huge financial risks.

With increasing frequency, injuries incurred during school-sponsored sports culminate in liability claims and suits that allege lack of supervision, inadequate instructions, or faulty equipment. What follows is an assessment of the risk of your district's liability due to negligence, and some guidelines to safeguard your district from potentially devastating financial risk.

The Liability Game

Without question, school systems have a duty to provide some level of care for their student-athletes. Although the degree of care may change as circumstances change, school systems must make plans and carry out procedures designed to provide reasonably safe environments.

One of the best ways to ensure that school administrators provide reasonably safe environments is for you to give them the information they need. Most failures to meet the degree of care required in school sports are due to ignorance; coaches don't know where they can go wrong. Coaches who don't understand where or how they can be negligent are at high risk of committing negligent acts.

All school sport programs need a full-fledged risk management program that covers loss-prevention and loss-control techniques.

However, providing the proper level of care doesn't guarantee an injury-free environment. It simply means that a reasonable person (or system) has done what's considered reasonable to prevent accidents and injuries under a set of circumstances. If, however, the level of care that should be expected isn't met, and any injury suffered is shown to have been caused by that violation, you can be fairly sure someone was negligent, either willfully or through oversight.

To state it more simply, once an injury occurs at a school-sponsored sporting activity, a superintendent or designee can determine whether or not legal liability exists against the school system and/or the coaching staff by answering four important questions.

1. Did the school system have a duty of care?
2. Was the school responsible for providing a "reasonably" safe environment?
3. Did the system not provide the level of care that should have been expected, considering the circumstances at the time of the injury and the relationship between the injured student and the school system?
4. Did the injury occur as a result of the school system not providing reasonable care?

If the answers to all of these questions is "yes," the school system probably will have a valid liability claim against it. The chances of a liability claim's landing in a court of law continue to rise. This rise isn't necessarily because of more negligent acts; it's just the direction in which American society is headed. Even if a particular claim doesn't make it all the way to trial, chances are good that the injured party will pursue the claim hoping for an out-of-court settlement. Because of the cost of prolonged legal defense in such cases, actual settlements to claimants often occur despite the lack of evidence of any real negligence on the part of a defending school system.

Whether there is a finding of liability, a settlement is paid, or the case is won, you still must pay your attorneys. The injury can be costly to a school system. Thus, it becomes extremely important to reduce your system's chances of being accused of negligence.

The Release-Form Dodge

Many public schools continue to obtain parent signatures in an attempt to release themselves from any future responsibility for injuries that happen during school-sponsored activities. In all likelihood, it's a waste of time. Increasingly, courts are refusing to recognize these "preinjury releases," even when they've been signed by activity participants. The courts' rationale is often that validating such forms puts the students at the mercy of the school system's future misconduct.

It's easy enough to understand the courts' reasoning. If the legal system accepted preinjury releases, there'd be little legal incentive for an activity's sponsor to do everything it could to protect the people participating in its activities. Let's face it, everyone's intentions may be commendable when it comes to students' health and safety, but if protecting students was as simple as having their parents sign release forms, what do you think would happen?

Despite that, parental permission forms—as opposed to preinjury releases—are necessary in public schools and are another way to help avoid negligence, if done correctly. Permission forms are mostly informational in nature and serve many purposes. The most common uses are for field trips and extracurricular activities.

Sports activities should also have a parent's or guardian's signature of permission. This is especially important if the activity has any element of danger that might be considered "out-of-the-ordinary," such as playing football, diving from a high board, swimming in the ocean, or sailing in the Bahamas. If a student-athlete is seriously injured during one of these activities, the coach, the school administrator, and the superintendent probably will be blamed. If the school system can show that a parent or guardian was aware of the activity's dangers and still gave permission, it can go a long way toward protecting itself and its employees from financial disaster. Without a signed permission form, and faced with the loss of a possible scholarship, even the most enthusiastic and involved parent will be "shocked" by the aggressive nature of football. They might very well claim that they had no knowledge that the sport actually involves athletes coming into contact with their opponents.

Many other school sports' issues need to be sweated by the superintendent's careful attention. These include:

- student use of personally owned protective equipment while engaging in school-sponsored activities
- student practice and participation rules
- use of equipment not owned by the school, such as pools
- team practices off school grounds, especially in the cases of track teams that run to the side of (or in) neighborhood streets, roads, and highways

These issues have some elements of liability that a superintendent can reduce if handled properly. Of course, each issue must be treated according to its own set of complex circumstances within your local environment. Generally speaking, applying the guidelines can help you get through the liability labyrinth.

Tackle Stadium Problems

Another issue is indoor and outdoor bleachers and stadium lighting. The National Federation of States High School Associations' motto is, "School Activities: The Other Half of Education." This is a far cry from the nineteenth century, when there were few activities and even fewer rules. Today, superintendents must ensure student safety and protect themselves from liability by having clearly defined and recorded sets of procedures for everyone to follow.

Stadium problems include proactive security that begins before an event and continues until it is over. School-spirit emotions can carry over from stadiums to postgame hangouts. The community does not separate the responsibility of the school from what happens after the game. A shared concern for many districts is not fighting or unruly fans but vandalism. The burning of a team name or class of "05" into the field causes permanent damage and can be very costly. The Lubbock Independent School District in Lubbock, Texas, has had success regarding stadium problems by posting the rules and responsibilities for crowds. Director of Police and Safety Services, Thomas Nichols, says that rules' violations are less frequent when fans know their responsibilities. He posts large signs around the facility and requests occasional announcements from the public-address system, reminding people that smoking is not allowed on school property.

Specific procedures for inspection of gymnasium and stadium bleachers are also needed. After establishing inspection procedures, training the authorized individuals, and following recommendations by the manufacturer, you should make the unpopular decision that bleacher boards will not be painted. An effective way to increase the life expectancy of bleacher boards, and to help identify unsafe and damaged boards, is to adopt this policy. The senior class or boosters clubs must find a substitute to express their individuality and leave their mark on the school. Painted boards cause moisture to be retained in the wood, and that contributes to splitting and rotting. A can of paint can mask rotting or other serious defects in boards, which in turn might cause the district more in insurance claims. Schools should find a more creative way of showing school spirit. The class rock or path have become popular substitutes.

Stadium lighting and the exterior around buildings can become a major headache for superintendents. Security is the main issue, but schools that are located in areas surrounded by homes often have complaints from neighbors that the lights are too bright and shine into their bedrooms. Schools want to be good neighbors but also want a safe environment. A lighting area that may "bite you" is that of the light-learning link. There are thousands of studies on the influence of light on the human body and how it affects student learning, behavior, self-esteem, and even IQ. If you do not have access to your own staff expert, and feel like a "dim bulb" when faced with "lumens, lux, and foot-candles," an excellent resource is the Illuminating Engineering Society in New York City. They can shed some light on these issues along with some bright ideas about the foot-candle average and mounting of security lighting.

FIELD TRIPS—EDUCATIONAL, BUT RISKY BUSINESS!

Field trips for public school children are not new. They are the result of teachers' wanting to teach students in an environment that is more conducive to learning a particular idea, concept, or theory. Or, they may be an attempt to expose students to something they might not otherwise have an opportunity to experience. In some cases, field trips are taken to accomplish some extracurricular objective.

Whatever the reason for a field trip, there is a need to constantly review them for appropriateness, especially in the litigious society in which we live. The vast majority of trips are for very commendable purposes. However, even these trips can be questioned when their agendas include activities such as hang gliding, caving, sightseeing on the Rhine River, or a helicopter ride over New York City.

A physics teacher plans a trip to an amusement park. Ostensibly, the trip is to test the students on information they have been exposed to in the classroom. The object is to see if they can apply theory to accurately calculate speeds, distances, times, and so forth, using amusement park operations (e.g., roller coasters). This method of testing students' learned ability is further enhanced by its being based on state testing procedures.

A question arises after the testing process is complete because the students are allowed to participate in the amusement park activities for fun as a reward. Should the students be allowed to enjoy the amusement park (after all, they have traveled some distance, and there is a time factor), or should this be considered an unacceptable risk for the school system?

The trip is for a very legitimate educational purpose, but once the purpose has been satisfied, activities occur that are risky, both to the students and the school system, and are not particularly educational. This is a fundamental issue, and one that has no easy answers for the superintendent.

PLAYGROUND SAFETY IS NO ACCIDENT*

It's no secret that most student injuries happen on the playground. But how can the superintendent enlist administrators, teachers, and students to join in recognizing that playground safety is everyone's responsibility? Robert (Bud) Spillane

---

Source: Adapted with permission from G.C. Forman and R.L. Webb, School-Based Risk Management for Playgrounds, *Public Risk*, pp. 15–17, Copyright © 1995, Public Risk Management Association.

was photographed on playground equipment, sliding down a tube slide, for a widely distributed safety poster reminding everyone that playground safety is no accident. He illustrated that it is a collective involvement. Superintendents are responsible for promoting playground safety through clear communication about accident prevention. It is an issue that parents of elementary age children frequently question.

Planning Safe Playgrounds

With myriad safety and liability issues that face school systems every day in our increasingly dangerous and litigious society, the playground and its attendant play apparatus remain persistent headaches. Each year more than 400,000 children are injured on playgrounds. The injured are mostly under ten years of age with boys outnumbering girls four to one. There are presently no federal or state guidelines for playground safety. The American Academy of Pediatrics and the Consumer Product Safety Commission are excellent resources for a superintendent.

Accident prevention prompts a variety of questions including proper adult supervision; protective ground cover following the Consumer Product Safety Commission's guidelines; blacktop usage; appropriateness of metal, plastic, and wood equipment; and routine inspections and maintenance.

Unfortunately, most questions are raised after an accident or injury has occurred, and the questions are raised most often by parents. For some concerned parents, those questions translate into legal action because they believe the school was negligent.

It's a given fact that school personnel care about the well-being of their students. It isn't so certain that they're always aware of the proper precautions they must take on playgrounds to ensure that well-being. Preventing reasonably avoidable playground accidents is crucial to reducing the risk of liability.

Inspections and Beyond

Superintendents should consider the following recommendations for all playground sites, regardless of size, to prevent accidents and protect the financial assets and integrity of their district.

- Develop a schedule for periodic inspection, cleaning, and routine maintenance. Assign someone to be responsible for following this schedule and for keeping written records of all activities. This schedule should include requesting repairs and following up to make sure they're done.

- Develop a list of the playground areas that either differ from each other in topography or have different specific uses. Include items to look for during inspections, such as uneven ground, missing or ajar manhole covers, and rocks and debris close to a playing area.
- Develop a comprehensive inventory of the apparatuses on the playground. List each facet of the individual piece of equipment that poses a potential hazard, and include what to look for during inspections. (Examples on swing-set chains include weak links and rust; examples on wooden slides include potential splinters and cracked or broken boards.)
- Develop a protocol for taking any area of the playground or any piece of equipment out of service when modifications or repairs are needed. This protocol may include posting signs and securely roping off an area or an apparatus so students won't use it.

Rethinking Recess Rules

It is important that a school district have rules specifically designed for recess. The Academy of Pediatrics offers the following guidelines with additions from practitioners.

- Adults on recess duty must be visible to all children at all times. They must position themselves around the playground and avoid standing in clusters.
- Once on the playground, children may not reenter the building except when given permission by an adult.
- Contact sports aren't permitted.
- Children should be encouraged to play actively without pushing, shoving, punching, pulling, or hitting other children.
- "Gangs" of children aren't permitted to march through the play area.
- Jump ropes may be used only for jumping and not for playing tug-of-war and other games. They should never be taken on the slide.
- Only soft balls are permitted on the playground during recess.
- Children shouldn't retrieve balls that are off the playground without permission from an adult.
- Snowballs aren't allowed.
- Children may not climb trees.
- Children on swings must sit in an upright position and may not twirl or jump off while a swing is in motion. They may not run in front or in back of the swings.
- Children must go down the slides one at a time, sitting in an upright position, and not loiter at the top or bottom. They must not climb up or down the slide.

- Children may not wear backpacks while playing on equipment.
- Students should leave objects such as pencils, pens, and markers in the classroom.
- Shoelaces should be tied at all times.
- Equipment should be used only for the purpose for which it was designed.

AUDITORIUMS AND STAGES

If your district is fortunate enough to have a school auditorium and stage facility, you'll find it is one of the more unusual areas of the school. Everyone is familiar with the basic features such as a stage platform, curtains, and seating for hundreds of people. What is not commonly known are the many special requirements that apply to the construction and operation of auditoriums and theaters. Because these facilities are designed to hold more than 50 occupants, they are referred to as public assembly areas in building, fire, and life-safety codes. Most high school auditoriums have four separate exits, each equipped with "panic bar" door hardware and an illuminated EXIT sign. At the start of an event that is open to the general public, an audio announcement must be made to advise the patrons of the location of all emergency exits, and how to proceed in the event of an emergency. A common myth is that it is permissible to block one or more exits with video cameras or other equipment if "it's only a dress rehearsal and we have no more than 30 people in the room." The fact is if just a single person is occupying the auditorium, the entire facility must be treated as if every seat were filled.

When Sir James M. Barrie wrote Peter Pan in 1904, he was fascinated with the creativity of the London stagehands and craftsmen. He constantly wrote new special effects into his play throughout the rehearsal period.

We no longer have Sir James Barrie with us to rewrite his play to match today's technology, but the creative genius of the theater technicians that he enjoyed in 1904 can be found in any high school today. Students are applying problem-solving skills and physics with carpentry, painting, and electricity. Their creativity needs to be encouraged but also monitored and sometimes denied. And just how did Peter Pan fly at two Fairfax County, Fairfax, Virginia, high schools without incurring an unacceptable financial and safety risk? The district contracted with Peter Foy, the creative genius who flew Mary Martin on Broadway in the 1950s to provide "in-flight services."

When a high school selects a script to present on stage, they must secure the production rights from the publisher by paying a royalty fee. What they get in return is a box of scripts—the playwright's written word. What is not included is detailed engineering drawings describing how to build flame-resistant stage scenery that will adequately support the actors. Nor is there information on how to create the lighting effects without causing a fire or overloading the electrical system. The task of designing the technical effects is usually shared by the theater-arts teacher and one or more students. The primary function of scenery and lighting is to help the audience transcend time and space, but physical laws cannot be ignored. A clear standard of safety must be in force to protect the actors, technicians, and audience. A superintendent must understand the specific hazards associated with auditoriums and stages. "Break a leg" must remain the superstitious way to wish an actor luck and not become a prediction of the inevitable.

ENVIRONMENTAL HEALTH ISSUES

It can't be repeated enough that the primary objective is to institute every practical measure available to eliminate injuries to students, employees, or others, and to prevent losses to district property. All superintendents should have procedures in place dealing with environmental health issues. Procedures include, but are not limited to, provisions in the following: The Safe Drinking Water Act; Resources, Conservation, and Recovery Act; Comprehensive Environmental Response, Compensation and Liability Act (Superfund); Hazard Communication Standard; Bloodborne Pathogen Exposure Standard; and Respiratory Protection.

The health department once sent a team of investigators into my school when three-quarters of a kindergarten class had an outbreak of a mysterious and unpleasant rash. The children had itchy, burning hives that became worse the longer they were in the classroom. The press coverage raised additional concerns about children being in danger from a mysterious illness invading the kindergarten. The culprit was simply bad housekeeping of the water table. Most developmental early-childhood programs use sandboxes and water tables. Soiled water in a water table can spread germs in the classroom. The table had not been drained and disinfected after each day's use. While sand is less likely to support the growth of germs, the practice of wetting the sand has also been discovered in classrooms to cause the growth of mildew that may adversely affect the health of sensitive children. The use of food products such as rice or beans in these tables is not an acceptable substitution. So when you are worrying about funding all-day kindergartens or meeting the needs of your at-risk preschoolers, sweat the small stuff. That "fungus among us" may be happening in your schools.

Sweat the Unexpected

A superintendent in California had his day disrupted after the custodians tried to freeze a gopher to death. The rodent, found in a utility room, was sprayed with a freezing solvent used to clean gum and wax off floors. After spraying, a custodian lit a cigarette that caused an explosion, injuring a number of people, mostly students. People were hospitalized and treated for minor injuries. The gopher survived and was let loose in a nearby field. How can you be prepared for the little things that might turn explosive? Have standard operating procedures for as many things as possible. A "No Smoking" policy would have helped here.

Indoor Air Quality

Nothing is as charged as the issue of indoor air quality. Not only does it put smokers against nonsmokers, but in educational settings, it places windowless classrooms, use of magic markers, chalk, and other art, science, and cleaning supplies on the list of concerns. The list of complaints can send the typical superintendent into a frenzied tailspin.

Indoor air quality (IAQ) concerns have escalated in recent years. A principal might lament, "We have a sick school building. Everyone is getting sick. The IAQ is very poor. What can be done about it?"

Indoor air quality should not be judged by perceptions of comfort. A room that is too hot or too cold does not necessarily have poor air quality. Neither can a cluster of cancer patients in a building be blamed on the IAQ. Yet, the concern or discomfort must be dealt with. A teacher complains of a headache every afternoon and many of the students fall asleep. Is this a simple IAQ problem, a warning sign of a major health issue, or is the subject matter being taught in an uninspired manner?

Indoor air quality may be better judged by the potential sources of pollution (art media, cleaning agents, pets, and even people) and the provision of mechanisms for source removal. Whether a room has an IAQ problem will depend on the common activities within, or adjoining, the room and the amount of fresh air that is either naturally or mechanically brought into the room to dilute pollutants. A classroom having operable windows is unlikely to have an IAQ problem, but a room that is inadequately ventilated is likely to be stuffy or have an unpleasant odor. Correcting a problem may require nothing more than improving ventilation or simply discontinuing the activity that is the source of pollution.

Often the problem starts as a minor nuisance, such as an uncomfortable temperature or a noisy ventilator. Instead of requesting proper maintenance, cardboard is taped over a vent or a fan is shut off. Before long the superintendent's office is contacted by the media asking about the emergency action plan to deal with the "health crisis." Fear of the unknown, and the concern created by that fear, can cause overwhelming psychological stress that may have its own adverse effect on health. For this reason, every IAQ complaint must be treated seriously and answered in a timely manner. The lack of an appropriate response on the part of the administration can cause its own problems.

In the spring of 1991, West Springfield High School in Fairfax, Virginia, had to call the local fire and rescue squads 63 times because of a rash of fainting, lightheadedness, and headaches among its students. This health crisis was blamed on a serious IAQ problem by community members, parents, students, and teachers. Experts were called in and the school was tested for carbon dioxide, carbon monoxide, temperature, relative humidity, air movement, respirable suspended particulates, and volatile organic compounds. The more reassuring the experts were that this wasn't an environmental issue, the less reassured people became. The parent leaders of the West Springfield High School believed that they were facing a growing health crisis that could potentially affect more people. They suggested steps to ensure that people are prepared in the future as well as a number of proactive measures to combat potential IAQ problems. People have become increasingly aware of the dangers of pollutants. Indoor air quality is a new science, but one with which the superintendent must have some familiarity.

Parents of asthmatic children are personally buying and asking to install air cleaners in their child's classroom. The use of these supplemental air cleaners may provide additional dilution of normal room contaminants in the immediate area of the device, but their effectiveness is limited, especially if the ventilation system in the building is working properly. This issue is monumental for a parent with an ill child attempting to do everything to keep him or her healthy. Be aware and ready to respond, or this could bite you.

Multiple chemical sensitivity/environmental illness (MCS/EI) is becoming more common, and you will no doubt have to handle it. At the University of Minnesota, the Disability Services Section has already established its internal guidelines for handling MCS/EI. They request that all offices and spaces used by disability services staff and their visitors remain free of chemical-based scented products. They request using nonscented body products (e.g., lotion, hair spray); refraining from the use of optional items in office areas that give off chemical-based scents (e.g., air fresheners, potpourri), airing out recently dry-cleaned clothing before wearing; and using the least toxic cleaning products, disinfectants, and paints that are commercially available and storing them in tightly closed areas away from traffic areas. These guidelines are not a ban from use, but a voluntary request to refrain from using chemical-based scented products to accommodate people who report chemical sensitivities. This may not be as uncommon in the future.[*]

---

[*]*Source:* Adapted with permission from the Statement about Internal Guidelines Regarding Multiple Chemical Sensitivity/Environment Illness for Disability Services at the University of Minnesota, Copyright © Disability Services, University of Minnesota.

Bloodborne Pathogens

Some public school employees, because of the nature of their primary duties, are considered to be at an increased risk of exposure to bloodborne pathogens, including acquired immune deficiency syndrome (AIDS) and the hepatitis B virus. These employees are protected from exposure by state regulation. Generally, those employees at greater risk include those who routinely administer first aid or care for students with special needs. Other employees are exposed only as a result of an accident or during the performance of a good-Samaritan act and only when blood is present. The overall risk of exposure to bloodborne pathogens in a normal school setting is considered to be small.

Exposure is not simple contact with blood. Exposure occurs only when the blood of an infected individual enters the bloodstream of an uninfected person through a cut or sore or when splashed into the eyes, mouth, or nose. Exposure does not occur through contact with other body fluids such as mucus, vomitus, or feces unless blood is present. The blood from any individual should be considered to be infectious. Exposure can, of course, be avoided by using universal precautions, including handwashing and using latex gloves in nonemergency situations.

Under state regulation, public school employees who are at an increased risk of exposure are eligible to receive hepatitis B inoculations and postexposure medical evaluation and follow-up treatment at no cost. Any public school employee who is exposed to blood should seek medical treatment as soon as possible and hopefully within 24 hours of the exposure incident. If the source is known, the school has the obligation to seek consent for blood testing to determine the infectivity status of the source. The source is under no legal obligation to grant consent.

Visitors, volunteers, and the parents of children who have been exposed should be instructed to seek the advice of their family physicians. The first suspicion of a child or staff member who is human immunodeficiency virus (HIV)–positive will bring community and press to your office door. Have a plan to handle it or they will take a big bite out of you.

Radon and Asbestos

The U.S. Environmental Protection Agency (EPA) has formulated guidelines to minimize radon exposures in schools and has developed guidelines to manage and control asbestos. Every school district should develop a thorough understanding of both radon and asbestos and become familiar with established EPA guidelines and regulations relative to each.

Radon is a tasteless, odorless, and colorless radioactive gas that occurs naturally. It is found in varying amounts in rocks, in soil, and in underground water throughout the United States. It results from the natural breakdown or decay of uranium into radioactive particles. The EPA has determined that radon is a serious environmental health issue. Since 1989, the EPA has recommended that districts test for the presence of radon, and, if elevated levels are found, measures to remediate take place.

Asbestos is the term used to describe six naturally occurring fibrous minerals present in certain rock formations. Adverse health effects associated with asbestos have been found in adults who had long-term exposure to asbestos in the various asbestos industries. On October 22, 1986, the Asbestos Hazard Emergency Response Act (AHERA) was signed into law. The act required the EPA to develop regulations for dealing with asbestos in public and nonprofit private elementary and secondary schools. Districts are required to develop a management plan that includes, but is not limited to, designating and training an individual to oversee all asbestos-related activities in the district, prepare a management plan for each school, conduct a thorough inspection of every school building, and notify the public about the asbestos activities in each school and the availability of the management plan. Radon gas molecules and asbestos particles are very small things that you have to sweat and cause some very big problems if left unattended.

Lead in Paint and Water

Teachers and parents are often concerned about lead poisoning from a pencil stab. Pencils contain no lead at all. They use graphite or powdered carbon bound together with a glue. Stabs are completely nontoxic, but if the "lead" gets under the skin, the mark becomes a permanent tattoo. This is the minor lead issue. You also have to deal with the major ones.

The Centers for Disease Control reported in 1991 that childhood lead poisoning, a preventable disease, is one of the most common health problems in the United States today. Children may have lead exposure at school from exposure to lead paint, both inside the building and outside on the playground equipment. Teachers wanting to make their classrooms comfortable, homey and inviting, will often contaminate the room with painted rocking chairs and bookshelves that contain lead paint. The old claw-footed bathtubs often used for reading areas are usually lead based. The lead content of paint was not regulated until 1977. Older school buildings have leaded paint that is peeling, flaking, and chipping. Children will eat the chips because lead paint tastes sweet. Dust from lead-painted surfaces that are sanded or drilled can easily be inhaled and enter into the bloodstream. You must have a plan for dealing with lead paint that uses any one or all of the following four methods—encapsulation, scraping or using chemicals to remove, removal of paint off-site, or enclosing a lead-painted area with paneling or drywall.

In 1988, an amendment to the Safe Drinking Water Act was passed. The Lead Contamination Control Act directs that water coolers that are not lead-free be identified, that water coolers with lead-lined tanks be repaired or removed, and that the drinking water of schools be analyzed for lead. Schools with their own water supplies are required to notify parents, teachers, school personnel, and the community that lead test results are available. Superintendents with buildings built before 1977, and those that have old plumbing, should investigate any potential source of lead poisoning.

SEXUAL HARASSMENT: TOUCHY-FEELY EMPLOYEES NOT WANTED

When school culture is mentioned, some people think not only about academic excellence, expectations, and celebrations but about warm and friendly individuals who care about one another and make the school a big happy family. "I really like the way your hair looks today." "That's a great looking dress you have on." "I really love the scent of your cologne." Welcome compliments from a principal or coworker, or sexual harassment in the workplace?

It may be either, depending on how it is delivered. If it is said while caressing the hair, touching the dress, or sniffing too close, it may be unwelcome by the recipient and considered a form of sexual harassment, especially if repeated with any frequency. The liability risks to an organization from sexual harassment claims keep growing. Following the airing of Anita Hill's allegations of sexual harassment during Clarence Thomas' Supreme Court confirmation proceedings, there was a dramatic increase in the number of sexual harassment claims filed with the Equal Employment Opportunity Commission (EEOC). What is sexual harassment, what is a school system's exposure to sexual harassment claims, and what can superintendents and others in your organization do to minimize its exposure?

What Is Sexual Harassment?

There are two types of sexual harassment in the workplace.

The first type is quid pro quo harassment, which is unwelcome conduct of a sexual nature where submission is a condition of employment or is the basis for an employment decision; e.g., sex in return for a promotion or for keeping one's job. Quid pro quo sexual harassment is easily recognizable and there is little dispute that such conduct is reprehensible and should not be tolerated in the workplace. It is the second type of sexual harassment, referred to as hostile environment sexual harassment, that has garnered most of the publicity and controversy. Hostile environment sexual harassment is sexually discriminatory behavior that is sufficiently severe or pervasive to alter the conditions of the victim's employment and create a working environment that a reasonable person would find hostile or offensive and that the victim subjectively finds abusive. Broad examples of hostile environment sexual harassment include unwelcome touching, hugging, patting, pinching, kissing, telling sexual jokes, making sexual innuendoes or gestures, and displaying sexually explicit materials. Sexual harassment includes a man harassing a woman, a woman harassing a man, or someone engaged in homosexual harassment.

Since only a supervisor has the ability to condition an employment decision in return for a sexual favor, all quid pro quo sexual harassers are supervisors. However, hostile environment sexual harassers can be coworkers, subordinates, or even nonemployees, such as vendors or customers.

The victims of sexual harassment are not limited to the persons who are the object of the harasser. A man or a woman who loses out on a job benefit, e.g., a promotion or a raise, that is given to someone else because he or she submits to the harasser's unwelcome demands, may have a valid sexual harassment claim. In a workplace where there is widespread consensual sexual conduct, even without the promise of a raise or promotion, the working environment may be considered hostile and offensive to those who are not involved in the sexual conduct, and they may be able to successfully claim sexual harassment against their employer. These "third-party" claims of sexual harassment by employees, who are not the direct object of the harasser, considerably increase an organization's exposure to liability.

Although any sexually harassing behavior is not appropriate in the workplace, it does not constitute unlawful conduct that will expose an organization to liability, unless there is a quid pro quo or the conduct is sufficiently severe or pervasive to alter the conditions of the victim's employment and create a working environment that a reasonable person would find hostile or offensive and that the victim subjectively finds abusive. Whether particular conduct is sufficiently severe or pervasive can be determined only by looking at all the circumstances, including the frequency of the discriminatory conduct, its severity (the more severe the harassment, the less need to show a repetitive series of incidents, and in patently offensive cases, such as the touching of intimate body parts, one incident is enough to make an environment hostile), whether the conduct was directed at more than one individual, whether the alleged harasser is a supervisor or coworker, whether others joined in the harassment, whether it is physically threatening or humiliating or a mere offensive utterance, and whether it unreasonably interferes with an employee's work performance. The effect on the employee's psychological well-being is relevant to determining whether the person actually found the environment abusive, but abusive environment harassment may be proven without showing any psychological injury. The EEOC takes the position that if the victim is a woman, then the reasonable-person standard is a reasonable woman; i.e, whether a reasonable woman would find the conduct hostile or offensive.

Often, it is the complainant's word against the accused as to what, if anything, occurred, and whether the complainant welcomed the conduct or considered it unwelcome and abusive. The EEOC and the courts will look at a number of factors in determining whether the complainant or the accused is more credible. Although sexually provocative attire or frequent use of profanity by the complainant may undermine his or her credibility on whether the conduct was unwelcome, the complainant's past sexual conduct with anyone other than the accused is usually not considered relevant. However, past harassment of others by the accused may well undercut denials by the accused that he or she harassed the complainant. Although contemporaneous complaints about the harassment (e.g., to a friend, spouse, or coworker) will substantially bolster the credibility of the complainant's story, the failure to tell anyone will not necessarily deprive a victim of prevailing on his or her claim. Though it is certainly preferable for the victim to tell the harasser in no uncertain terms that the conduct is unwelcome and should cease, all that is required to prove a claim is that the victim's actions (e.g., she turned, or walked away) indicated to the harasser that the conduct was unwelcome.

The Employer's Liability for Sexual Harassment

The EEOC's position is that a company is absolutely liable for quid pro quo sexual harassment by one of its supervisors and is liable for hostile environment sexual harassment by a supervisor, coworker, or a third party if the company knew of the harassment, or upon reasonably diligent inquiry should have known, and failed to take immediate appropriate corrective action. Some courts have refused to hold an employer liable for quid pro quo sexual harassment where the company took immediate and effective corrective action.

Under Title VII of the Civil Rights Act of 1964, a company whose employee proves that he or she was sexually harassed by a supervisor, coworker, or other person at the workplace is liable for any back pay lost, interest, compensatory damages for future pecuniary losses, emotional pain, suffering, inconvenience, mental anguish, loss of enjoyment of life, and other nonpecuniary losses, plus punitive damages in cases involving malice or reckless indifference. There is a cap on such compensatory and punitive damages that ranges from $50,000 for a company with 15 to 100 employees to $300,000 for a company that has over 500 employees. Title VII claims are often combined with other causes of action, such as the intentional infliction of emotional distress, for which there are no caps on the amount of damages a judge or jury may impose against an organization.

Minimizing Your District's Exposure to Sexual Harassment Liability

Although there is no way to completely eliminate the liability risk to sexual harassment claims, there are a number of things you can do to minimize the extent of your district's exposure.

It is essential that your management team be educated to understand the broad scope of activities that constitute unlawful sexual harassment. Management must make a commitment and undertake the effort to eradicate, as much as is humanly possible, sexual harassment in the organization. If management does not take the matter seriously ("let's not sweat this one"), its employees won't either, and a six- or seven-figure jury award may not be far behind. This commitment and this effort must be communicated to all employees. Supervisors should be trained and sensitized to understand what sexual harassment is, how to properly investigate claims of harassment, and when and how to impose appropriate and effective corrective action. All employees should be assured that sexual harassment in the workplace won't be tolerated.

The district should formalize a written sexual harassment policy that defines sexual harassment, gives examples of it, and includes a procedure for employees to report harassment claims. At a minimum, the procedure should allow a claim to be made to someone other than the employee's supervisor, who often may be the accused harasser. It would be advisable to include a woman among those to whom a sexual harassment claim may be reported.

All claims should be thoroughly investigated. Confidentiality should be maintained to the greatest extent possible. The complainant, the accused, and all persons who could possibly corroborate or contradict the claim should be interviewed in detail. If there is insufficient evidence to substantiate the claim, the complainant should be so informed and advised to report immediately any further problems. Even without sufficient corroboration, the system should consider any feasible steps to ensure that the complainant is protected from any future potential problems. All parties should be made aware that any retaliation for the filing of the claim will be immediately and severely dealt with.

If there is reasonable cause to believe that the claim has merit, the company must take whatever action is necessary to remedy the situation and ensure that the harassment ceases. There are a number of court decisions against companies that took action that proved ineffective. Each situation differs. Effective action may merely require a warning, or it could include a transfer of the offending employee, or it may require discharging the harasser. The complainant should be fully advised of the action that will be taken and be asked for any recommendations he or she may have. To minimize potential claims for defamation, only those with a need to know should be privy to the reasons for the action taken against the offender.

As a superintendent, it is vital to your district's welfare that you be sensitive to the broad scope of unlawful sexually harassing behavior and undertake procedures to minimize your organization's exposure to sexual harassment liability.

The importance of responding promptly and fully to an employee's claim of sexual harassment is illustrated by a case filed by a school custodian against the school board in Lima City, Ohio. The school custodian claimed that immediately after being hired, the school principal invited her to get together after school, made numerous sexual comments to her, followed her around the school, watched her work while he ate lunch, and rubbed his hand across her back.

The custodian said that a month after being hired, the principal forced her to go to the basement boiler room with him where he fondled her and rubbed against her in a sexual manner. The custodian said she protested against his actions and he released her after she vomited. Later that day, the custodian reported the incident to the head custodian, who shortly thereafter notified the assistant superintendent. The school superintendent was then informed of the matter, and the school district retained a law firm to conduct an investigation.

After concluding its investigation, the law firm recommended that the principal be dismissed. A hearing was held; the hearing referee recommended dismissal and the school board dismissed the principal. The principal appealed and the local state court upheld the dismissal. The custodian then sued the school board for sexual harassment in federal court.

Although the court found that the principal's sexual assault constituted extreme sexual harassment, it said that the school board was not liable for the harassment because it took immediate and appropriate corrective action by promptly investigating the matter and terminating the principal as soon as it had been notified of the harassment. The court found that there was no evidence that the school board knew or should have known that the principal may have had a history of sexual harassment.

Like the federal court in the Lima school board case, most courts now hold that an employer will not be liable for hostile environment sexual harassment, whether committed by a supervisor or a coworker, if the employer did not know and had no reason to know about the sexual harassment and took prompt and appropriate remedial action upon first learning about the harassment. It should be noted that in quid pro quo sexual harassment cases (i.e., where submission to the harasser is a condition of employment or is the basis for an employment decision) the courts are currently divided on whether prompt remedial action by the employer will relieve it of liability or whether the employer is strictly liable.

Federal civil rights laws also cover student-on-student sexual harassment. School districts are under increasing pressure from courts to effectively respond to complaints of student-on-student sexual harassment as illustrated by the following cases:

- A six-year-old first grader in Lexington, North Carolina, kissed a classmate on the cheek. A teacher who observed the kiss reported the child to the principal. The school principal decided that the child should be denied certain privileges for violation of a school rule that prohibits unwarranted and unwelcome touching of one student by another.
- Another first grader, a seven-year-old boy in Queens, New York, also kissed a classmate "because he liked her" and took a button off her skirt because he was reminded of a book about the bear who wears overalls with a missing button. The school suspended the child for five days for sexual harassment.
- A California jury awarded a 14-year-old girl $500,000 in damages after ruling that, in 1993, officials of the Antioch Unified School District had ignored the student's complaints that a fellow classmate subjected her to frequent vulgarities, insults, and physical threats.

Failure to prevent student-on-student sexual harassment could cost a school district federal funding under Title IX of the federal civil rights law.

TRANSPORTATION: THE BUS STOPS HERE

Students start and end the school day with the bus driver. This individual has responsibility for moving kids safely while maneuvering a 15-ton vehicle through traffic in all kinds of weather. Whether the buses are owned, leased, or contracted for, the bus driver must undergo specific screening and training.

Keeping the Buses Rolling

Recruitment and retention of a sufficient number of school bus drivers is a continuous problem throughout the country. Good pay and great benefits are essential. Other proven inducements are allowing drivers to take their own preschool children on the bus and offering a bonus or a bond to drivers who recruit other individuals. One of the biggest problems in retaining drivers is the lack of summer work, or a summer paycheck, and the lack of a set number of guaranteed hours so drivers know they can count on a specific amount in their paychecks.

Driver training is one of the most important facets of a transportation operation. As a minimum, initial driver training should be conducted in addition to recertification training every five years, first-aid and cardiopulmonary resuscitation (CPR) training, driver improvement for all who have a preventable accident each month, bus attendant training, and defensive driver training. Statistics should be kept and measured against the overall operation on all accidents to try and predict what emphasis should be placed on existing and future driver training.

The U.S. Department of Transportation (USDOT) along with the Federal Highway Administration administers a federal law entitled the Omnibus Transportation Employee Testing Act of 1991. The law requires drivers to have a commercial driver's license (CDL) and subjects drivers to random drug and alcohol testing with physical examinations. The CDL law requires separate driver testing through the Division of Motor Vehicles (DMV) in each state and is required for drivers who operate vehicles in excess of 26,000 pounds referred to as gross vehicle weight (GVWR), designed to carry 16 or more passengers (including the driver), or of any size, which is used in the transportation of a placardable amount of hazardous material. The GVWR includes most standard and transit style–sized school buses of 64 or more passengers.

Bus Standards

States and localities have varying laws regulating school bus transportation for students. In some instances, distance from school is a criteria. Safety considerations may make it impossible for students to walk any distance in certain areas. Special-education transportation is also required as a related service and is sometimes included in a student's individual education plan (IEP).

The USDOT sets mandatory standards for school bus transportation, particularly construction standards. Have you ever wondered why all school buses nationwide have the same exact shade of yellow paint? Long ago a group of transportation safety specialists were asked to sweat the color for school buses. The yellow that you see on any school bus is the national standard, adopted because of its high visibility and easy recognition. The National Highway Transportation Safety Administration (NHTSA) is within USDOT and is the agency that reviews, studies, and recommends construction standards for school buses. The National Transportation Safety Board (NTSB) investigates major accidents involving school buses and other passenger conveyances and submits recommendations to NHTSA for construction standard changes, and to states for operational changes when utilizing school buses.

Fuel for Thought

Superintendents should consider a continual replacement program for aging school buses. This is necessary to prevent a fleet that costs an excessive amount per mile to operate. For all intents and purposes, if the policy is to maintain a 12-year-old fleet, a continual replacement program for aging school buses is necessary. Then for planning purposes, one-twelfth of the fleet should be replaced annually. It is also very important to study the type of buses to be purchased. If the fleet continues to get older and the 12-year-old policy is not followed, it is essential to specify buses that will have heavier duty components that will last longer. Many floors are currently being replaced in buses that are over 12 years old. This is very expensive. Another issue is the size of the buses to replace the existing fleet. If the school population continues to grow, then the replacement buses should be sized in a larger capacity to help handle the growth so additional buses will not always be necessary. Most buses are for 64 passengers. In a rural area or for special-education transportation purposes, smaller capacity buses may be sufficient.

Bell schedules are key elements in determining the number of buses required; hence the cost of transportation. The transportation department needs to have the authority to suggest the most efficient beginning and ending times for each school within state requirements for length of school day. Ideally, the best approach would be a four-tiered approach to bell schedules or four distinct morning and afternoon schedules to maximize the use of the bus fleet. Unfortunately, in most cases only two or three distinct time schedules are used. This requires more buses. Factors that impact multitiered scheduling include the following:

- Elementary students should not start so early that they walk or wait in the dark in the winter months.
- Some think no students should start school before 8 a.m.; starting later puts everyone in the afternoon rush hour traffic and darkness in winter months.
- Day care needs must be considered.
- High schools are often scheduled in-first and out-first due to sports schedules, after-school jobs, and other individual reasons.
- The length of the school day may vary by level.
- Opinions and/or rulings by school boards, administrative staffs, principals, teachers, and parents on school hours affect scheduling.
- Facilities problems of not being able to house all students from a given community in a local school cause longer bus runs across the area.
- Changing previous schedules often meets with resistance due to impact on personal schedules.

Automated transportation systems provide many benefits, particularly in large school districts. After inputting the number and names of students at each bus stop, an automated system can be used to maximize the riding capacity of each bus run and determine the optimal bus routes using the fewest buses. Computer-generated bus routes need to be reviewed carefully and tested on the road before they are implemented. Having the names of students in the database is of great assistance in an accident situation.

Having two-way radio-equipped school buses is very important to the total operation. It is not icing on the cake as some budget-conscious officials think when a driver can instantly call in an accident, medical emergency on a school bus, a lost child, a fight, weapons at a bus stop or on the school bus, or even a bus breakdown. Prior to installation of two-way radios in all buses, a school bus in a Virginia district was caught in heavy traffic on an interstate highway. A medical emergency occurred, and the driver had no way of communicating for assistance. The student died. Naturally, parents and school officials are concerned about the safety and well-being of the children being transported. A two-way radio-communication system assures them that students are in good hands. Drivers communicate with other drivers to help stranded buses or students and to reroute buses due to adverse weather conditions. Drivers have notified the schools and police as a preventative measure if a strange adult is following the bus or is seen talking to students at a bus stop and possibly interfering with their overall safety.

Long before strings, straps, key chains, bookbags, and coats became a matter of concern for the NHTSA and state departments of education, I had a fourth-grade student who stopped on the playground while walking home from school. Unsupervised and alone, his backpack caught in the slide and he was strangled. Today drawstrings and backpacks persist in causing injury and death across the nation, especially as related to school buses. The strings can become caught in bus doors and handrails. Students have been dragged to death because the driver did not notice the string was caught and students could not get free. Sweat the small strings, remind drivers of added safety measures, and work with garage facilities to make all needed modifications to bus handrails and doors.

"Buses are overcrowded," is a complaint that schools or parents use from time to time. School bus capacities are rated by bus manufacturers based on a standard 39-inch seat and using a state definition of average "rump" size of 13 inches. Therefore, for elementary-level students, three children are expected to be seated per seat on a 64- or 78-passenger school bus. However, middle and high school students are only expected to sit two to a seat, which brings the capacity down to 45 on a 64-passenger bus and 55 on a 78-passenger school bus. Students are expected to only carry on the bus what they can hold on their laps for space and safety considerations. Some states do not permit any standees on school buses after the first 30 operating days of the school year, except in an emergency. The safety design inherent with school bus construction is violated when passengers are not properly seated.

Why don't school buses have seat belts? The Department of Transportation (DOT), at both the federal and state level, do not recommend seat belts on school buses. The DOT studied the most severe school bus accidents and found that seat belts would not have prevented any injuries or accidents, and that belts could have caused more injuries or deaths. Compartmentalization, however, requires reinforced seats, more padding, and closer spacing. This combination helps absorb shock from an accident without serious injury to the passengers. Seat belts require supervision by drivers, but compartmentalization does not. Compartmentalization works equally well for one, two, or three passengers per seat, whereas seat belts become entangled and need adjustment for small to large passengers every day, requiring readjustment as the bus is reused. Another concern is that students on buses equipped with seat belts might experience an increase in concussions from other students' swinging belts with the heavy buckles at the end. Compartmentalization leaves the passenger free to escape the bus, whereas seat belts leave passengers strapped in, even upside down, in burning or flooding buses. Compartmentalization is most affordable as it is required on all school buses and is built in; whereas seat belts require stronger seat structures. Materials cost between $1,300 and $3,000 extra per bus based on the bus size and manufacturer.

Buses are always in a state of picking up or discharging students or traveling empty between one bus run and the next. Some school buses appear to the public to not always be full. Buses may be full on a high school run, pick up a shuttle of a handful of vocational students to deliver to another school, then have a full elementary run. Due to time or distance constraints, the bus is utilized at its best during that time, but has some seats available during the shuttle run. Afternoon high and middle school runs sometimes appear lighter due to after-school activities for some students. Some elementary schools have half-day kindergarten runs that crowd buses in part of their geographic boundary for the morning runs, then those students go home at noon and those same buses appear lighter loaded in the afternoons. The opposite occurs in the remaining geography of the school boundary where the students come in at noon on the kindergarten run and go home on other school buses; thus crowding them in the afternoon only. In addition, special-education buses may appear large on the outside, but the inside is configured with smaller seats or no seats at all so wheelchairs can be transported. These buses often seem to have seats available when viewed from the outside. Also, parents may drive students, some students may drive, or some students may be ill, which makes a bus appear to not be full.

BE COOL—EAT AT SCHOOL

You have brains in your head.
You have feet in your shoes.
You can steer yourself
Any direction you choose.
                    –Dr. Seuss (1990)[*]

Dr. Seuss is right on target. As superintendent you can go any direction you choose. Choosing a food service operation will influence students' future health and eating habits.

The National School Lunch Program is over 50 years old. In 1946, President Harry S. Truman signed the National School Lunch Act into law. At that time, parents sent surplus garden produce to be used in the lunch preparation, and students furnished their own silver and china, which they took home each day to wash. The price of lunch was ten cents.

The philosophy of feeding students now runs the spectrum from contracting out to fast food to running a district operation. As the superintendent, in determining the role food will play, you should remember that the purpose of schools is to prepare students for the future and that proper eating habits should be reinforced at school. A food service program should be an extension of the educational program, operating under the federally funded National School Lunch and Child Nutrition Acts. The program must be run in accordance with federal and state laws and regulations and your district-established policies. The objective of the program is to improve the health of students and to promote nutrition education by providing appealing and nutritious food at a minimum cost. If a district participates in a National School Lunch Program and Child Nutrition Program, they enter into an agreement to provide free and reduced-price meals to eligible children in the schools. Eligible children may not be required to work for their meals, enter the lunchroom through a separate entrance, or go through a separate serving line; and they can't be required to use a separate lunchroom or eat meals at a different time.

Penny McConnell, the past president of the American School Food Service Association, and president of the School Food Service Foundation, says that "the cafeteria is the nutrition lab of the school." She cautions superintendents, that in order to run a successful school program that is nutritious, you must be competitive. The individual who oversees the program must be a manager whose exper-

---

[*]*Source:* From OH, THE PLACES YOU'LL GO by Dr. Seuss and copyright © 1990 by Dr. Seuss Enterprises, L.P. Reprinted by permission of Random House, Inc.

tise includes safe handling of food, menu planning, garnishing, allergies, and all the business challenges. McConnell cautions "that you don't need to go branding if you're in touch with your clientele" (personal communication). McConnell, who turns a $2-million profit for her school district, says that the superintendent, who supports food service, is an important part of the school day and will do the best for his students. When a district contracts out, it no longer deals with nutrition but only with turning a profit.

Competitive foods is a major issue since everyone is vying for the same dollar. The sale of candy, chips, and soft drinks causes a conflict with teams and clubs who want to raise funds. Districts should have a competitive food regulation that states that "junk" food, called low nutrient–dense food in the industry, cannot be sold during the school day. You can't eliminate the foods completely, but you can regulate.

Breakfast plays an important role in student health and school performance. Many districts have breakfast programs but must be sensitive to certain religious groups who find that breakfast programs conflict with both family values and religious observances. Research can help a superintendent formulate his philosophy on feeding students.

School Health Alert frequently reports on student health issues. A study done by Dr. N. Vasmeer showed that students who ate breakfast 30 minutes before taking a test made higher grades than children who ate breakfast two hours before the test (Andrews, 1997). Dr. Vasmeer tested 560 fifth- and sixth-grade children from different neighborhoods and income levels. Cognitive functions tested were memory and visual-word recall. Results showed that children who ate breakfast at school about 30 to 60 minutes prior to test time performed better. Other studies that Dr. Vasmeer references demonstrate improvement in test scores of children who drink a glass of orange juice prior to testing and that poorly nourished children score lower on tests if they have no breakfast. For districts trying to improve test scores, a mid-morning snack of carbohydrates might provide the mental prowess needed to achieve some improvement.

If you are considering contracting out your food service, you better do your homework. Be certain you know what you are taking over in the kitchens. Are you still responsible for the equipment or is the contractor? Are the employees your responsibility or theirs? Will they handle worker compensation claims? Who is going to oversee the free and reduced-price lunch programs? School superintendents have been bitten with outsourcing when the company came in and handled nothing but the preparation of the food. Be certain you are clear about all the details. McConnell points out that every state has a chapter of the American School Food Service, and they will act as a resource and send in a peer team whenever asked.

BIDDING AND PROCUREMENT: USE IT WISELY

Most states have laws regarding public procurement of goods. As superintendent, you must familiarize yourself with the requirements. Be certain that the person to whom you delegate the purchasing understands and follows the law and provides guidance to schools on the rules and regulations for purchasing goods and services with both public and nonpublic monies.

No one can deny that competition in purchasing is good and should be used to ensure the best possible goods and service at the best possible price. Competitive bidding is used when you know what you want to purchase and price will be a determining factor in awarding the contract. When competitive bidding is used, the award must be made to a responsible firm submitting the lowest responsive bid. Responsible means that you have reason to believe that the lowest bidder can perform according to the contract. Responsive means that they submitted a bid for that which was requested.

Competitive bidding is the preferred method of procurement because it eliminates the subjectivity contained in the other methods and helps avoid any appearance of impropriety by school personnel. If your state has no rules for competitive bids, you might want to establish a district policy directing your schools in how to sweat the small stuff in terms of legal purchasing. In Fairfax County, Virginia, competitive bids for items estimated to cost up to $5,000 may be obtained by telephone. Two firms must be contacted to obtain bids. For bids with an estimated cost greater than $5,000, requests for bids must be submitted by mail to at least three firms and a notice of solicitation posted in the school.

Competitive negotiation is another means of obtaining competition. Competitive negotiation is used when you need to consider factors other than price in awarding a contract. Many states allow schools to use competitive negotiation for the acquisition of class rings, yearbooks, pictures, and graduation announcements. The advantage of competitive negotiation over competitive bidding is that it provides much greater flexibility in determining contract award. Unlike competitive bidding that requires that you award the bid to the vendor with the lowest responsible and responsive bid, competitive negotiation allows contract awards to be based on factors that you decide are important and relevant to your needs. The competitive negotiation process recognizes that you will be making subjective decisions about vendor proposals and that one is superior to another.

However, the following situations and circumstances dictate the use of noncompetitive purchasing.

- Small purchases. This method of procurement establishes a dollar-value level up to which no competition is required. The basis for no competition for small purchases is that any cost benefits to be gained by competition would be outweighed by the administrative costs of obtaining bids.
- Sole source. This method of procurement is followed when there exists only one practical source for the required goods or services. The basis for these decisions must be documented. An example of a sole-source purchase is when you acquire textbooks directly from publishers. These textbooks are not available from any other source but the publishers.
- Emergency purchases. Emergency purchases are allowed when required to avoid a diminution of public services. The basis for these decisions must be documented.

Dean Tistadt, a certified public purchasing officer, offers these critical elements to competitive negotiation (personal communication).

- You *must* issue a written request for proposal (RFP).
- The RFP must contain the following information as a minimum:
  - scope of the RFP
  - specific requirements
  - basis for contract award
  - deadline for submission of proposals
- The proposals must be evaluated consistent with the requirements and the award must be made on the basis stated in the RFP.
- Once you have determined the ranking of vendor proposals, you have the right to negotiate changes with the top-ranked vendor as a part of the process of executing a contract.
- After contract award, vendors have the right to see the contract file (by appointment).
- You should be very cautious in making any statements to vendors about your decisions regarding the award of the contract. (You should never say, for example, that you have awarded the contract to another vendor with whom you have been doing business for many years because they have always done such a good job.)
- It is recommended that you write to all vendors who submitted a proposal, thank them for their interest, inform them that their proposal was excellent and received serious consideration, but that a decision was made to award to another vendor. State that you hope that they will continue to respond to future solicitations. In other words, accent the positive, not the negative.

YOU'RE ASKING FOR WHAT?

Constantly changing conditions necessitate continuing revisions in all nuts-and-bolts policies. Dangers lurk everywhere. As superintendent, you cannot run from dangers. You must confront them and provide the necessary leadership. Being known as the so-called safety and health superintendent, as well as the instructional leader, will provide a healthy educational environment for students and staff. My Italian grandmother who spoke little English used to say, "trying to do the impossible, we obtain the best possible." Don't be afraid to do the impossible while sweating the small stuff.

REFERENCES

Andrews, R. (1997). Timing of breakfast affects test results. *School Health Alert, 12*(6), 4.

Dr. Seuss. (1990). *Oh, the places you'll go!* New York: Random House.

Office of Juvenile Justice and Delinquency Prevention. U.S. Department of Justice and Office of Elementary and Secondary Education. (1996, September). *Creating safe and drug-free schools—Action guide,* Washington, DC: Author.

SUGGESTED READING

78 American Law Reports. (1986). *When is work environment intimidating, hostile, or offensive, so as to constitute sexual harassment in violation of Title VII of Civil Rights Act of 1964, as amended.* Rochester, NY: Lawyers Co-operative Publishers.

American Bar Association. (1980). *The model procurement code for state and local governments recommended regulations.* Chicago: American Bar Association.

Bravo, E., & Cassedy, E. (1992). *The nine to five guide to combating sexual harassment.* New York: John Wiley & Sons.

Environmental Protection Agency. (1995). *Indoor air quality tools for schools.* Pittsburgh, PA: Superintendent of Documents.

Equal Employment Opportunity Commission. (1990, March 19). *Policy on sexual harassment.* Washington, DC: Author.

Equal Employment Opportunity Commission. *Policy guide on employer liability for sexual favoritism under Title VII.* Washington, DC: Author.

Furr, K. (1990). *Handbook of laboratory safety.* 3rd Ed. Boca Raton, FL: CRC Press.

Lindermann, B., & Grossman, P. (1996). *Employment discrimination law: ABA section of labor and employment law.* 3rd Ed. Washington, DC: Bureau of National Affairs.

Lindermann, B., & Kadue, D.D. (1992). *Sexual harassment in employment law: ABA section of labor and employment law,* 3rd Ed. Washington, DC: Bureau of National Affairs.

Minor, J., & Minor, V.B. (1991). *Risk management in schools: A guide to minimizing liability.* Newbury Park, CA: Corwin.

Slote, L. (1987). *Handbook of occupational safety and health.* New York: John Wiley & Sons.

Zenz, G.J. (1994). *Purchasing and the management of materials.* New York: John Wiley & Sons.

Appendix 6–A

ORGANIZATIONS

AAA Foundation for Traffic Safety
1440 New York Avenue, NW
Suite 201
Washington, DC 20005
(202) 942-2050
(202) 783-4788 Fax
http://www.aaa.com

Centers for Disease Control and Prevention
National Center for Injury Prevention and Control
4770 Buford Highway, MS K63
Chanblee, GA 30341
(770) 488-4652
(770) 488-1317 Fax
http://www.cdc.gov/ncipc/ncipchm.htm

Kidsnet
P.O. Box 56642
Washington, DC 20011
(202) 291-1400
kidsnet@aol.com

National Alliance for Safe Schools
344 Lanham-Severn
Suite 102A
Lanham, MD 20706
or
P.O. Box 30177
Bethesda, MD 20824
(301) 306-0200
http://www:safeschools.com
nass@allware.com

National Association of School Safety and Law Enforcement Officers
P.O. Box 118
Catlett, VA 22019

National Highway Traffic Safety Administrators
Safety Countermeasures Division
400 7th Street, SW
Washington, DC 20590
(202) 366-1739
(202) 366-7149 Fax
http://www.nhtsa.dot.gov

National Institute of Government Purchasing (NIGP)
Reston International Center
11800 Sunrise Valley Drive
Suite 1050
Reston, VA 20190-5303
(703) 715-9400
(703) 715-9887 Fax
http://www.nigp.org
fabu-taleb@nigp.org

National School Safety Center
4165 Thousand Oaks Boulevard
Suite 290
Westlake Village, CA 91362
(805) 373-9977

National School Transportation Association (NSTA)
P.O. Box 2639
Springfield, VA 22152

Nonprofit Risk Management Center
1001 Connecticut Avenue, NW
Suite 900
Washington, DC 20036-5504
(202) 785-3891
(202) 833-5747 Fax

Public Risk Management Association (PRIMA)
1815 N. Fort Myers Drive
Suite 1020
Arlington, VA 22209
(703) 528-7701
(202) 528-7966
http://www.primacentral.org

School Foodservice & Nutrition
ASFSA Member Services
1600 Duke Street
7th Floor
Alexandria, VA 22314-3426

CHAPTER 7

People Are Everything

Marlene C. Holayter

Except in a few lingering evolutionary backwaters, the autocratic, my-way-or-the-highway type of superintendent is obsolete. Where such boss-type know-it-alls are not becoming extinct by an advance in understanding among school leaders themselves, they are being rapidly fossilized by the concerted action of feisty teacher unions, aggressive community groups, bellicose business people, and cantankerous school boards. The old archetype has flown the coop as surely as the carrier pigeon no longer takes wing. Further, only a few are left and they may be jawing around the cracker-barrel, mourning the passing. Yet others are imagining that the high-performance, high-standard, information-explosive world will just fade away.

Enter the metaleader—evolved and fit for survival and success in the twenty-first century. The more enlightened, visionary, and collegial breed of superintendent, who is today's model, embodies the core understanding of the new-school world order, which simply is this: In educational leadership, as in life, people are everything. The most valuable asset possessed by public education in America walks out the doors of the nation's 15,500 school districts every night after school. Try imagining a school system without them. Impossible. As educators, our business is people.

This chapter is about the people dimension. It explores changes where the people element in businesses and organizations is successful and presents an approach to creating and sustaining the best in people. This is not a how-to manual with easy answers. Building the human element requires that each leader in a school district struggle with the dilemmas inherent in the individual organizations. It explores why the superintendent as the metaleader must reach out and get the best people, expect the best from people, and keep the best people. This role calls for a person who embodies the qualities everyone wants in a leader. To thrive in this environment, school leaders must embrace the new reality and turn it to everyone's advantage.

This will rarely be easy. Schools are not only people-intensive places, but they also summon up in people's minds parts of the past as well as the future. Everybody has a preconceived notion about what is good for schools. They get it from newspapers, television, and radio talk shows. They are experts about schools because they went to one. They are accomplished in diagnosing schools' ills because they've heard all about what's wrong from the news media. Amidst their deep and broad skepticism about everything else they see on TV and read in the papers, they seem to believe that education is the one topic where pundits, politicians, and reporters finally get it right. They hear what the news media say is wrong with the schools and accept that it must be true.

The school system is the one place where parents, guardians, uncles, aunts, and grandparents send their children—and expect miracles. Fair enough, and sometimes we do perform miracles. We know that all the families in our communities send us the best children they have. And it is our fundamental duty to give them the best we have. A good superintendent does this almost by second nature. But many questions prevail, such as, Have you ever thought about what a profound role the school leader has? Who is at the core of this person who is called superintendent? Why have you chosen to lead a learning community, to be responsible for such a large number of children? What is your role as a superintendent? You, the superintendent, must not only equip these young lives to succeed in an uncertain future, but you must see that they are fed, transported, and protected. More importantly, you must accurately mobilize your staff to excel in everything they do for the students.

There are many other things that the school board, the lawmakers, governmental agencies, and the community want you to do to fix other societal problems. Yet, your job is educating students and making certain that your schools provide the best educational path they can find to excel in the twenty-first century—after all, they only get to cross this path once in their lives. More profoundly, this is the educational foundation for the rest of their lives.

These responsibilities have long been the opportunities and obligations of the superintendent, but now the climate is rapidly changing and is even more demanding. Being a superintendent today is complex and even more challenging than in the past when parents, who eagerly worked with the schools and factories, were a vital part of American industry. Remember when television portrayed perfect (as in "Leave It to Beaver") and we thought life was that simple? Remember when everyone trusted the doctor, everyone believed the clergy, and everyone liked the superintendent? Not anymore. Superintendents are challenged by the news media and on Main Street. No wonder a superintendent's tenure often lasts only a few years!

Simple routine, leave-it-to-beaver, and hierarchical leadership styles are passé except for a few attempts to copy the old version by those longing for the past.

Schools today need leaders who excel at the very core definition of human management: getting things done through people and modeling that behavior. The role now is a humanitarian one, taking serious responsibility for every child and every staff member. The complexities of today zero in on people and find every human way possible to help people achieve their maximum capabilities. Impeccable human values and strong leadership skills must guide every decision throughout the school system as well as direct the action of the leader of children—the superintendent—the person who has the power to shape the future through his or her staff.

Often overlooked is that many of these staff members come from the local community, so there is no hiding from the community what goes on in the district. Informal public-relations comments from staff can often be a powerful vehicle for communication. These employees can either be ambassadors or critics. How they are treated as part of the system determines how they relay messages back to their families, neighbors, and other community members, who can build support for schools or jettison it. Indeed, since many school districts depend on the communities for financial support, informed public relations can be an important avenue for making certain your people are valued and your community supports your vision.

An understanding of the unique culture of the community, the people, and the symbolic system of the community must be respected, and at the same time, the school system is expected to be academically competitive with national and international achievement levels so students can achieve at the highest levels. Within the larger community, schools must cooperate effectively with the other components of the community, working in tandem on a host of key issues, yet retaining the unique character and purpose that distinguishes a public institution from private enterprise. The superintendent must be a valuable and productive part of this greater community while, at the same time, being the visionary leader for the school system. The district's vision shared with the clearly articulated and accepted higher-order mission, general principles, and norms and goals carries the message through the system and into the community.

The problem, according to Paul Houston (1995), former superintendent and current executive director of the American Association of School Administrators, is that schools in the last few years haven't been very clear about what they are supposed to be accomplishing. He states that they used to know what their jobs were. They were supposed to set the course for children to work in a differentiated workplace. In other words, they picked the winners and losers, trained them accordingly, and thus provided workers and managers for a powerful industrial complex.

Houston believes that some insightful leaders today say that many schools still are doing just that, and better than ever: Too many schools are doing a better job of educating children of the 1990s for the society of the 1950s. His is a clear message: Superintendents must articulate the mission of education and demonstrate a willingness to transform these institutions called schools to be result oriented. The message for the current structure is focused: Either change or get out of the way. America needs schools that are focused on high standards for students and can still survive in a rapidly changing, highly technological world.

The problem is that schools in the last few years have not been very clear about their mission and what they are supposed to be producing. As Houston (1995) puts it: Our old task was to preside over a 100-yard dash and give out ribbons for first, second, and third place. Our new mission may be more like organizing a marathon race and seeing that everyone finishes.

It is now the job of the chief educator, the chief executive officer (CEO) of schools, to lead politicians, business partners, parents—whole communities—in discussions about the important mission of their schools and then to develop a consensus about how you, as a visionary leader, are going to deliver the results. So today, the superintendents must draw on multiple strengths in a grueling series of unique challenges and still achieve victory when all the disparate components come together for sustained, coordinated achievement.

The other CEOs, the chief executive officers of the private business sector, have been faced with critical issues that have forced them to change the way they do business. If we knocked on certain doors of the private sector and school districts, we would find examples of exceptional leaders on journeys to building successful organizations on vision and results by maximizing the human potential.

THE GOAL: A PEOPLE-BASED VISION FOR SUCCESS

Building for success through a clear direction and vision comes from Kerry Killenger (1997), a CEO in the banking industry. As I listen to him, I know his vision is based on the needs of the people—and getting results is a lesson he executed to survive in the new global environment. As CEO of Washington Mutual Savings, one of the nation's largest and most profitable savings banks, he knows all about the Darwinian theory and its value as a metaphor for survival in the marketplace.

Just before a major takeover, he said that the most successful organizations are those that expect change and embrace it. Those institutions will not disappear. Under his leadership, the bank's assets have grown at a phenomenal rate. If financial institutions like his had not undergone a dramatic revolution, he says, they slowly died or became part of a merger. Without upheaval, he says, institutions can stay mired in old thinking and never realize how ineffective they have become. Nine-to-five banks are a remnant of the past. Because banks are in the people business they have to reach out to everyone and do so in convenient places such as shopping malls and airports. They are in the service business and reaching out has paid big dividends for them. Assets have gone from $6 billion to over $44 billion in a decade.

Reflecting on the similarities between education and banking, Killenger finds a cautionary tale. Both need to transform themselves. Education today is a business, he says, and educational leaders need to use the same simple messages business people do to create action and results. The steps are easy, necessary, and succinct. People want to hear clear, direct, and concise language. They want answers to questions such as, (1) What is your vision? (2) What is your clear mission? (3) How will you achieve results and know when you have?

Killenger's type of vision and leadership are what separate the dying organization from the dynamic one. Organizations of the past, steeped in business theories of the 1950s, focused on capital, money, and power. Organizations that survive and thrive today focus on people, change for the better of the organization, and the dynamics of survival.

The example that follows demonstrates that this CEO superintendent put in place the vision and leadership to thrive and achieve at a level that engaged everyone for the children, for service, and for education.

"You are here because your grandchildren asked you to be." This poignant line directed to the students by a teacher captured the media, the community, regional directors, and the high school students who were in the class. That statement motivated the superintendent to change a dying school system into a dynamic learning community. She embarked on this journey with a passion to turn around a grumbling, unsupportive, dying lumber community in a depressed area. Today people want to be part of this dynamic system. She knows how to get the best people to get the job done.

She could see beyond the confining walls of the schools to the rich land around the district, and she broke tradition. She had a vision to turn the rich land at the foot of the school district into a living science–educational laboratory. Wetlands, the wasteland of the past, became the rich estuary that students use to study real science. The adjacent sacred Native American land contained relics of the past that were moved from a museum to the environmental science laboratory display area. Outside are the new totem poles carved by Native Americans. Over 23,000 acres of a state park have become a classroom learning center because one woman rallied people to be part of the dream. The park is used by students from the high school to hold lessons for elementary students and to learn new science skills. The new class of seniors are exploring environmental engineering, environmental science, marine biology, and teaching.

The stakes are high in this school system. People are proud. Everyone is expected to meet success. The lumber jobs are almost gone in this community, but the vibrancy in the school system extends to the community as well as to state agencies and departments. This school system has engaged everyone in its community and beyond in preparing the students for tomorrow and surviving in the dynamic marketplace.

These types of actions are ways to encourage and support a common shared vision and shape a common mission. The leader sets the vision and puts a metaphor into action as the most powerful belief statement of the school district, which transcends the mundane in the system by engaging and empowering all the people in the system; encourages a system for risk-takers; and develops a system of expectations and appreciation.

THE GOAL: ACHIEVING RESULTS BY INVESTING IN PEOPLE

The competitive world around us is nipping at the heels of educators, challenging them to better prepare students. Corporate leaders are frustrated with having to remediate our students. Schools and school systems are the foundation of democracy and the institutions that must be held accountable for results. We need visionary people with a mission and passion to lead with an eye to the future. They will be the true leaders of school systems in the twenty-first century.

Chief Executive Officer Frank Shrontz, as the powerful past chairman of the Boeing Company, continues to champion education and the need to transform schools. He has taken his message into all arenas that are looking for leaders—the political field, the business domain, and the school world. He does not mince his words. As a world-class business leader, he knows the mission of education must change. We simply cannot accept the extinction of schools as a vibrant institution—a message I often hear from him.

Shrontz is well versed in what happens when a business or institution does not address the needs of its environment—the marketplace for a corporation: It becomes a takeover target, or it falls under its own weight. In fact, his challenge to educational leaders at a symposium with representatives from over 50 states in 1994 was, "Making Education Work for All Children" (Shrontz, 1994). In today's world, he knows, companies that expect to keep pace with their global competitors must continually strive to improve quality and productivity.

Shrontz tells us that corporations want people who are motivated and who can motivate others; people who can work together as a team, and who treat their fellow workers with respect and concern. In short, we need employees who not only have good skills but who also have good values. He calls upon superintendents, as the leaders of today who most affect the business environment of tomorrow, to heed his concerns. He clearly worries about the impact of a poorly educated work force, and he knows the importance of education goes far beyond that.

Our democratic institutions, if they are to function well, depend on an educated, informed electorate. Shrontz believes that the crisis in education won't be solved overnight but that we are moving in the right direction. He, along with other business leaders, expects that it will be superintendents who advance the educational enterprise. For education as for business, he says, the keys to revitalization are to strive to improve quality, pay attention to expenditures of time and energy, and, most importantly, to develop human resources.

Today, many of the chief educators, the superintendents, are working at a rapid speed to motivate others to ensure success for the students. They have a vision, and their teams of leaders are positioned ahead of the curve to achieve results. One superintendent leader told me recently how he told his community, "We will have high standards, we will change, and we will hold the system accountable for students' learning." Above all he inspired that belief in his staff. At the start of the following school year the innovative educational leader was using more than rhetoric. He implemented a pilot program for capable at-risk students who were failing. These students would normally be assigned to the high school. He was not willing to waste that young human potential. He wanted to motivate these young people toward success. The students were reassigned to the middle school with the staffing reconfigured. Motivated high school teachers began teaching these capable students to overcome any obstacles. This brief intervention brought results at a critical time. The media carried the story and applauded the superintendent for moving out of a status-quo position into positive action. Many important questions were asked of parents, teachers, and others having influence on children. The focus was on helping students achieve success.

The actions described in this section are focused on achieving results and expecting the best from people through training, involvement, and high expectations. In most cases, delivering results is what others expect of us. A system empowers teams and individuals to be result oriented. Included in the equation are not only those who work for us but also our customers: community members and parents. Making the important link that businesses know well: Without satisfied customers people will go elsewhere for better services. We must rethink how everyone in the system plays an important role in our work, and we must accept the most fundamental reality of managing people: People are everything.

THE GOAL: CHANGING THE PROTOTYPE TO MAXIMIZE THE HUMAN POTENTIAL

Leadership today is based on maximizing the human potential rather than the old tell-them-how attitude. The factory and in-line production models are behind us. Top-down management was suited to the production line and the factory floor. The boss used to be poised in a crisp shirt and tie, sitting sagely above the toil and din, monitoring progress and issuing orders to fine-tune performance. Today's society is too complicated for that. The plain fact is, few people genuinely know what is the right thing to do. And in the rare instance when somebody does know exactly the proper action to take in a given situation, the value of such knowledge is limited. It's circumscribed by the certainty of change.

Chief executive officers at IBM and General Motors operated under old bureaucratic rules and they suffered accordingly. They were battered in the competitive marketplace and deteriorated economically because they were reluctant or unable to change. Like coldblooded dinosaurs lumbering into a cold, cruel world, they lacked the mental agility and internal warmth that would keep them alive. They kept looking for the lush vegetation that had sustained them for so long and were unable to find or adapt to new resources perhaps right under their snouts. They clung, in other words, to a noxious, sometimes lethal, reaction to an altered environment. They refused to relinquish a comfortable but often fatal adherence to the old term "management by entrenchment." Just pick up a copy of the *Wall Street Journal* or look at the business section of your local newspaper. We see frequent examples of sluggish companies being gobbled up by stronger, smarter competitors. We see others sliding into bankruptcy under their own massive bulk.

Too often, we fail to recognize such symptoms and trends in our school systems. True enough, public education is not private enterprise. And until only the last decade or so, no serious rivals stood eyeing our franchise with a lean and hungry look. What once was a virtual monopoly looks a lot less so today. Serious competitors now circle public schools, and the tall grass of the public sector is dying. The $200-plus-billion-a-year public education field is as susceptible to takeover and extinction as the buggy business was. It's about time to turn our buggies into Ferrares or maybe Saturns.

Maximizing the human potential is a lesson learned from Saturn, since timing is everything. An example of a corporation that did a quick turnaround just in time and changed its focus from the old-factory way to the dynamic-people way is Saturn. It emerged not a moment too soon for a staggering General Motors. Just as the pundits and polls were polishing up the last drafts of their obituaries for the American automobile industry, along came Saturn to offer the paradigm shift, the radical change from business as usual to a bright new answer to nagging old problems. Even difficulties subsequently encountered by Saturn are perhaps just a valuable testament to the fact that the status quo is a formidable adversary. The day-to-day performance of each individual adds to—or subtracts from—achieving results.

Since we can't waste precious time filling a child's head with erroneous information, using outdated learning models, and accepting lack of performance, I listened intently to a presentation by the Saturn employees about why General

Motors once again is a winning competitor. Saturn employees are in demand from school districts to answer questions about their new-found successes. Saturn employees explained how they helped transform a dying segment of a major automobile corporation into a dynamic, successful enterprise by putting people at the heart of its production unit.

The employee presenters were not the usual executive types but rather a floor manager and team worker who work side by side in the plant. The person representing labor talked about the huge learning curve he had to climb just to be ready to make a presentation for the company. Such responsibility, however, was indicative of the worker's role at the plant where workers assume a leadership role—even to the point of being able to call a halt to the entire production line if that's what it takes to ensure zero defects.

In an informal interview, the worker told me of the evolution of the firm that made his team determined to do what they had to do to be the best. The greatest transformation for him was when he realized he doesn't go to work just to pick up a paycheck anymore because now he is part of the corporation and feels responsible for the company's future. Speaking with pride, he told me about being an integral member of the team and how each person becomes an even more valuable member of the Saturn team because of his or her capacity to seek out new information, to be a constant learner, and to be always ahead of the market to serve their customers. This reinforces the concept that with higher value as a person comes higher productivity.

The group of excited educators in this progressive district regrouped to find ways they could work as a Saturn-type team and continue the open dialogue with their superintendent who encourages all employees to find ways to transform their part of the educational system into a dynamic enterprise. She reminds them often that knowledge is seamless; understanding comes with looking at the whole and connecting at different levels in the system.

I thought of a less-dynamic situation and questioned the structure of schools and what has to be done to put people at the core of action while pushing away the bureaucratic structure that blocks people from being part of a true learning venture. The evening before, I had attended one of the usual elementary school reunions in a neighboring district. Everyone who worked there or attended as a student had been invited. The cook whom all the kids loved was all dressed up, and the faithful custodian was there in his best suit, smiling but stooped over with age and hard physical work. I reflected on the contribution they had made to the school and, most importantly, to the children. The vivacious cook made lunch a treat and because of her no child went hungry. I thought of the excitement that was pending as we would hear the success stories of those who had made a difference and the experiences of the students who were now on the road to success.

Instead, the presentation began with the usual program—the principal welcoming everyone, a too-long history of the district and the school, the accolades for all the past administration. Then all past and present teachers were honored. During the final closing, I noticed the cook and the custodian quietly leaving, unacknowledged, with the smiles of the audience fading away.

The Saturn presentation made me question how many times staff meetings provide real collaboration among all of the staff. Who is honored, who is empowered to halt the educational system when it is not working or learning is misguided, or who has the power to transform learning beyond the classroom? How often do dying systems just continue to follow the pattern of the past, like the factory floor?

The ideal of the Saturn Corporation represents a new model of corporate excellence—a model that recognizes the core fact of management: People are everything. Everyone works together, and everyone on the team is learning empowered and ready to accept responsibility. The work for each one must be interchangeable.

Even the Saturn contract book (called a "Memorandum of Agreement") is condensed for wide distribution. Its 33 pages are designed to fit in a pocket. The booklet codifies Saturn's philosophy of shared leadership. It sets forth agreements, covering decision making, consensus guidelines, conflict resolution, code of conduct, and more. The burden of the contract book is to underscore the Saturn philosophy and culture, which strives to reduce the differentiation among people in a successful organization.

Within the organization, everyone is a corporate member. The person who was once called "the worker," now is a new kind of learning executive—one who comes to work prepared to spot mistakes and change the course if necessary. A core concept of the Saturn model is that the worker is not undervalued but is equal to and part of the decision-making team. Employees of Saturn are valued and are expected to contribute their knowledge and expertise, not just their muscles.

Imagine sitting at the table in the deep mahogany boardroom with other CEOs—from Saturn, Boeing, Washington Mutual, Nordstrom, and Microsoft—asking you the following key questions. Use these questions to query yourself, a leader of people who has a vision based on success, investing in people and maximizing the human potential. These are questions that leaders in education must be able to answer to lead schools from the past to the present.

- Do people consider you a visionary leader?
- Do you have the high-quality people skills, inner structure, and ingenuity to transform schools into dynamic learning places?
- Do you hold people accountable to high standards of performance?

- Do you invest in your people by preparing to excel?
- Is your mission clearly focused on your business—students and learning?
- Are your people customer oriented?
- Do you model high performance and expect your people to excel?

Key to answering these questions and attaining achievement is for everyone engaged in education and everyone who influences it to understand that we are living in a dynamic postindustrial society. Dynamic organizations need leaders. They don't need people whose primary training and aptitude are focused on telling others what to do, checking up on them to see that it's been done, and rewarding and punishing performance based on the degree of strict compliance with detailed orders.

The superintendent archetype for the twenty-first century is a people-oriented thinker who looks at all sides of the organization to measure human productivity, capacity building, and ways to create successful programs and procedures.

Yet, even the best-intentioned, most-enlightened superintendent would do well to reflect briefly from time to time on being a leader. I have found that what you expect of yourself is often what you will get from your people. Few school leaders, even among the best of them, have a nature so elegant and fine as not occasionally to stray from the paradigm of leadership. In real life, the struggle to be a leader and not just a manager or boss is never completely over. Those old 1950s leadership books may still hold a prime place on many superintendents' and central office people's bookcases from management lessons learned long ago on how to be a good boss, but they won't work to motivate people in today's society.

Dynamic people do not stay in boxes—they think beyond the box. They are focused on value-added results, and on effectiveness and quality. The ineffective might have been myopic about the future and, rather than grasping opportunity, liked to say, "This too shall pass," or "We have seen this before," so change could be avoided. But there is no room for them today in dynamic learning organizations.

Today's society is too complicated for that. The plain fact is, few people alone genuinely know what is the right thing to do. And in the rare instance when somebody does know exactly the proper action to take in a given situation, the value of such knowledge is limited. It's circumscribed by the certainty of change. By tomorrow or next week, that set of circumstances no longer applies. That which was the right answer on Tuesday can become exactly the wrong answer by Thursday. Nobody alone can have all the answers. In fact, nobody alone can even see all the questions. Synergy, team dynamics, and collegiality aren't merely the best answer for school leadership and for people. They are the only answer.

If it takes a village to raise a child, it takes a community and a faculty and a transportation department and a food services department and a maintenance team and a PTA and a student council and a school board and a superintendent and a thousand other key elements—all of whom are people—to educate one. And when an enterprise so plainly depends for its very survival on so many people, it just doesn't make sense for somebody to sit in a big chair or drive around in a big car giving orders.

The complexity of today's modern society means an organization needs to have every brain engaged, every ear attuned, every eye unblinking in the search for solutions and direction. The art of leadership lies in finding a way to orchestrate an entire symphony of talented and accomplished players and to guide them, by mutual consent, into the rich harmony of common purpose. The value of a leader is his or her ability to pick the music, show everyone the beauty of the score, and help them imagine what it could sound like when every note is played with perfect pitch.

Being a full-time visionary leader is the challenge of a lifetime. And, fortunately, in our lifetime, we've had the privilege to witness genuine leaders and watch them work. True leaders always have a vision for a better tomorrow and a message that transforms people and moves them toward a greater good. Great leaders have changed the course of history. Martin Luther King Jr. had a vision for peace and a message to end inequality. John F. Kennedy had a vision to engage the nation in the American dream. Gandhi had a vision to lead his people through spirit and wisdom. Mother Teresa's life-long vision was to eradicate poverty and oppression—a quest to erase the inequities among people.

Each of these visionary leaders focused on the people they served. They had the courage and strength as visionaries to give hope to their people, and they were purposeful leaders. They, too, had a time in life, a path to follow to make a difference for people, and so does the superintendent. It is all in how we accept the challenge. The superintendent of today must be a visionary leader, the person who has the courage to carry the dream forward for the children. The overarching statement for the school system is the articulation of that dream.

When people are empowered to believe and can see the greater good, they will commit their own resources and actions. This is a common scenario in people-oriented, dynamic education systems. Educators often have a unique sense of purpose in what they do. Most enter education with a sense that they are responding to a calling.

A few years ago, an elementary school in my region was experiencing white flight. The population had shifted and the primarily all-white school was now culturally rich with ethnic diversity. With that came a shift in test scores because of immigrant children new to the ways of America. Resources were limited and more and more parents and children needed to call on the school for help. The community was in an uproar with the world of change.

A transformation happened when I was able to reconstitute the school into an arts and science magnet school. A team of transformational school and community leaders designed the framework for the success of the school. The principal could see the potential. The current staff was invited to become part of the transformation. It meant hard work, thinking about providing learning in multiple new ways. Some welcomed the challenge and others transferred.

The principal and staff reached out to every corner of the community for help. They rearranged the school day to provide more learning programs, before- and after-school programs, and programs in the summer. A partnership was formed with the Smithsonian Institute. Immigrant parents were invited into the school to learn with their children in the evenings and on weekends. The school became a rich cultural center for the community. Today, there is a waiting list to get into the school, the test scores are up, the teachers want to be there, and this school is a hub of the community. The school has won national recognition.

Vision can be the catalyst that brings the reawakening, galvanizes it throughout the system, and moves it forward. If people believe their voices have been heard and that they can serve the children, they can satisfy their desire for a commitment to the greater good.

I have found that educators will support and work for a system more readily if they feel they are keeping a promise they made at the beginning of their careers. We know that people, in general, will commit if they can understand its purpose, believe they can make a genuine contribution, and see their energy making a positive impact and difference. When people believe in a worthy mission and align themselves with a unique sense of life purpose and become part of the spirit of the schools, their role in the system can create energy, purpose, and a life.

It is the job of the superintendent to influence, change policy, convince business leaders to support schools, and engage parents as partners—whole communities—in discussions about the mission of schools and then to develop a consensus about how he or she, as a visionary leader, is going to get them there. In our business, we are surrounded by people. Our job is to engage them. So, today, perhaps our mission is like a decathlon in which we must draw on multiple strengths in a grueling series of unique challenges and achieve victory when all the disparate components come together for sustained, coordinated achievement.

The superintendent can change the structure and shift the power to set a higher standard for the school system, a level where all can strive to be part of the spirit for the children, service, and education. The leader sets the vision—puts a metaphor in action—as the most powerful belief statement of the school district, which transcends the mundane in the system by engaging and empowering all the people in the system.

A leading headhunter who assists school boards with searches explains that a superintendent today must be like a diamond—solid to the core, with a bright moral facet and shining self-awareness. Even the brightest jewel of a superintendent knows about his or her flaws. Successful leaders know themselves pretty well and are smart and honest enough to magnify their strengths and minimize their weaknesses.

The smart ones create new assets by surrounding themselves with people of high quality and expertise who complement their own strengths and offset weaknesses. Superintendents with a realistic sense of humility know they alone are not the powerful organization but that the real power lies with their abilities to maximize human capital. Successful superintendents must be able to see strengths in others and know how to draw out and amplify these strengths. They know that teamwork and collegiality are not merely the best answer for leaders and for people.

In a recent random sampling of people in a large educational organization, I found that people were disinclined to follow a leader who did not communicate the vision of the organization regularly and consistently, who did not walk the talk, and who made decisions primarily for political reasons or to serve their own self-interests. Those surveyed said they felt estranged from such an organization, even though they believed their primary mission in life was to work for children. In general, I found that people will not follow a leader they do not have confidence in, respect, or trust to keep promises. It can be a humbling and worthwhile experience to step back and take the time necessary to catalog one's strengths and weaknesses as a leader to more effectively work with others. Such insights aren't easily acquired. Asking the next in command how you're doing as a leader might elicit an answer of "Just fine" and might even be an honest one, but such a limited perspective probably isn't much better than addressing the question to your mirror.

Prodding each corner of a person's leadership skills and abilities, through leadership institutes or seminars, can be more informative than checking with the mirror. It can be a cornerstone or anchor in tough times to know where your inner strength lies. Knowing who you are, what you stand for, and what is important can be a gift. It provides strength to know your qualities, but even more importantly, it can help you improve potential areas and analyze areas of weaknesses to determine where you need others with different sets of skills to maximize the people power in your organization. Certain qualities stand alone and continually provide the foundation for leaders in the organization.

Credibility is often identified as one of the most valuable leadership characteristics. It's a quality that must be proven before people will give a leader their absolute confidence and trust. With high credibility, a superintendent can begin to establish a sustainable foundation for the school district and the education community in general. When the superintendent has gained credibility, people know they are ready to make a commitment to an organization based on values that can be trusted.

A leader's credibility becomes a positive political force because people will align with someone they trust but will disengage from and shun a superintendent they have no confidence in. Unfortunately, for today's highly mobile superintendent, credibility is not immediately transferable. A superintendent with rock-solid credibility in one school district must often start at ground zero in the next one.

Moving to implement even the most inspiring vision is a careful maneuver between credibility and timing. Waiting too long to implement a visionary plan and not keeping a promise can cause unrest and loss of trust in a system. Yet, visionary leadership, based on a foundation of credibility, and with strategic moves, is often the key to establishing and sustaining a lasting purpose and synergy throughout the system.

People often will accept change if they believe the system's most fundamental principles are based on learning and the welfare of students. The superintendent has the power to create this dynamic by transforming every person in the district into a valuable, vital part of the vision as well as a corporate partner in the educational enterprise.

A model for accelerating credibility and building on good customer-relations skills with a community of people is through what is called the Future Search process. The process is simple, people intensive, productive, and has wide-reaching possibilities, especially for leaders new to a system or organization. I worked with community leaders to activate a Future Search process in a community that had lost faith in their schools due to lack of trust. We needed to pass a school levy. Our target group was the most influential people from across the community, the people with a voice that would be heard. We formed a small group of leaders from the community that helped us select the who's-who list. People were invited formally, and the meeting was not open to the public. That got the attention of the community. We started receiving calls from others who wanted to know why they had not been invited. In fact, in a short time, it is truly amazing what happened.

On Friday night we identified the historic and cultural aspects of the community that needed to be honored, we addressed the critical issues of today and where the community wanted to be in ten years. If the schools continually spiraled downward, people realized that the community's economy would be affected. More reduction in staff meant less revenue, which meant fewer people to purchase goods and services in the community. Everyone knew we would have to lay off some of our best and brightest, and we needed their support to build this quality school system. The community leaders rallied for the first time in three years to support schools and the vision of the district because it was in harmony with the mission of the people in the community.

By Saturday morning robust, innovative thinking and dialog among the 50 participants meant serious and meaningful exchange from leaders across the community. A mission statement, distinctive goals, critical success factors, and the date for the follow-up conference had been accomplished.

By Saturday afternoon the vision for the community was in sync with the mission of the schools, and credibility was being regained (and yes, the levy passed the next month). Credibility for the superintendent comes from the community and from within the school system. Perhaps a new role for the superintendent is always being in the eye of the storm, moving forward, not going off course.

Throughout the Future Search conference, we were faced with the critical role of the school leader. It was evident that the superintendent needed to be consistently authentic in the face of pressure and media scrutiny. The crucial characteristic of an authentic leader is his or her being unwavering when it comes to principle and truth. The superintendent today is often called on to move with the political wind or with self-interest rather than to stand steadfast. This may be one of the most difficult times for a superintendent to stand steadfast for children. School leadership is never exercised on a landscape of black and white. The genuine challenge often is to determine how your unshakable principles apply to a given situation. Sometimes the test of authentic leadership is not a matter of linear analysis at all. A wise advisor once explained it this way: "If you are not authentic, you will feel it deep inside. It will cause a wrinkle in your soul." Do not falter on your belief system. This is the time for your passion to influence the media and other pressures and for you to take a stand for children.

Even so, we still see school systems where superintendents have failed to understand the relationship between being authentic, being honest, and being effective. A superintendent I observed recently had a deliberate strategy to signal authenticity and had put into place a process that was fair and that only hired the best. The search reached wide across the system and those with the highest degree of respect in their field were sought after and joined the team. The flags that signaled quality, competence, action, and innovation started going up the poles. An immediate reaction followed. The energy inside the system quickly shifted to a high level. A transformation was beginning.

Transforming a system requires having people who are highly qualified and who have the ingenuity to advance the system. The best, the brightest, and those who focus on people will send a message rippling through the system that the people are expected to do their best. A new "transformational" energetic superintendent recently had the luxury of bringing on a new leadership team. He immediately provided the nucleus of energy for the system, and signals moved throughout the departments and schools that quality was a key factor.

That type of leadership is the opposite of the tired, old, ineffective style of management. It involves restructuring or reinventing the system in ways that engage each staff member and each stakeholder, and align each person with the mission of the system. They are in sync with the people they lead. They also extend the support necessary to give the people they lead the security necessary to perform effectively in furtherance of the mission.

One example is the kind of support that occurred when I was dealing with 29 boundary changes as the area superintendent for a region of a county. The boundary changes caused major concerns among some disgruntled parents, and they set up a meeting with the division superintendent. The parents' objective undoubtedly was to have my head roll. When I arrived for this meeting, the division superintendent began by saying: "I want to start by telling you that I'm here to make sure this superintendent is successful. I know that's what she wants for her community. What can we do together to make this happen?"

Putting trust in the people you work with and letting them do the job at a high-performance level is a hallmark of effective transformational leadership. To look for faults or to be afraid to step forward and support your staff undermines their confidence and their ability to implement the vision of the leader.

If people are empowered, they will excel to their highest ability. If they are intimidated or expect to be left without leadership support, they either will retreat and do as little as possible or look for employment elsewhere. As one employee said, "Sometimes we feel like big kids with large responsibilities and a need to know our work is important and how we are part of the bigger system." She said that, often, school systems encourage and sponsor staff members to get new training only to have them come to a dead stop when they seek to implement what they have learned. The improved methods encounter the old paradigm, and resistance to change overpowers innovation. The smart leader knows people are an investment and that it takes a toll on time, energy, and morale when people cannot work to their full capacities.

Superintendents who inspire the people they work with to feel trust demonstrate that they respect their staff members. The intuitive, unconscious self responds to how the message is being received. The better that people are treated in human terms, the better they perform.

Empowerment pays genuine dividends. The function of the leader is to empower others to use their knowledge and creativity to accomplish goals that are emerging in the organization and that are part of the vision.

Whatever the term, *transforming*, *reinventing*, or *reforming*, leaders must look deep into the system and ask high-quality people questions. If we want world-class schools, we must expect high standards of our students. Across this nation a tidal wave of rising standards for students is on the move. As the wave gets closer to your shore, have you as a superintendent hired, trained, and motivated your people to be ready, or are you ignoring the wave and preparing for the crash?

Progressive school districts know that raising the standards means improving results. Results-oriented thinking is not just for businesses or students. Future-thinking systems have put in place comprehensive selection, training, and evaluation models to achieve high-performance targets for their people.

Enlightening was the only way to describe my experience as the director of a university center that sought to assess the performance of school leaders (primarily principals and aspiring principals). I had never had a chance to study school leaders' behavior across such a wide spectrum. The evaluation project was comprehensive, and it identified the areas of strengths and weaknesses through an extensive process often using real situational problems they would handle as school leaders.

Dealing with the people dimension was a problematic area for some participants. Using a group process to do problem analysis was a difficult task for some who prefer to make decisions on their own behind closed doors. Unfortunately, that type of decision-making process is often based on the N of 1 (their own experience and a narrow viewpoint), not on relevant information. I found that when a person studied the issue, considered all sides, and made the decision based on the best interest of the students, the decision was usually unbiased and fair.

Human relations, a skill that we would expect of school leaders, was glaringly absent at times as I observed participants who lacked tact and were insensitive to others even under the eyes of a video camera. Role-playing with a teacher or support person, such people would consistently interrupt. They would not listen to the message and would verbally override the other person, showing that they were in charge of the meeting. Yes, they were wearing the big-boss hat.

Judgment was assessed through case studies, review, and observing taped mock situations. During that time, and since, I have found judgment to be a problem that hinders success for school leaders, often with unintended but serious consequences. Examples are: the person who lacked tact and who wrote a caustic letter to a parent or newspaper as the way to respond to a problem; the person who told a racial joke at a staff meeting; the person who inappropriately discussed a personnel issue. Problems arise out of making a decision based on a prediction rather than the consequences of the action. Problems also arise when using unreliable resources and data to make a critical decision. Logical conclusions, based on a high-quality decision is a must for a successful leader. Too often, leaders choose the wrong battles and lose the bigger battle for students.

Communications, a necessary skill for those who are in the people business, and the key to interacting with others, was not an easy skill for many. The skill of guiding and facilitating a conversation in order to achieve its purpose often needed refinement. Too often, good oral communication skills, such as paraphrasing ideas and eliciting enough information, were set aside as the person dominated the conversation. Even in written form, some participants would forget the audience and carry on without thinking of the ramifications.

Educational values were evident when the participant possessed a well-reasoned educational philosophy—placing a high price on the needs and welfare of students. The person who scored high in this category had a clear perspective of the role of education in society and set personal high-performance standards.

Often, seasoned principals were not trained in the instructional process and ways to help teachers improve their teaching. Their knowledge focused on parts or a specialized expertise they had around management, such as scheduling or time management. This left them with limited ways to truly assist teachers as well as a simple pat response that they were doing a poor job of teaching. No explanation, no ways to improve, and no professional growth plan were offered. This highlighted the need for school leaders to be highly trained in their business of learning and teaching.

During a final session of reviewing the results, one principal halted the process. He wanted to tell me that, because of that process, I now knew more about him than anyone, probably even more than his spouse. I chuckled at the time. A few years later at a leadership conference, he let me know how much he valued the assessment program and that he now worked for a people-oriented superintendent, someone he could emulate. He had left the previous school system because the superintendent had used the university assessment information in a punitive way. Too often, supervisors can quickly spot a problem but either lack the expertise in human dynamics or a system to evaluate and help correct a problem area for an employee. We know from the business world that it is cost effective to retrain and assist current employees—investing in your own—before hiring new employees.

The simple premise is to put in place a system that finds the best people, trains them once they're in the system, and evaluates all staff against high-quality standards. As the chair of the committee to develop and implement a high-performance and evaluation program in a large school system, I had the challenge of establishing the performance standard-setting process for school-based administrators. In prior years, the district had established performance standards for teachers but not for administrators. The school board called for a set of standards for administrators.

As the assistant superintendent for personnel, I knew the quality impact that a new-teacher evaluation plan had on the system. Outstanding teachers were excited to be recognized for their achievements, and, on the opposite side of the spectrum, teachers who lacked skill, ability, and motivation were threatened and knew they had to change or find another profession. Often as I visited buildings, teachers welcomed me into their classrooms to show student progress and then beam with pride as the students shared their excitement for learning.

Albeit, one very arrogant teacher was so sure of himself that he challenged the curriculum specialist and the principal to videotape him, so he could prove to the world that he was a good teacher. That video and a team of specialists helped him realize that he had the potential but that his dictatorial manner, his lack of understanding different cultures, and his lack of good classroom management skills to match his students' needs were hindering his teaching. The children were afraid of him, and indeed he had a lot to learn. He wanted to be a top teacher, and, with help, he achieved his goal. Five years later he was recommended to be the teacher of the year. The same transformation occurred with the school administrators' performance evaluation program.

Across the system, the vision was set and the mission was focused. The name of the game was high standards targeted on high performance. The message was clear, the standards were set, and everyone knew what was expected. The comprehensive evaluation system crossed all areas to be evaluated. All written materials, all reports, and all activities were based on the standards. Even the parent newsletter took on a new, friendly, professional look. There were no surprises, and everyone was trained. The guesswork was gone. It gave permission to the real leaders to be superstars, employees raised the quality of their work, and those who thought they could still slide by made other choices.

Later, as the area superintendent for one of the regional areas, I realized when it comes time to make hard decisions that the process is simplified if high standards, clear expectations, and a fair evaluation system are in place for all employees. During the evaluation cycle, I recommended areas for improvement and worked with the principals and other administrators on an improvement plan related to high performance. Each person had an improvement plan that capitalized on or enhanced certain areas considered as strengths but needing improvement or areas that were identified as weaknesses. The action plan was time specific, and a major component was in professional development. The school system coordinated professional development and training to match the criteria within the standards and provided opportunities to assist the principals. The previous status-quo system had been replaced. People were excited to "step out of the box" and to prove that they could excel and meet the challenge of higher standards. The learning curve for adults was on an upward spiral.

Too often, unfair evaluation systems rely on whether the boss likes you or not. We all hear about the horror stories of capable dynamic people who are punished with a bad evaluation by a boss who is threatened or professionally challenged. This system eliminates that process and encourages all people to excel. The engagement of each staff member to be a stakeholder in their own professional growth made a difference for the individual, for the school, and most importantly for the students.

The problem with an external human evaluation system is in the follow-up and the purpose of the evaluation. An internal school system model let me match performance standards with the needs of the school or departments for finding the best people, then helped them achieve their goals through professional development.

I remember searching for a dynamic, charismatic high school principal with exceptional communication skills to lead a high school that had a changing population due to an increase in families representing the Hispanic community. The performance standards were set and certain qualities within those standards were identified. The candidates were interviewed using an assessment center process: responding to in-basket activities, writing a letter to the new PTA president, videotaping the opening address to the school community, and the usual panel to interview the candidate with questions based on the performance questions.

The candidate who was chosen met every beginning step we set for him. Within the first month, we knew his interest in areas of growth and had a professional development plan ready for him with plenty of assistance from the central office to ensure his success. Unless growth components are identified and linked to criteria or standards, people are not as intrinsically motivated to change.

Yet, we still see school systems where superintendents have failed to understand the relationship between empowerment and effectiveness. If people are empowered, they will excel to their highest ability. If they are intimidated or expected to be left without leadership support, they either will retreat and do as little as possible or look for employment elsewhere.

Building rapport and trust is a tremendous interactive human skill that pays huge dividends. I can't remember the hundreds of calls I got from principals and other administrators who just needed someone to listen, someone they trusted whom they could use as a sounding board to resolve a tough situation. Many times it was a 24-hour-sleep-on-it decision that did not seem so serious the next day; the hurt or anger had disappeared and reasonableness had returned. It took time to establish rapport, but my goal was for staff to know that their smallest foibles and biggest confidences would be held in my trust.

I believe that leaders who inspire the people they work with to feel trust do so by demonstrating that they respect staff members. The intuitive, internal self responds to how the message is being received. I can recall one organization in trouble where the superintendent said that if anyone was concerned about the morale they had a problem because he wasn't about to make any changes. Obviously, the turnover in employment was extremely high. The better that people are treated and respected, the better they will perform and respond to the organization. Empowerment pays genuine human quality dividends. The power of the vision to create the potential to accomplish goals that are emergent in the organization is to maximize the people power.

Customer-oriented exemplars and advocates for high quality are achievable through expectations, training, and evaluation. To have world-class schools, we must move the system forward with a can-do vision, innovative thinking, and the right people. If we want students able to be technologically smart and lifelong learners, we need to rethink our delivery of services beyond the walls of the current system. This means pushing beyond the edges and finding creative ways to find the best people to teach our students to be world-class citizens. If the expectation is to change schools and know what the world beyond school is like, then the leader must provide training and experiences toward that goal. If students need to work as a team, then we need to shift the paradigm inside the schools through new models.

Finding highly qualified staff begins with clear, high-level questions, intensive interviewing procedures, and training. Working with universities and businesses in innovative ways is necessary. Capitalizing on a strong teacher performance plan can identify high-performance teachers who then became mentor teachers. Teachers must have the skills and expertise to prepare the students for the twenty-first century. I formed a joint agreement with credible universities to hire their best and brightest students for one year as permanent substitutes. This allowed us to match future teachers with our best teachers and not only train them to meet the expectations of the system and learn the curriculum but also to be able to evaluate their performance before hiring. We were growing our own highly capable teachers—not losing a year with them in the system before we could evaluate their effectiveness and lose a year in the classroom with the students. Learning is too precious to lose a moment.

We can become more sophisticated about external needs in the workplace areas, as identified by Saturn, for our staff and our students. Areas such as decision making, consensus guidelines, conflict resolution, codes of conduct, and empowerment are areas of need not only in the business sector but definitely in the school systems. High-quality schools are of immediate benefit to local employers. Excellent schools attract high-quality employees. These employees are attracted to the community because they want the best education they can get for their children. The schools, as they deliver the high-quality education that the current employees came for, also simultaneously provide local businesses with prepared, high-quality employees for the world of work.

If it takes a Saturn approach of empowering everyone as a learning executive, it takes a signal from the leader as to what is important, and putting the message into action. In fact, when left to human ingenuity it is surprising what people will do. I realized through a survey that the community felt our schools were too institutionalized, and school climate was part of the evaluation criteria for principals.

Because each of the principals had the power to create an environment for their school, they created far beyond what I had imagined.

One morning as I drove into one elementary school, I found the principal in the school driveway with a bright umbrella in hand, opening the car door for the student and saying good-morning to the parent, as the parent drove off. The principal was not at the front door looking stern. It set the tone. Students and parents were welcome. It was a customer-friendly environment.

At the next school, I met with the new high school principal. He had taken home the school annual and had memorized the students' names. He greeted each of the students as they came in the door, and when the first assembly was held, he scanned the audience and called on individual students section by section. That school leader had put his vision in place—students were his priority. The students were not just faces in the audience, they were important as people and as potential leaders. Creating a buy-in for change can yield results beyond the superintendent's greatest expectation when people are given support and freedom.

The leader for the twenty-first century is not without the greatest challenge when it comes to people. The new millenium will be a time of high, rigorous standards for students with the goal of government, business, state departments, and communities being improved student learning and higher standards. It will also be when this nation will need two million new teachers. It will take a meta-leader—a confident, humanistic, visionary leader who understands that people are everything and that every source of human capacity needs to be expanded to lead these schools. The capacity-building process in many districts has already began.

As a state leader, I have worked with and watched 296 school districts prepare for statewide high-performance standards and an accountability system. The leaders who are building the bridge for students to be world-class citizens in the twenty-first century have opened their school gates to universities and businesses to help them build the capacity and to ask the hard questions. Every avenue is being explored. They are building the finest system possible for students, and they are maximizing the staff to be highly results oriented. Throughout the system, the expectation is on unleashing the human potential for students and staff through energy, creativity, and spirit. The superintendent knows every trend that could impact the schools and has a plan, a niche, or a creative way to meet the needs of the students by finding ways to enrich the system through learning for students and staff.

Today, we can still find schools that are organized in ways that can block student and teacher learning. Many districts have not focused on their business of students and learning. Many have limited curriculum goals, limited teaching materials, and outdated ways to teach and lead. Many districts have either ignored or lacked focus on student learning. Often, financial sources have been directed away from the learner. Many districts are reacting out of fear—afraid of high-performance standards—and are becoming fossilized.

Other districts have moved into planning for the next decade, preparing the road for the kindergarten student of today. The change is not on how many minutes the child is in class but on new paths to learning. Student and teacher internships in specialized areas, businesses working with staff to understand what "core learnings" are on demand, on-site technology training by high-tech firms, summer programs for teachers to learn the business side, technology grants, and blue-ribbon committees of community leaders helping the schools are just a few of the ways metaleaders are unleashing the potential that lies behind the walls of schools.

These superintendents are already extending the human capacity to excel by instilling continuous improvement strategies and high-performance standards systems and through creating an environment where people want to work, and grow, and be respected. They are on the move, exploring and learning. They are on the floor of the tool company or in the boardroom asking what we need to do to have world-class schools; they are learning what businesses do to motivate their people; they are exploring how Microsoft teams work together; they are asking Nordstrom how to improve customer relations; they are asking how to hire the best people and keep the best people. They are learning from Saturn how students need to improve their decision-making and conflict-resolution skills. They are asking what code of ethics businesses expect of their employees. They are asking questions at every turn in the road and learning new ways through technology on how to collect and disseminate information, to improve and provide continuous feedback.

And yes, they have teams from their schools asking the same questions at every turn on the road to success. The custodial service teams are not only learning new techniques and the bus drivers new technology, but everyone is learning ways to help the students learn and provide a positive difference for the children in their districts and in their communities.

In the infinitely complex, rapidly changing environment of current times, effective superintendents will be those who are honest enough to know they can succeed only by engaging the advice and support of fully empowered staff members and community. They need to know their strengths and weaknesses and act without ego or insecurity to augment and overcome their shortcomings. When they know everyone deserves their respect and they extend it willingly, then they will find common ground without compromising core principles. Then they will realize they do not have all the answers, but by working together with others, they can overcome any obstacle and ultimately fulfill their lifelong commitment to education and the children.

REFERENCES

Houston, P. (1995, April 15). Education outlook: learning to play leapfrog in a new world. *American Association of School Administrators Leadership News.*

Killenger, K. (1997, January 21). *Partners in change.* Remarks at the Washington State Commission on Student Learning Conference, Ellensburg, WA.

Shrontz, F. (1994, April 13). *Making education work—For all our children.* Remarks at the National Center on Education and the Economy Symposium, Washington, DC.

SUGGESTED READING

Block, P. (1993). *Stewardship: Choosing service over self-interest.* San Francisco: Berrett-Koehler Publishers.

Bolman, L.G., & Deal, T.E. (1991). *Reframing Organizations: Artistry, Choice, and Leadership.* San Francisco: Jossey-Bass, Publishers.

Capra, F. (1993). A systems approach to the emerging paradigm. In M. Ray & A. Rinzler (Eds.), *The new paradigm in business: Emerging strategies for leadership and organizational change.* New York: Jeremy P. Tarcher/Perigee.

Corcoran, Elizabeth. (1991, August). "Ordering Chaos: Researchers Are Beginning to Harness Systems." *Scientific American.*

Covey, S.R. (1989). *The seven habits of highly effective people.* New York: Simon & Schuster.

DePree, M. (1989). *Leadership is an art.* New York: Doubleday.

DePree, M. (1992). *Leadership Jazz.* New York: Doubleday.

Gardner, H. (1995). *Leading minds: An anatomy of leadership.* New York: Basic Books.

Gellerman, W., Frankel, M.S., & Ladenson, R.F. (1990). *Value and ethics in organizations and human systems development: Responding to dilemmas in professional life.* San Francisco: Jossey-Bass, Publishers.

Greenleaf, R.K. (1977). *Servant leadership.* New York: Paulist Press.

Haas, R.D. (1993). The corporation without boundaries. In M. Ray & A. Rinzler (Eds.), *The new paradigm in business: Emerging strategies for leadership and organizational change.* New York: Jeremy P. Tarcher/Perigee.

Heifetz, R. (1994). *Leadership without easy answers.* Cambridge, MA: Harvard University Press.

Kouzes, J.M. & Posner, B.Z. (1993). *Credibility: How leaders gain and lose it, why people demand it.* San Francisco: Jossey-Bass, Publishers.

Nanus, B. (1992). *Visionary Leadership: Creating a compelling sense of direction for your organization.* San Francisco: Jossey-Bass, Publishers.

Peters, T. (1988). *Thriving on chaos: Handbook for a management revolution.* New York: Alfred A. Knopf.

Ray, M., & Rinzler, A. (Eds.). (1993). *The new paradigm in business: Emerging strategies for leadership and organizational change.* New York: Jeremy P. Tarcher/Perigee.

Rost, J.C. (1993). *Leadership for the twenty-first century.* Westport, CT: Praeger Publishers.

Senge, P.M. (1990). *The Fifth Discipline: The art and practice of the learning organization.* New York: Doubleday.

Terry, R.W. (1993). *Authentic Leadership.* San Francisco: Jossey Bass, Publishers.

Wheatley, M. (1992). *Leadership and the new science: Learning about organization from an orderly universe.* San Francisco: Berrett-Koehler Publishers.

CHAPTER 8

The Community— You Work for Them and They Pay the Bills

Robert R. Spillane and Paul Regnier

Nothing happens in the school system without at least tacit support from the community, and no significant changes can be made without willing support. Developing and maintaining this support is one of the most important things that a superintendent does, but many superintendents do not see this as part of the job description. As educators, they see themselves as professionals, whose work should be respected as such. After all, you don't see doctors and lawyers out politicking for public support. However, public education is very different from the medical and legal professions in a number of ways. One way is that public education is directly supported by taxes paid by the community whose children are educated in our schools. As superintendent, you do work for the taxpayer, and they do pay the bills.

This means that you are responsible to, and should be accountable to, all the taxpayers—not just the parents. As strong believers in public education, we believe that education is a public good, which means that it benefits the whole society not just the parents of children in schools. To a large extent, arguments for "privatizing" education (e.g., through vouchers or tax credits) are based on the underlying premise that the only good provided by education is to the students and their parents. This view is dangerous to the future of public education and should not be furthered by supporters of public schools. There is substantial evidence that excellent schools increase the value of housing in the schools' attendance areas (Jones, 1996) and attract business investment, but more important are the long-term economic and social advantages of an educated citizenry. Every superintendent needs to aggressively argue this case and mobilize public support for his or her schools—not just support at the polling booth but in the schools and the school system.

What comprises the community? Every community is diverse and includes diverse interests, many of which require special efforts to reach. Make the efforts.

A community consists of, at least, the following: parents, homeowners, renters, senior citizens, small businesses, larger (corporate) businesses, the news media, the arts community, civic associations, service clubs, youth sports leagues, ethnic organizations, religious groups, political parties, labor unions, and other special-interest groups. Almost all these groups overlap with others. A superintendent needs to target all of them as well as any others in his or her particular community. What's more, you need to stay alert to discover other groups that you may have missed or that may arise.

In most communities today, voters and taxpayers without children in school vastly outnumber parents, and the ethnic make-up of the community is likely to be much less minority than the ethnic make-up of the student body. This means that you cannot contact most of the community by working through the schools. You must reach out to civic associations, business and labor, ethnic organizations, service clubs, political organizations, churches, senior citizen organizations, and other places where the rest of the community can be reached. Get out on the street. Find out face to face what people are thinking; answer their questions; tell them what is going on in the schools; listen to their suggestions for improvement. Does this sound like political campaigning? You bet!

The belief that "professional" education could be kept aloof from politics was probably never viable, and it certainly isn't today and will not be in the future. This distinctly does *not* mean that a superintendent should get involved in partisan politics, but it *does* mean that the superintendent must continually work on having a public presence in the community so that, when he or she needs support for specific policies, he or she can go to the well of public support. Ongoing efforts to achieve and maintain community support and special efforts to get support for specific policies are essential; politics isn't just for politicians anymore.

Parents remain, of course, the schools' essential base of support. If they are unhappy, support from no other community group will provide a substitute. Increasingly, parents are going directly to school board members rather than through the school administration. If your board gets heavily involved in this kind of "constituent service," you, the superintendent, will lose control over the system. You need to keep the board from the kind of micro problem solving that will get everyone in trouble. The best way to do this is for you and your staff to do an excellent job of solving the problems right away. This means that your entire staff needs to keep you informed of any parent issue that might cause a problem so that you can tell a board member, when he or she calls about the issue, that you have dealt with it and how. Some parents will still go to the board, but it will be mostly malcontents who will give the board members so much trouble they will beg you to handle them.

Beyond parents, the community needs to be looked at holistically. As superintendent, you should be able to "feel the pulse" of the community. In spite of the competing demands, there is still a common ground or universal purpose to education. Even those who are the furthest removed from schools recognize that excellent schools attract people to the community and maintain property values.

There are three reasons that people in a community support a superintendent.

1. They like your aggressiveness and support your making everyone in the school system toe the line.
2. They like your thoughtfulness and the inclusiveness of your style, especially when it involves them in the process.
3. They admire your focus on the main thing (see Chapter 2), your statesmanship, your leadership, your knowledge of learning, your ability to get things done, your patience with everyone, your smooth manner, and your rising above the fray.

All of these need to be used at different times under different circumstances.

Business! Involving business in the schools is an underused strategy but is critical to the success of the superintendent of the future. While there will be people in any community who feel that businesses have interests that are contrary to the interests of residents, it is largely the private sector that sustains the economic health of a community, and this has at no time been truer than it is today. Even many communities that, in the past, have had large public-sector economic presences (e.g., military bases) are now being forced to substitute private businesses as the bases and other establishments are eliminated. Both of us have spent the past 10 to 12 years in suburban Washington, D.C., and are very aware of the need for private-sector support. Without strong business support, public institutions such as schools are likely to be underfunded and will eventually wither, leading to business pull-outs as public services decline.

One of the things that is important here is to gauge the economic interest that a given type of business has in schools. For instance, land developers have a fairly direct interest in excellent schools, since they are selling houses to families or renting office space to businesses whose employees may be looking for homes in the community. High-technology firms have a less direct financial interest in excellent schools. They are not "tied to the land," as are land-owning developers and can conceivably move their businesses elsewhere if their taxes get too high. They are not "selling" good schools to their customers. Nevertheless, they do want to be located in places where schools emphasize science, math, and technology. Their employees are likely to want schools with very high academic expectations. And the companies themselves are likely to want strong universities nearby that contribute to the high-technology synergy on which the firms depend; schools that prepare students for such universities also contribute to the synergy.

There is one thing to remember about involving the business community: They expect to deal with the chief executive officer (CEO), and that means you—the superintendent. If you need to ration your time, make it a high priority to personally meet with the business community. And, as is the case with all community groups, listen to them, think about what they have to say, and let this be an important part of the input you consider when you develop your policy proposals. In general, businesses understand your role as leader and are not interested in the details, which they will expect you to take care of. They do, however, want to influence the overall direction of the schools. Perhaps equally important, they can provide substantial assistance to schools. In both Boston and Fairfax County, Virginia, R. Spillane has been able to use his contacts with the business community to secure political support and to provide material assistance to individual schools and to school systems.

The Boston Compact helped unite a community, which had largely given up on its schools, behind a plan that eventually made the schools accountable (financially and for student learning) to that community instead of to the political structure that had held back reform for many years. Boston businesses badly wanted to stay in Boston, but they also wanted Boston to provide the kind of place they wanted to stay in, including school graduates who were employable. The deal that Spillane made was that the businesses would contribute assistance, employment opportunities for school graduates, and (perhaps most important) political support, and the schools would guarantee employable graduates. In Fairfax County, Spillane established and fostered many business connections, including school–business partnerships for individual schools and a systemwide Business/Industry Advisory Council (BIAC) reporting to the superintendent (and a systemwide director of business relations to coordinate these activities). He also established the Fairfax County Public Schools Education Foundation, which raised money from the business community and provided money, expertise, time, and commitment for projects such as a high-technology magnet high school that had more merit scholarship semifinalists than any other school for seven years out of eight; a program to identify middle school students who might not go to college and to mentor and otherwise work with them through high school into college entry; and a program to provide appropriate technology for special-education students.

But the business community is far from being the entire community, or even being entirely representative of it. As superintendent, you not only need to speak with and work with community groups such as civic and homeowners' associations, you need to have your own advisory group that represents the community; *and you need to listen to them.* In his book, *Is There a Public for Public Schools?* David Mathews (1996) says that "many Americans no longer believe the public schools are their schools," and, unfortunately, that "when educators talk about public engagement or community involvement, all they mean is using more effective ways of telling the public what's good for them." Today and in the future, school systems that prosper will be those that listen to their communities. This does not mean doing what the "squeaky wheels" in the community want, nor does it mean waiting to hear from the community before proposing anything.

Community members are more likely to offer good (or at least informed) advice if they are familiar with your schools. A volunteer school program that reaches out beyond the usual parent teacher association (PTA) types to older people and younger people without children can build a constituency of informed voters/taxpayers who recognize what the schools are doing and why and how well they are doing it.

Opening up schools to community visits on a day when many community members have a holiday but school is in session (in some cases, election day works for this) and getting substantial publicity for the event can really showcase your program to those who matter. But many people will never visit a school during school hours. There are, however, 24 hours in the day, and there is a great deal that a school system can do to be part of the everyday lives of its community. Just getting voters and taxpayers into schools will inform them and make them more likely to recognize the value the schools have for them. Elderly people can be invited to schools for lunch and for activities after school, and some will even become volunteers. In some places, religious groups without their own buildings can use paid school facilities on weekends, thus participants can get a sense of what the school is doing. Schools provide some of the best recreational facilities available in most communities, and community use of these can build knowledge and support. Schools can be open to the public for many other purposes, including civic association meetings and college courses. Every school system ought to have a community-use policy for school facilities that charges appropriate fees to pay for maintenance, security, and other legitimate expenses.

Besides bringing the community into the schools, it is important that you and those who work for you go out into the community. This may mean membership in service clubs and other community organizations, a speakers' bureau offering expertise that is available on the school system's staff, and use of all the connections you and your staff have in the community to network for the schools. All these and other networking strategies that may be specific to your community should be used consciously to build that constituency. And once again, it is at least as important for you and your staff to listen—and to bring the messages back to the rest of the school community—as to explain what the schools are doing and why and to check out and scotch rumors. As superintendent, you should accept every invitation you can, and listen to as many types of people as you can. Whether it is a black-tie affair or talking with people at the diner on Saturday morning, you get a different perspective each time, and the more diverse the people you talk with, the better everything hangs together and the better decisions you make.

At the same time, it is important to recognize that the community can be very fickle. Many a superintendent has taken an issue that started with solid community support and has gotten out in front with it only to find that the support has substantially diminished as other groups (e.g., teachers unions, the business community) have provided their own takes on things to the community. This is why it is so important to listen, to listen to many groups of citizens, and to keep listening as things develop. We have been bitten by this fickleness on a number of issues. In the late 1980s and early 1990s, Spillane tried to extend learning time at the elementary and secondary levels in Fairfax County. At the beginning, there was solid community and board support for both proposals—a seven-period day in secondary schools and a uniform day (ending a traditional early Monday closing policy for teacher planning) in elementary schools. After much *Sturm und Drang*, the high school proposal was approved and is still providing benefits for thousands of students, but the uniform elementary school day went down because the teachers (who opposed it for obvious reasons) convinced enough parents. The issue, which had once been the community's, had become "the superintendent's" (Spillane, 1991).

If you do not have a clear mandate from the community, special interests can drive the agenda. Parents and others who become deeply committed to a particular program in which their children participate can mobilize substantial pressure to keep or expand that program at all costs. Several years ago, when deep budget cutting was imperative in Fairfax County, parents whose children were involved in the swim and dive program mobilized demonstrations of support for this program. They did not care what else was cut—staff development, supplies, library books; their only goal was to retain their program. Since the vast majority of parents (and other members of the community) were not involved in any demonstrations, the swim and dive demos of a few hundred looked pretty massive, and the program was kept. This is a very bad way to do business for a number of reasons, not least that it provides a model for supporters of any other program to get what they want. What is needed is to develop a clear public mandate on budget priorities in advance of any special pleading.

How do you develop this mandate? The short answer is by clearly and forcefully presenting a statement of what is most important, and working relentlessly to explain and build support. Of course, the school board must be with you on this. We can even tell you what that vision has to convey—that academic learning and the academic achievement of *all* students is the very highest priority and that everything else the school system works on is secondary (see Chapter 2). This is a vision that every community and every part of every community will buy into if they clearly understand what it is and that you and the school board are willing to stand by it. Conveying and explaining this vision is probably the most important thing a superintendent does. Again, listening to people in the community and making this vision relevant to their concerns is part of what you need to do. If this vision is clearly explained and understood in a community, issues such as swim and dive will be clearly seen as peripheral to the main thing and the rest of the cart will overwhelm the squeaky wheel.

But a clear mandate from the public is not always achievable. Several years ago, the Fairfax County school board spent many hours of public meetings (not to mention untold hours answering questions on the phone and in person) over the issue of whether elementary gym floors should be carpeted. Carpet was better for the kids but not for the youth and adult basketball teams that used the gyms at night. This seemingly minor issue pitted the interests of students against those of members of the larger community who did not have children in elementary school but who also benefited from the schools. As we have said above, the support of this larger community is important to the continued survival of public schooling. Nevertheless, when the chips are down, schools are about educating youngsters, and their interests are paramount. When a conflict such as this arises, the superintendent who has built an ongoing relationship with the larger community and has conveyed to the community his or her vision and priorities will be in a better position to assert the priority of the students.

The best superintendents are risk takers, and this will be even more true in the future when those who take no risks to create the future will be overtaken and discarded by events. But risks should be taken in the service of ideas whose time has come, and these will be ideas that have broad public support. Even though (as in the case of the uniform elementary school day, described above) public support can turn, over time, into opposition, an idea whose time has come will outlive an early defeat. A good example of this is teacher merit pay. In Fairfax County, we managed to develop substantial community and staff support for a Teacher Performance Evaluation Plan (TPEP) that included merit pay. Over 2,000 teachers eventually qualified for substantial bonuses, but eventually a combination of teacher union and budget pressures led to the discontinuance of the merit-pay portion of TPEP, although the strong evaluation system (that for several years resulted in over 100 terminations per year) continues (Spillane, 1992). We believe that in the future, when accountability will be one of the most important forces in education, merit pay will be back as a viable option for superintendents and school boards. Today, merit pay (extra pay for excellent teaching) has broad public support; retaining that support through to implementation, while some teachers oppose it, will be a challenge and an opportunity for superintendents of the future.

Because public support is not enough, PTAs are often not willing to come out publicly in favor of something that the teachers of their children strongly oppose, even though these same PTA parents may complain loudly about the lack of achievement of students in particular teachers' classes. It is inevitable that many who have worked for many years under a given system will resist changes, even when their clients or customers are demanding change; very few people are instinctively risk takers. Public support is one major pillar in the edifice of educational progress; other pillars include strong evidence of efficacy, the resources to make the thing happen, and the support of enough opinion leaders among employees to get the project through to implementation. After that, the entire edifice must be constantly maintained until enough people look on the changes as part of "the way we do things around here."

Sometimes the public thinks it knows what it wants but does not understand what it thinks it wants. School-based management (SBM) is an example. Almost everyone these days believes in putting decision making at the level closest to the students and teacher in the classroom. Usually, this means devolving central office decisions to the school level. There is (or at least there was) an actual example of fairly radical SBM in Edmonton, Alberta, where most central office functions continued only as long as individual schools were willing to pay for them out of their school-based budgets. However, SBM raises numerous questions that most supporters in the community haven't asked themselves, questions ranging from whether school-based purchasing undermines economies of scale, to whether parents want principals and other school-based personnel spending their time on fund-raising and purchasing rather than instruction, to hardware compatibility if all schools purchase their own computers, to curricular differences among neighboring schools. This is an example of an issue whose complexity almost precludes broad public understanding but whose innate appeal builds support. Explaining such an issue is a challenge in community relations.

In a time when the public, politicians, and pundits are focusing on education as never before, the superintendent's relationship with the community and with every segment of the community is and will be more important than ever. Accountability to the broader community (beyond the parent community) will be a major feature of education in the twenty-first century, and the superintendent of the future had better prepare for it. Building community relations day after day, every day, is the only way you will survive.

REFERENCES

Jones, D. (1996, May 15). Location, location, location. *USA Today*, 18.

Mathews, D. (1996). *Is there a public for public schools?* Dayton, OH: Kettering Foundation Press.

Spillane, R. (1991). Restructuring the school day in Fairfax County. In M. Cetron & M. Gayle (Eds.), *Educational renaissance: Our schools into the twenty-first century* (pp. 130–135). New York: St. Martin's Press.

Spillane, R. (1992). Pay for performance in Fairfax County, Virginia. In L.E. Frase (Ed.), *Teacher compensation and motivation* (pp. 413–424). Lancaster, PA: Technomic.

CHAPTER 9

School Boards—Partners in Policy

Jacqueline P. Danzberger

Effective leadership and governance of a school district requires the school board and superintendent to forge and sustain an effective partnership. While each has separate roles and functions, each is dependent on the other for success in their respective roles. Tension is inherent and natural in the relationship. Superintendents bring their professional expertise and school boards their knowledge of community history, values, goals, student needs, and public expectations of the schools to the partnership. Ideally, where mutual understanding and respect for each other's role and functions exist, policy direction and oversight and professional recommendations and management will ensure steady, community-supported progress toward improved achievement for all students.

Unfortunately, assessment of school board–superintendent relationships in the late 1990s documents more and more conflicted and broken relationships, increasing mutual suspicion of motives and purposes on the part of both parties to the partnership, and the not uncommon compromise of going along to get along ("peace in our time"), particularly if there has been a great deal of conflict in the relationship between a prior superintendent and the school board.

This chapter is intended to help superintendents better understand the institution of school boards, the social and political contexts that affect how boards govern, the expectations of constituencies, documented problems of school boards (or why so many behave as they do), superintendents' roles in the relationship, how school boards might be restructured by states and why this is not likely to occur, and what superintendents might do to forge and sustain effective partnerships with their boards. Some history is provided to explain the increasing politicization of school boards and Americans' growing skepticism and distrust of professionals and experts. The case for urgency for finding ways to rebuild school board–superintendent partnerships is made through the lens of decreasing public confidence and support for the public schools.

THE IMPACT OF SOCIAL AND POLITICAL STRESSES ON THE
SCHOOL BOARD–SUPERINTENDENT RELATIONSHIP

School superintendents in the foreseeable future will face more, not fewer, challenges in their relationships with their school boards. Many problems result from conflicts arising in the larger society and in individual communities. School boards, as political institutions, bring the public's unresolved issues, group conflicts, special interests, frustrations, and fears to their governing practices and relationships. This is not to say that the superintendent–board working relationships cannot become more productive but rather to emphasize that these relationships are not formed, nor do they play out, in a vacuum.

School boards and superintendents, in their individual and collaborative roles, are not simply victims of political and social forces but frequently contribute, through "sins" of omission and commission, to intracommunity conflict about the schools and the absence of an engaged and supportive public. These problems, in turn, provoke self-defeating professional and political behaviors from superintendents and school boards that poison their relationship. Trouble between the roles precludes stable leadership to improve the schools and reinforces disenchantment and anger among members of the public about the leadership and accomplishments of their public schools.

The next step in what has become an all-too-common vicious cycle is usually the firing or voluntary departure of a superintendent and new faces on the school board at the next election. Experiences in this decade document the futility of simply changing the faces—superintendents or school board members—either for forging a productive relationship or for meeting community expectations for educational improvement from a new team. Superintendent tenure in the nation's 45 largest school districts is now less than three years, and has dropped, on average, to five years or less in other types of school districts. One-third of school board members turn over each year. Further, successful efforts of community members and leaders who have elected "reform" boards (that select new superintendents) in such cities as Cleveland, New Orleans, and Chicago proved sorely disappointing.

Much more is at stake at the end of the twentieth century than the professional and political fortunes of superintendents and school board members. The problems among members on school boards and between boards and superintendents result in an untoward amount of time and energy invested in problem relationships and issues of control and turf rather than in providing direction for schools' and school systems' educational improvement to meet students' needs and public expectations. Americans, even divided as they are about the means for reform, believe in public education and want good public schools. But, Americans' patience is wearing thin.

The erosion of public confidence in the public's schools and a growing, seriously dysfunctional gap between members of the public and educators are realities well documented in public-opinion research over the past several years (Immerwahr, 1994; Johnson, 1995). In a study conducted in 1995, almost 6 in 10 parents with children in public schools said that they would take their children out of their schools and send them to private schools if they could afford to do so (Johnson, 1995). And, 47% said they did not believe that a diploma from their own local high schools guarantees that graduates have even mastered basic academics and skills (Johnson, 1995). Research conducted in Connecticut for the Graustein Memorial Fund in 1995 documented that members of the public believe that educators have broken the contract with the public in terms of the public's basic expectations of the public schools (Immerwahr, 1994).

Public confidence in the public schools and with that, public support for educational reform and improvement, will be revived, supported, and sustained through actions taken and results demonstrated in the nation's 15,000 school districts and the individual schools within them. How well the schools are governed and professionally led will determine the future of the public schools. An ineffective school board–superintendent partnership cannot provide the kind of leadership required to meet the educational and political challenges to the public schools.

Superintendents and school boards, irrespective of whether they are in rural, small town, suburban, or urban school districts should take heed of steps taken by state officials and mayors when they lose faith in the traditional local school district leadership roles to govern and manage for improved educational results. The state of Ohio took over the Cleveland schools, Connecticut ousted both the superintendent and the school board in Hartford, and the mayor of Chicago eliminated the school board and replaced the superintendent with a noneducator. As of 1997, Maryland and Baltimore will now share control of the governance and management of the Baltimore schools, and the traditional superintendent role has been redefined and will probably be filled by a noneducator. A retired general now leads the Washington, D.C., school system, and the elected board is basically ceremonial. States legislatively empowered to take over failing school systems are less and less reluctant to exercise their authority to do so.

The nature of these actions—removal of both superintendents and boards, turning to professional leaders outside of education, and taking over the political governing role and functions—underscores recognition of the interrelatedness of the two roles as well as boards' and superintendents' joint responsibility for success or failure of school district leadership to produce expected educational results.

FROM FAITH TO DISENCHANTMENT: ORIGINS OF THE DECLINE OF AMERICANS' LOVE AFFAIR WITH THEIR PUBLIC SCHOOLS

Americans have historically turned to their schools not only to develop new generations of citizens to sustain and complete the great work of creating the republic begun with the American Revolution but also to prepare their children to enter the economy successfully. They have also turned to the schools to instill and/or reinforce certain beliefs, values, and "virtues," such as our basic freedoms, individualism, and individual success, hard work, self-reliance, and moral-ethical behaviors rooted in the Judeo-Christian tradition. All of these, taken together, and reinforced by the belief that our aggregate national success was the result of individuals' success, defined for most what it meant to be an American.

The nation's explosive economic growth beginning after the Civil War, the ability to absorb and inculturate massive waves of immigrants, and the rise to preeminent world power all reinforced Americans' belief in the nation's political and economic structures and in the institutions supporting them. The role of education, delivered through free, common public schools governed locally, enjoyed enormous credit for the rise of the majority of Americans into the middle class, as well as for the nation's world dominance in the post–World War II era. Public-school educators, while never in the revered position of educators in some other developed countries, nevertheless benefited from Americans' faith in education and in tangible results from their public schools.

Americans' commitment to education and to the public school system they established did contribute greatly to the rise of the nation in the world and to the astonishingly quick development of America into a nation of the middle class. However, availability of land, a relatively classless society, and an industrial economy that, for a while, had an almost unlimited ability to absorb uneducated and low-skilled workers, were also essential to the economic success of masses of the people.

Americans did not set out to establish public schools to produce a highly educated populace. Educating all children was viewed as necessary for responsible citizenship in a democracy; for economic self-reliance; for moral development; and, beginning in the latter part of the nineteenth century, for the absorption of immigrants into the mainstream of American political and cultural life. The majority of Americans, then and now, carry a deep-seated distrust of highly educated people and continue an unfortunate bent toward equating high levels of academic attainment with elitism. In a 1995 public-opinion study, members of the public, parents, and teachers rated "getting along with people" as more important to career success than high academic achievement (Johnson, 1995).

All Is Not Well in the Public Schools: Americans Read the Headlines and Wrestle with the Evidence

Since 1950, Americans have endured not only a fairly constant stream of reported crises in the schools but also failures of public education. The terrible inequities between public schools serving whites and blacks in segregated systems were real and unconscionable—not the fault of the public schools per se but of American society. Fears that the Soviet Union would outstrip the United States in science and technology found culprits in science and math curricula and teaching. Drops in U.S. worker productivity, that were real at one point, and even shifts in U.S. world economic dominance in certain industries were blamed on the workers' education and less emphasis on hard work in the public schools.

The Scholastic Aptitude Test (SAT) and American College Testing (ACT) scores did in fact drop, but there were no headlines telling the public that this was an inevitable downside of the public schools' positive effort to extend access to college to formerly excluded populations. Judged by reports of student achievement, urban schools began a slide down into failure that, so far, appears impervious to all reform efforts. Enrollment in remedial, basic academic courses by 50% or more of entering college freshmen has become the norm in public colleges and universities. Reports in the last decade about college students' entering teacher education programs scoring in the bottom percentile on college entrance examinations did little to engender confidence in the profession among leaders in the political and for-profit sectors. School boards' and educators' policies and practices are largely blamed for broadly reported breakdowns in discipline and safety in schools. It is important to understand that all of the above are processed by the public in the context of wrenching shifts in the economy, in fears about adults' own employment and economic prospects, and in even greater concerns about children's futures.

In short, we have a public with a legacy of belief in the dependence of adult economic success on the institution of the public schools, but we have a public that increasingly questions whether that institution, particularly for a growing percentage of the school population, is up to the job. Compounding the erosion of faith in the institution is an increasing skepticism about what seems an unending stream of reforms that the public is asked to support but that appear to have little impact, particularly on achieving the public's basic priorities and expectations of the schools.

Whom To Blame

Obviously, many of the problems that appear as school problems are societal problems and are neither of the schools' doing nor solvable by the schools. But, there are improvements that leaders and policy makers external to the schools and the public deem under the control of teachers and administrators in school systems and the boards that govern the systems. By turn, the culprits, and therefore the focus of reforms, have been high school graduation and course work requirements, teacher competencies and salaries, administrators, curriculum and assessment, teaching methods, mismatches between the culture of students and the culture of schools, lowered parental involvement, the structure of schooling, the locus of decision making in school systems, academic standards, school and classroom discipline and order, safety, and so forth.

The school boards' governing and making decisions about many of the above largely avoided culprit status in their communities until recently, even though state reform initiatives in the early 1980s often stemmed from lack of confidence in local boards as well as in local professional educators. Highly visible urban boards' problems and their conflicted relationships with their superintendents certainly heightened awareness among the public of the relationship of boards' governing behaviors to educational change and improvement. In suburban, rural, and small-town communities, school boards have increasingly become the battlegrounds for philosophical control of the schools and for deciding who will win among special interests; thus heightening public awareness of boards' political role in these communities. And, even while conflicted about objectives and means and electing board members with narrow interests and objectives, increasing numbers within the public are making the connection between how school boards govern and possibilities for progress toward educational improvements.

COMING FULL CIRCLE: THE EVOLUTION OF SCHOOL BOARDS IN THE TWENTIETH CENTURY

Superintendents, along with the national education reform community (foundation boards and program staff, academicians, business leaders, and many highly placed state policy makers) decry the politicization of school boards in the late twentieth century. School board members, particularly in urban and changing inner suburbs, increasingly define their roles as representing and responding to the immediate interests and demands of their constituents, and they allow constituents to define not only the priorities of board members they elect but also how they play the role. Frequently, vocal constituents' interests are narrow and/or conflicting, reflecting the demographic, philosophical, and political conflicts present in all but a few American communities.

The expert "class" must also contend with growing public skepticism about experts. Nowhere is this more evident than in the dysfunctional gap between the public and educators. While one might assume that school boards could bridge or narrow this gap, this proves unlikely given changes in those seeking to serve on school boards in many communities. Increasingly, board members do not have extensive community leadership experience, and are not broadly recognized and respected community leaders with access to community power structures as were the majority of school board members in the past. More individuals achieve school board membership based on their advocacy for a particular population group, special interest, hot issue, or political position.

What has caused the escalating politicization of school boards over the past 30 years? How did we get to this point from what superintendents might consider the halcyon days of school boards composed of members with a trusteeship notion of the role who were recognized as moral and cultural leaders of their communities? Admittedly, the great social, economic, and political changes in the nation are major contributing factors. However, reforms of the early part of this century, which generally placed the experts in charge and ultimately isolated the grass roots from the schools, carried the seeds for a repoliticization of school boards.

In large measure, the political volatility of school boards over the past 30 years reflects the grass roots trying to take back the schools. However, this populist movement sends conflicted messages. On the one hand, constituents want strong leadership to produce successful students. This requires school boards able to forge the necessary consensus to give strong and sustained policy direction to their communities' public schools. On the other hand, constituents put individuals on school boards who tend to define their roles more as mirror representatives of constituents' interests than as members of governing bodies that must reconcile differences to provide strong policy direction and oversight accountability to the public.

School board behavior, today, has much in common with urban school boards in the late nineteenth century. While there were multiple school boards in cities tied to ward politics at that time rather than the central boards of today, school board members were elected then, as they increasingly are now, with the expectation that they would respond to the particular interests of their constituents and reward the faithful. At the turn of the century, the rising intellectual class, drawn from the newly emerging business and professional classes across the country, saw nothing but chaos and public schools that could not respond to the needs of a country coming to a position of world prominence through its economic power. The new intellectual leadership groups across the country, driven mainly by industrial leaders, began to lay the foundations for their own interpretation of education reform. A fundamental change in the decision-making structure was the primary objective of the reformers. To do this, they eliminated the urban ward systems, established a system of small central school boards, and set about to replace the decision makers. Hoping to gain control of the schools and bring order, the new elite sought to insulate education from the vagaries of political influence and partisanship. For the leaders of the movement, the rationale was simple: school board members in the cities were basically politicians and could not or would not reform the schools—this, from their perspective, could only come from the leaders of the intellectual and business life of communities.

Arguments to the public were couched in slightly different language. The reformers argued that school board members elected by individual wards tended to represent parochial interests at the expense of those shared by the entire community. At-large elections would guarantee the election of board members who had the needs of the entire school district at heart. In reality, school board representativeness came to mean representation of the views and values of the financial, business, and professional communities (Spring, 1984). This reform of local-education governance really was a return to the beginnings of school board membership in the country when community-recognized moral and cultural leaders were expected to make up school board membership.

The industrial and professional reformers established this new governance system in concert with the major education reformers in the early part of this century. In this restructured system, the leadership role of the superintendent was elevated to parallel the leadership role of a corporate executive, and superintendents' role relationships to their school boards were essentially the same as chief executive officers (CEOs) to their corporate boards. The new governance system was also grounded in the, then, newly prevailing theory of scientific management and the efficacy of bureaucracies.

Members of these reformed school boards were frequently heads of businesses and busy professionals and were therefore constrained in the time they could give and in their ability to participate actively in school policy debate. These boards increasingly depended on their superintendents, which was consistent with these board members' belief in scientific management.

The selection of the superintendent became the critical function of school boards. University leaders allied themselves with the industrial and professional reformers and began to give specialized attention to school administration, giving birth to school administration as a "learned profession." Over time, the school board role became mainly that of buffer between the public and professional administrators and of provider of official approval for the actions of the education professionals. This structure and governing philosophy, which began as a reform of urban governance, ultimately became the dominant definition of the board–superintendent role relationship in all school districts. This was particularly true in terms of superintendents' expectations of their roles in relationship to the roles of school boards. These expectations were and, in the opinion of this author, probably continue to be reinforced in the institutions that train school administrators.

Centralization of school board elections made it difficult for average citizens to seek board election because they lacked power bases, access to the press, and sufficient financial means. The new, small central boards and district-wide elections produced little diversity among school board members. Detachment from the pulse of the people, exacerbated by the changing face of the nation, eventually led to troubles for the reformed school board and, consequently, for the board–superintendent relationship.

The Civil Rights Movement in the 1960s was the catalyst for what might be termed the school board counterreform movement. As with the turn-of-the-century governance reforms, demands for change began because of concern about urban public schools, but the grass roots became the reformers demanding change. Urban school boards were attacked for failing their students and for not representing the rapidly growing minority populations in the schools. Minority parents questioned whether white school boards could respond to their children's needs. This period also gave rise to the politics of difference and the demand for representation with the implicit assumption on the part of constituents that differences and particular interests would define behaviors of those elected.

Change in the governing structure of schools began in New York City with the establishment of community school districts, each with its own school board empowered to select the superintendent. In the 1970s, state legislatures at the behest of major cities began to break school districts into single-member electoral districts for school board elections. This local governance reform is spreading rapidly to medium and small urban districts and county districts. In most instances, single-member electoral districts produce school board members who define themselves as politicians with separate loyalties controlled by constituents. And, while communities ultimately have little respect for constant bickering and fighting among board members, there is rarely sufficient consensus about expected governing behaviors among the community to send a compelling, consistent message to change behaviors.

The governance counterreform began to ensure that school board members were representative of population groups served in urban schools. It was and is, in essence, a grass-roots reform that fairly quickly escalated to a more general expectation for electing individual board members to represent special interests and political factions, and, with increasing frequency, for electing those opposed to particular education reforms. In the current climate of general distrust and lack of faith in government and big public institutions and, more specifically, a sense among the public of loss of control of its public schools, the politicization and overall volatility of school boards is not surprising. School board members now are much more likely to be elected to represent and help various population differences (geographic, racial, ethnic, class) and factional positions prevail within a community. For many board members, this means that they must get into every facet of their school systems and be ever vigilant in order to demonstrate faithfulness to their constituents. In particularly diverse and/or conflicted communities, this is a major cause of micromanagement.

THE IMPACT OF EDUCATION REFORM ON SCHOOL BOARD GOVERNING BEHAVIORS AND THE BOARD–SUPERINTENDENT RELATIONSHIP

Changes in the governing behaviors of school boards and the motivation for school board service parallel not only demographic, social, and political changes over the past 30-plus years but also the evolution of the nature and focus of education reforms since the publication of *A Nation At Risk* (National Commission, 1983). Certainly shifts in the purposes and strategies for reform posed major challenges to professional educators. However, as difficult as changes in the reform agenda have been for educators, the changes have posed and continue to pose even greater difficulties for school boards. These political bodies represent a public that is not only divided but also feels like the victim of top-down imposed reforms; has little understanding of many reforms; increasingly distrusts particular reforms; believes its basic priorities and expectations of the public schools have not been met; and frequently are not respected by educators, many policy makers, and other leaders of the national reform movement.

Over the past 14 years, the philosophy, objectives, and strategies for public school reform evolved from strengthening the structure, system, pedagogy, and curricular content assumed and experienced in common by the public to promulgating reforms that questioned and attempted to change many underlying assumptions and practices. School boards (and superintendents) found themselves contending with escalating expectations and state mandates for implementation of more complex and less understood reforms that would or could have a profound impact on the known system. School boards, particularly, are frequently caught in the middle between the reformers and the public—a public that defines improvement of the public schools as a high national priority but that has not had civic opportunities or political leadership to come to informed and workable public consensus to give direction to the governing bodies for the schools.

Superintendents, frustrated with the seeming inability of their school boards to provide consensual leadership for school improvement, need look no further than to the lack of public consensus to understand much of boards' behaviors. Exercising effective governance, that is, setting goals, establishing policies for steadily guiding a school system toward achievement of the goals, and determining means for assessing progress and corrective strategies, requires that a governing body be able to make decisions based on valid assumptions of commonly held core values, beliefs, and expectations among those on whose behalf a representative political body is empowered to govern. Historically, school boards could govern with much more certainty about what these basic commonalities were and that they even existed in their communities.

The dramatic escalation of superintendent turnover, which began in large urban school districts, has spread to affect superintendent tenure in all types of districts. This parallels the escalation of demands for profound change, particularly in failing or changing school districts, and of conflicting political pressures on boards in all types of school districts arising from changes in the direction, means, and expectations of education reform.

Concerns, misunderstanding, and opposition manifest themselves across the great middle of the national political spectrum, not, as may be comforting to believe, just within organized conservative Christian coalitions. Isolation of the public from the reform of the public schools is a root cause of the inability, thus far, to build sustainable, proactive political will for reform of public schools among a majority of the public. This political reality, coupled with minimal or no improvements in the educational outcomes for the nation's most difficult to educate students in relation to the promises for reforms instituted and resources invested, produces increasing public skepticism. This, in turn, breeds a feeling of powerlessness among average Americans who do not identify themselves with either extreme of the political spectrum.

Absence of a politically involved and proactive middle in most communities creates opportunity and motivation to elect sympathetic school board members among those who have strongly held beliefs, for and against, the philosophy and content of current major education reforms promoted by academe, the "national reform community," and many local professional educators. Thus far, the political middle appears to have become galvanized around school board elections only to correct extreme swings in political control of a school board. Littleton, Colorado, provides a case in point. A school board and superintendent worked in close partnership to develop major changes in schooling structure, curriculum, and assessment intended for initial implementation at the high school level. Community lack of understanding and resistance resulted in the election of a school board that voted to throw out all the changes. This, of course, made the superintendent's position untenable. The political middle that contributed to the election of the new board found its actions too extreme, and subsequently elected school board members in the next election who worked toward compromise and implementation of some of the reforms.

The Littleton example offers powerful instruction about the political responsibilities of superintendents in the relationship with their boards. A strong board–superintendent policy partnership, mutually supportive in the direction and strategies for reform, will achieve as little as a conflicted relationship in the long run if the board, as the community partner, is not in touch with all community perspectives and able to integrate these into their guidance of the school system. This example also underscores the increasing political role of superintendents. Gone are the days when the major political challenge for superintendents was limited to reading the politics and probable political behaviors of board members.

SCHOOL BOARD PROBLEMS AND THEIR IMPACT ON THE IMPROVEMENT OF PUBLIC EDUCATION

This section focuses directly on the governance and leadership responsibilities and failures of school boards for which they can and should be held accountable. Not all, but too many, school boards give evidence of serious governing problems. And, it is difficult to find an exception among the school boards that are governing the nation's large urban school districts. One need look no further for evidence of serious troubles than to the states and mayors of certain urban school districts who have taken over the school boards.

Those calling for school board reforms, including this author, do not necessarily agree about what would be most effective, but all do agree that the evidence of problems, reports in the media, turnover among superintendents, continuing low student achievement among poor urban and rural students, and performance data from school boards can no longer be ignored. Critics agree that school boards all too commonly*:

- fail to provide farsighted and politically risky leadership necessary for education reform
- have become another level of administration, often micromanaging school districts and blurring accountability for results
- are so splintered by members' attempts to represent special interests or meet their individual political needs that they fail to govern to meet the needs of the whole district
- are not spending enough time on educating themselves about education issues or on education policy making
- have not provided necessary leadership to mobilize other agencies and units of government to meet the human and social service needs of students and their families

---

*Source: The following list is reprinted with permission from J.P. Danzberger, Governing the Nation's Schools: the Case for Restructuring Local School Boards, *Phi Delta Kappan*, p. 369, Copyright © 1994, Jacqueline P. Danzberger.

- do not exercise adequate policy oversight, lack adequate policies for accountability and intervention strategies throughout their school systems, and fail to communicate problems as well as successes of schools and the system
- place greater emphasis on improving their public relations than on providing opportunities for open public dialogues and engagement of members of the public with the schools
- honor devolution of decision making on schools more in rhetoric than action
- exhibit serious problems in their capacity to develop and sustain positive and productive relationships with their superintendents
- tend to make decisions in response to the "issue(s) of the day" or the loudest constituents
- pay little or no attention to their performance and their own education and training needs (Danzberger, 1994, p. 369)

The Data Confirm Superintendents' and Critics' Observations

Findings from three studies conducted by the Institute for Educational Leadership (IEL) from 1985 through 1992 and reinforced by direct assessment and development work with a variety of school boards over the past five years confirm critics' observations. The governing behaviors and problems noted in the first study have, in the observation of this author and other external critics, increased over time. The findings from the first national study during 1985 and 1986 documented an institution in trouble but an institution with very strong grass-roots support (IEL, 1986). This support for the institution rarely translated into positive perceptions (including perceptions of school board members themselves) among interviewees of their own local boards in the nine case study school districts. In addition to broad-based interviews in the case study districts, the study included survey data from more than 400 school board chairs in the nine metropolitan areas, as well as data collected from school boards in three rural states in the Midwest and West.

School board members in the study communities confirmed the observations of community and school system interviewees that the boards were spending too little time on major educational concerns and too much time micromanaging their school districts. Board members noted conflicts on their boards about the role of the board and the absence of policies and strategies for developing strong working relationships with their superintendents and for resolving conflicts among themselves and with their superintendents. The study data exposed increasing concern about a shift in the concept of board service away from that of trusteeship and leadership to a more politicized notion of reactive representation of special interests and/or constituent groups. These trends exacerbated interpersonal tension on school boards and were making it difficult for members to function as corporate governing bodies. Changes in the concept of the board and board member role were beginning to change the concept of the board–superintendent relationship to what is all too common now—an expectation on the part of many board members that the superintendent should primarily relate to individual board members and service their individual political needs.

The Institute's second study, *Governing Public Schools: New Times, New Requirements* (Danzberger, Kirst, & Usdan, 1992), revisited earlier findings in the then new contexts of systemic education reform, increased recognition of the noninstructional needs of a growing percentage of the school-age population, and new players in the education policy arena. This report provided evidence of increasing governing problems, documented in self-assessment data from approximately 300 school boards across the nation that participated in a three-year demonstration of IEL's School Board Effectiveness Program (Danzberger, 1998). These data provided powerful evidence of an institution in trouble. Self-assessment data from school boards using the IEL instrument over the past several years is consistent with the earlier findings.

Individual members of the participating boards anonymously rated their boards' effectiveness on a six-point scale. The instrument has 15 sections corresponding to the "indicators of school board effectiveness" developed from the first study. Each of the indicator sections has from 7 to 15 assessment items. The 300 boards in this sample (large urban; urban; suburban; and rural, small town) generally rated themselves least effective in the core areas of governing responsibilities—the areas in which boards are widely criticized. These included leadership, planning and goal setting, policy oversight and accountability policies, involving parents and the community, relating to and influencing others (agencies and institutions whose policies and actions have an impact on students and their families), and board operations and board development. Boards' ratings for key items within the sections documented, for instance, that a majority of board members believed that their boards were not very effective in developing a common definition of the role of the school board, resolving conflicts among board members, spending time on and learning about major education issues, developing education policy, providing effective orientation for new board members, or in ensuring well-developed measures of accountability to assess the progress of their districts and individual schools.

While the majority of boards in this study rated themselves "somewhat effective" overall in the two sections of the instrument pertaining to working with superintendents, boards' ratings of certain specific assessment items within these sections portended nationally escalating problems in board–superintendent relationships. Generally, boards rated themselves less than effective in the following: the superintendent evaluation process; opportunities for superintendents to give input to boards about the working relationship; processes for regularly assessing the working relationship and for resolving conflicts; and working with their superintendents to define roles, to continuously clarify policy and administrative responsibilities, and to agree on the gray areas between the two.

One of the most compelling findings (and, again, a portent of escalating board problems in the 1990s) was the remarkable consistency among the boards in all types of school districts. For example, in the planning and goal-setting section, each of the subsamples of boards rated itself highest in having district goals and lowest in communicating progress toward goals to the community. This latter piece of data about boards' communications responsibilities is but one piece of the study data correlating boards' governing practices with the increasing alienation of the public from its schools. And, like several of the findings about the board–superintendent relationship, these boards' data pertaining to parent and community involvement and communications portended current problems of the public's separation from its schools (Danzberger, 1994).

In 1991 and 1992, IEL conducted a field study of six urban school boards in school districts then enjoying high national visibility for system restructuring. The study probed the role of the sitting and prior boards in initiating, implementing, and sustaining the reforms. A school board had played a definable role in initiating reforms in only two of these school districts, and one of these boards was a prior board. The boards in these cities were unsure about how or even whether to devolve greater authority on the schools even when they had adopted such policies and their districts were supposedly instituting this change. These boards had not specifically addressed how their central governing role should be redefined, had not embedded many of the major reforms and structural changes in board policy, and had not adequately defined the new roles for participants in school-based decision making or the locus of accountability for structural changes.

Most of these boards gave too little time and attention to coherence among reform initiatives to ensure consistency with the goals and objectives of restructuring. This, in turn, prevented articulation of clear messages to the community and within the system about how many reforms and new programs related to overall goals and objectives. Their inability to shift the focus of their boards' work from immersion in immediate problems and crises to exercising more community leadership and longer-term governing responsibilities frustrated many members of these boards. But, board members could not envision how to change board behaviors and practices, nor did they feel they "had the time" to analyze what they were doing or for consequential and sustained board development. At the time of the study, some of the boards struggled to maintain a bare majority in support of highly touted reforms and the superintendents appointed to reform the systems. By 1995, all these superintendents (all of whom were initiators of these districts' reform efforts) were gone (voluntarily or through mutual consent). School board majorities have been overturned, have backpedaled support of many reforms, or, new majorities are addressing different constituent pressures in four of these school districts.

Help for School Boards: A Framework for Restructuring Roles and Responsibilities

School boards, except for the rare state in which they exist in the state constitution (e.g., Florida), are creatures of the states and are controlled by state codes and mandates. States should assume responsibility to help boards redefine their roles and responsibilities. It makes no sense (other than for state legislators' and governors' desires for election and reelection) for state policy makers to enact reforms, encourage and provide incentives for local district reforms, and create leadership coalitions for statewide education reform while, in all but a few instances, ignoring the local governing bodies.

Institutions in all sectors rarely reform themselves; indeed, it is almost impossible for political institutions to do so. There are few incentives and many disincentives so long as individuals are elected and reelected. State action can help all school boards to govern better. Redefined and clear expectations of the role and responsibilities of boards are also critical to changing constituent perceptions of the school board as just another political body whose members are judged on how well each reflects and serves his or her most vocal constituents.

IEL developed a framework of recommendations in 1993 for comprehensive and coherent restructuring of boards to help them become a positive force for reform and improvement of the public schools. The intent of these recommendations is to transform local school boards into true "education policy boards" able to focus on development, implementation, and oversight of policies; to improve the academic achievement of all students; and to provide leadership to rebuild public engagement with and support for the public schools. Except for few of the recommendations, which would require state actions, school boards, themselves, could redefine themselves using this framework. However, as has been stated, the incentives are few and the disincentives many. Superintendents whose boards feel they are not spending the majority of time on important issues and responsibilities might suggest their boards use this framework to think about what they are and are not doing, define what they believe are their most important governing responsibilities, and determine what must change to bring what they are doing in line with what they believe they should be doing.

The Recommendations

States should repeal all current laws and regulations that specify the duties, functions, selection, and role of school boards: Rename the school board the "local education policy board."

There are 14 recommendations for school boards. They are*:

1. develop the vision for the school district and engage in short- and long-term planning to reach consensus on district- and school-level goals and objectives, school performance indicators, and student assessment objectives
2. be responsible for hiring, evaluating, and defining the role of the superintendent and, with the superintendent, define roles and evaluation policies for cabinet-level administrators; establish personnel policies to guide hiring, evaluation, and dismissal of other district personnel; not be involved in individual personnel decisions
3. approve school district budgets, ensuring that spending priorities are consistent with the systems' goals and objectives; establish policies to exercise their fiduciary responsibilities for oversight of system financial management but not be involved in approval of expenditures and contracts consistent with board policies and board-approved budgets
4. determine policies and guidelines for negotiation of employee contracts, and approve negotiated contracts; not negotiate directly with representatives of employee bargaining units
5. approve curricular frameworks and standards for student achievement
6. provide policy coherence by linking policies and reform initiatives to student achievement objectives, curricular frameworks, and assessment
7. establish policies for staff development to ensure coherence with educational goals and objectives
8. develop a system for a substantive review of individual school performance on a periodic basis
9. hire administrative law judges (or another type of qualified third party) to hear and decide complaints and appeals of individual students and staff members
10. establish a procedure (external to the board) to hear and decide complaints from individual constituents
11. convene community dialogues to discuss major education policy issues and provide leadership for public education

---

*Source: The following list is *A Framework for Redefining the Role and Responsibilities for Local School Boards*, Copyright © 1993, Institute for Educational Leadership.

12. establish policies and procedures to facilitate their own and staff cooperation and collaboration with appropriate units of general government and other agencies serving children and families
13. conduct regular and periodic self-assessments, securing superintendent (and ideally community) input
14. commit to an ongoing process of learning and development (IEL, 1993, pp. 6–7)

This framework would actually strengthen and re-create local boards so that they might become influential forces for change and improvement of schools and for ensuring there is a public for the public schools.

Obstacles to Restructuring School Boards' Roles and Major Functions

Since 1985, the Institute for Educational Leadership (IEL) has conducted studies of school boards, worked with boards across the country, participated in other national organizations' studies of local education governance, and worked with communities in long-term, community-based dialogue processes to reform school governance. IEL has worked hard to raise local governance reform higher on states' reform agendas and among national leaders of education reform. A few states—Kentucky, Massachusetts, and Texas (to some degree)—have redefined powers and functions of boards. However, legislation requiring a few hours of board training is as much direct school board reform as other states have risked in the current political climate. Obviously, state legislation requiring greater school site autonomy affects the span of control of boards. Unfortunately, few states have seized the opportunity such legislation presents to redefine the role and functions of local boards or even to help boards rethink their roles and functions.

State policy makers avoid tackling comprehensive local governance reform, even though it is critical to achieving states' own education reform objectives. The political risks appear too great. Political coalitions have not formed for reform of local governance, and leaders who are not in the political sector, such as business leaders strongly involved in states' reform efforts, appear as reluctant as politicians to initiate local governance reform and for many of the same reasons. There certainly is no broad grass-roots pressure to reform local school boards, but there are those who would organize quickly, or use existing organized networks, to fight any change perceived to weaken the power of a representative body close to the people and strengthen the power of professional educators. Legislative leaders in Indiana early in this decade learned this when they introduced legislation to redefine the roles and functions of school boards.

A major obstacle to development of community pressure on boards to govern more effectively arises from general lack of understanding of the role and legitimate functions of school boards. Interviews with a broad range of parents, community members, and leaders in the nine case study school districts for IEL's mid-1980s national study revealed little understanding of the role of the school board, as differentiated from central district administration. Many among the public do not understand that individual board members have no authority and that decisions can only come through members' collective actions. This misunderstanding about what an individual member can do is obviously exacerbated by the increasing number of board candidates who promise they will do specific things, e.g., keep a program, get rid of a program; support the superintendent, get rid of the superintendent; and so forth. Such constituent expectations and the candidates they spawn are not unique to school boards. Increasingly, candidates for city councils, county boards, state legislatures, and Congress are elected by appealing to narrower interests and discrete groups within the public.

PERSPECTIVES ON BOARD–SUPERINTENDENT RELATIONSHIPS: THE PROBLEMS ARE NOT JUST THOSE "PESKY" BOARDS

Tension between school boards and their superintendents is neither new nor surprising: Tension is inherent in any lay governing board and/or professional CEO relationship. Boards of trustees and university college presidents have growing concerns about their relationship, as do boards of directors and executive directors of voluntary and not-for-profit organizations. Lay board members, irrespective of the type of organization, institution, or agency, frequently come to their positions with minimal understanding of the policy role of the board or the role of individual members of a governing board.

Over the last 10 years, particularly, natural constructive tension between the role of the board and that of the superintendent more often escalated into tension that destroyed the relationship. Increasingly, boards and superintendents play out their respective roles and their relationship buffeted by strident and conflicting external demands. These demands challenge the professional leadership of superintendents and the ability of members of boards to exercise effective consensual policy leadership to give direction to their school systems. The fact that the relationships among board members and the board relationship with the superintendent must basically play out in public compounds the difficulty of resolving role and relationship problems.

Superintendents' professional education may perpetuate what were generally accepted definitions of the roles in the past—superintendents administer school systems, and boards only make policy. In fact, today, the increasing complexity of public education and shifting constituent expectations blur the separation of policy and administration so that there are many gray areas. Most board members know that they are supposed to set policy, but they also know that boards are legally responsible for everything that occurs, or fails to occur, in their school systems. Neither boards nor superintendents pay sufficient attention to the need to work at developing their relationships to adjust to new demands and the fraying of the boundaries of responsibility between the two roles. The evidence from highly visible urban districts suggests two stages in the relationship: the honeymoon with a new superintendent when all seems possible, and the divorce, when one or the other party becomes sufficiently frustrated and disenchanted to terminate the relationship.

Defining root problems in the relationship depends, to some extent, on where one stands. Observers outside the relationship can see problems arising from shortcomings in both boards' and superintendents' performance in their roles and in their capacities to develop effective working relationships. In urban districts and in districts with rapidly changing demographics, there are enormous pressures on both parties to improve the educational attainment of students who are among the most difficult to teach and whose noneducational needs may be critical determinants of school success. Pressures for visible short-term improvements in educational outcomes are exacerbated by increasing divisions among the public. When one adds to these realities the seemingly immovable bureaucratic organizations peopled by principals and teachers who will stay on to outlast board after board and superintendent after superintendent, the tumult in the superintendency in these districts is not surprising. Communities vent their frustration by turning over school boards, school boards seek solutions by changing superintendents, and superintendents express their frustrations by leaving.

Problems of the relationship, once mainly apparent in urban and demographically changing school districts, are spreading like a fungus to small-town and traditional suburban school districts. The political pressures in these school districts may arise from different reasons, e.g., deep philosophical conflicts about the direction and substance of schooling, public frustration with educators' responses to the public's priorities, and so forth, but the effect on boards and superintendents and their relationship is the same.

Superintendents cite the characteristics and motivations of those serving on school boards and the politicization of education governance as hindrances to exercising their professional leadership and to forming and sustaining effective partnerships with their school boards. However, superintendents also cite problems of the superintendency, itself, that affect the relationship and thus the effectiveness and longevity of superintendents.

In an IEL telephone interview survey of veteran superintendents in large and small school districts, and of aspiring superintendents, working with school boards surfaced as one of the major problems (IEL, 1992). However, responses to the survey and meetings with superintendents indicated that the difficulties stem from the institution of the superintendency as well as from behaviors of school boards. There was consensus among those surveyed about the inadequacy of current and past professional preparation for the superintendency and about the lack of developmental and support mechanisms for superintendents. The following are illustrative comments of those interviewed.*

"We must look at brand new ways of preparing urban school leaders; we don't know how, and university programs are irrelevant."

"Probably the most important thing is not to take a degree in administration."

"Deficits in academic training include not enough help understanding organizational theory and dynamics; weak focus on leadership and leadership issues."

"Human relations skills and conflict management skills are vital."

"It (the superintendency) is a political position, yet decidedly nonpolitical course work was provided."

"There's nothing about social organizations (in preparation)—the nature and culture of bureaucracies and how to change them."

"We need human relations skills to build coalitions, to work with the board, with the community, with parents."

"Among the biggest problems—dealing with collaboration, this is something new and we have no training or support in this."

"Written and oral communications are a problem in dealing with the board and others."

"Need extensive component in training on working with school boards."

"Need educational leaders with broadly gauged backgrounds; broad knowledge, interpersonal skills and strong background in organizational development."

"A major problem is knowing how to respond and be receptive to all diverse groups in the community. Each interest group has its own agenda—need help in problem solving with conflict resolution and good communication skills."

*Source: Critical Problems of Superintendents, Copyright © 1992, Institute for Educational Leadership.

When responding to questions in IEL's studies about problems in the board–superintendent relationship, school board members frequently pointed to issues of information access and information flow as problems contributing to the erosion of the relationship. Superintendent behavior that evoked complaints included, "burying us in information." The possibility that this is a strategy to keep the board busy was not lost on board members. School board members also cited unevenness of information flow, with the "group always supporting the superintendent" getting more information or quicker action on requests than those who frequently opposed or questioned superintendent positions or proposals. Board members complained about superintendents "counting the votes" and disregarding minority viewpoints. Such behaviors erode trust.

Theodore Kolderie of the Center for Policy Studies in St. Paul, Minnesota, suggested in an informal observation that the increasingly political and "intrusive" behavior of boards in managerial and administrative matters, particularly in urban and conflicted school districts, may be a consequence of boards' greater responsiveness to the real politics of their communities than superintendents'.

In the foreseeable future, the probability is slim to none for substantive state action to restructure and strengthen boards in their legitimate and important governing role and functions. And, superintendents, themselves, say that their professional preparation all too frequently inadequately prepares them for what the job has become in the late twentieth century. Given these realities, what hope is there for increasing the possibilities for effective board–superintendent partnerships focused on learning and high achievement for all students? The possibility and the responsibility lie with individual boards and their superintendents.

IMPROVING THE RELATIONSHIP: SUGGESTIONS FOR SUPERINTENDENTS

The majority of the difficulties in the school board–superintendent relationship are behavioral and are, therefore, within the control of one or both parties. Many problems arise from sins of omission. Too much is assumed about what the working relationship will be, and too little reality is anticipated. Too few prevention strategies are put in place at the beginning of a board–superintendent relationship. External pressures and conflicts are real and do have an impact on the relationship. But, these realities too frequently become excuses for conflicted relationships. School boards and superintendents can improve the possibilities for productive working relationships. Both parties must be forthright and decide that negotiating, developing, and sustaining a positive and effective relationship are core responsibilities of each.

An effective school board–superintendent relationship is much more likely if the expectations of each are paid careful attention during the selection process and the initial months of the relationship as well as during the maturation of the relationship. This requires candor and initial clarity on the part of both parties about how they view their own roles and how those will relate in the partnership.

The following suggestions for superintendents address the preappointment, initial, and sustaining stages of the relationship. Some of these suggestions may appear rudimentary, i.e., what were the successes and problems in a board's relationship (and why) with its last superintendent, but frequently receive little attention. The suggestions are not all-inclusive, but rather focus on critical and/or inadequately addressed factors affecting the relationship. There are 7 steps for before accepting an appointment, 10 steps for the initial stage of the relationship, and 8 steps for sustaining an effective partnership.

Before Accepting an Appointment

1. Board preparation for selecting a superintendent—*Determine if the school board has taken itself through any process to clarify its expectations of the relationship and its operating behaviors in respect to working with its superintendent.* If it is a conflicted board, how do the members play out their conflicts in the relationship? Are the members willing to admit and take positive steps to relate as a board to a superintendent? Study data and experience with school boards suggest to this author that school boards, when selecting a superintendent, pay too little attention to how the dynamics among board members and conflicted definitions of the role of the board will affect the relationship.

2. Board self-assessment and development—*Determine whether there is commitment to board membership and board development as evidenced by participation in appropriate activities.* Has or will the board commit to developmental activities to build and sustain its working relationship with a superintendent?

3. Processes for sustaining the relationship—*Identify established processes or assess the willingness of the board to agree to establish processes for anticipating and resolving conflicts in the relationship.* Will the board commit to periodic mutual assessment of the relationship? IEL study data and empirical evidence suggest that few boards practice mutual assessment of the relationship nor have processes for resolving inevitable tensions and conflicts with their superintendents.

4. Expectations of a new superintendent—*Identify a board's priorities.* Are they clear? Will a board support its new superintendent when he or she takes action? Superintendent candidates and school boards should antici-

pate better the sources of strain and conflict that may develop. For instance, when board members interviewing superintendent candidates say, "We want someone who will clean out the 'deadwood' in the system," how many candidates ask what a board will do if community pressure develops to retain certain individuals? Superintendent candidates might take a board through some simulations of the consequences of such a board directive and determine how the board members might respond to political fallout.

5. Board relationship with the community—*Assess the board's relationship with its community and the various sectors within it.* Is the board generally respected for its efforts and governing behaviors? Is the board providing effective leadership for the public schools with the community? Does the board understand and carry out its critical bridging role between community and professional educators in the school system? Does or will the board establish processes for public dialogue and improved engagement of the public with its schools? Rebuilding the public's relationship with its public schools and closing the gap between the public and professional educators are essential to achieving goals for high educational attainment for all students. A superintendent's professional goals and objectives for students will not be realized in the absence of a critical mass of involved and supportive community members and community leaders.

6. Board collaboration with general government and other agencies and institutions—*Identify the board's policies or intent to establish policies for its own, the superintendent's, and other appropriate school system staff's relationships with external governmental units and organizations.* A candidate for the superintendency of a school district that serves large numbers of students with critical noninstructional social and human needs must be particularly concerned about the importance a board places on external collaborative relationships. A candidate should also determine how a board defines its and the superintendent's role in establishing and sustaining collaborative relationships.

7. School board member turnover and community politics—*Assess how long the board or a majority of a board that is hiring a superintendent is apt to be in place.* Are there community political elements organizing to change the board? How powerful are they? Do they want to change the direction of the school system? Do they want to strengthen support on the board consistent with the superintendent's professional leadership of the system, or do they want to change direction? Given the increasing political volatility of even historically stable school districts, these are difficult questions to answer with any certainty. But, if for instance, a superintendent candidate

finds growing organized opposition to the hiring board or a majority of its members, and a school board election is imminent and another will occur in two years, a new superintendent's tenure may be very short lived.

The Initial Stage of the Relationship

As most experienced superintendents know, the mutual "euphoria" that characterizes the hiring of a new superintendent rarely lasts. But, if there is a mutual commitment, a productive and positive partnership is possible if a board and its superintendent have thoroughly assessed the potential for a good match, been honest about their expectations, and realistic about probable ambiguities in the roles as the relationship evolves. Two major mistakes boards and superintendents make in the new relationship are avoiding anticipation of the natural stresses, strains, and possible conflicts that will inevitably arise and failing to establish processes for dealing with differences. The following are suggestions for superintendent behavior and actions a superintendent might initiate with a board if not addressed in the hiring negotiations.

1. *Respect the school board's role (even if you question the motives of some of the members) and understand the pressures on the board and its individual members.* Superintendents choose a profession in which they know they will serve at the pleasure of a lay, political governing body. Work to strengthen a board in its legitimate role and functions—a strong body can help, not hinder, a superintendent's professional role.
2. *Treat all board members equally.* This is essential to building and sustaining trust in the relationship. For instance, if a superintendent is hired on a split vote, it should not be assumed that those opposed will stay opposed. A superintendent bears an equal responsibility with a board majority for trying to make the relationship effective with all board members.
3. *Encourage the board to establish expectations for board member behavior with input from the superintendent.* Written expectations should address, among other areas, board member communications with staff, how the board requests information from the superintendent (only on full board request or from individual members), board member handling of constituent complaints and/or requests, visitations to schools, individual board member communication with the media, individual board member differences with the superintendent, and so forth.
4. *Establish a process for clarifying board and superintendent roles in anticipation of major issues and initiatives.* Boards and superintendents should regularly clarify the policy and administrative roles and functions.

5. *Establish an evaluation process.* This includes superintendent input to the board about the board's governing behaviors and its impact on the achievement of objectives for the superintendent.

6. *Determine who will be the spokesperson for the school system in what circumstances.* Some boards leave much of this to their superintendents, and some do not. Who is spokesperson is not really so important as agreement about the spokesperson responsibility.

7. *Clarify in policy the roles of the superintendent and the board in relationships with external agencies and institutions.* A good rule of thumb is that the board, as the political body, has the lead in relating to other political bodies, e.g., the city council. An often-observed mistake on the part of external bodies, including elected ones, is to relate primarily to the superintendent—if you have heard from the superintendent, you have heard from the school board. While this is frequently so, when there are political issues, and political relationships are key, the school board may not only be most effective but also may provide some protection for the superintendent's professional leadership.

8. *Encourage participation in developmental activities with the school board and board commitment to its own development.* Suggest a retreat to help in developing the working relationship in the initial months. This will help a board to integrate attention to the relationship as a "way of life," rather than only to address problems. Mutual learning of conflict-resolution skills— useful among board members and in the relationship—is important.

9. *Propose establishing processes for resolving conflicts that may arise and encourage board and superintendent anticipation and early identification of problems.* For instance, a board might establish a policy for quarterly discussions of the relationship—what is working well and what aspects may need attention or better communication. A board might also have a policy for bringing in an external facilitator for resolution of what might become serious problems.

10. *If the board does not have a process for setting and periodically reviewing its priorities for its work, help it to establish such a process in policy.* The board will be and will feel more effective, and community perceptions of a board's effectiveness will be enhanced.

Sustaining an Effective Partnership

First and foremost, never take the relationship for granted. A superintendent and board should commit to paying continuous attention to their working relationship. Even the most stable partnership will probably be sorely tried at some point by external, if not internal, issues. And, there will be turnover in board members. The following suggestions assume an effective and mutually satisfactory beginning relationship and are intended to assist a superintendent as the relationship matures and inevitable changes in board membership occur.

1. *Continue to revisit the roles, the relationship, and mutual expectations periodically.* It is imperative to do so when a new member comes on a board. Few persons coming on a school board truly understand the role and many have potentially troublesome ideas about their role as an individual board member.

2. *Alert a board early to any potential problems or "bad news."* Work with a board to solve problems and to determine how they will be communicated.

3. *Ensure there is an effective new board member orientation program.* IEL data and experience document that most boards feel they do not have effective orientation programs and that the board is insufficiently involved in new board member orientation. Superintendents have a major informational role to play with new board members, but only the board can make expectations of members clear and transmit the governing culture of a board.

4. *Be alert to political trends in the community and their possible or probable impact on individual board members and/or the board.* Periodically, with the board, assess the effectiveness of school-system communications with parents, community, and system staff, and recommend new strategies as indicated.

5. *Respect a board's knowledge of its community and what will and will not "play."* Exercise the patience required to win battles and be willing to lose a few skirmishes.

6. *Help a board to stay current and knowledgeable about major education issues, research, and trends so that they might make informed policy decisions for the school system.* Data from an overwhelming majority of boards in IEL's studies and work with school boards document that boards pay very little attention to their own learning. This has an impact on policy making and on boards' leadership for education reform in their communities.

7. *Convey a belief that the public schools belong to the public and help a board to establish inclusive (yes, including the naysayers and opponents), open, and ongoing community dialogues.* Such dialogues, along with open and forthright communications, are the basic tools for developing informed public opinion and engaging the public with its schools.

8. *Set a standard for and exercise effective collaborative leadership within the system and with external institutions, agencies, and organizations necessary to develop and support successful families and students.*

FINAL THOUGHTS

School boards and their superintendents are responsible to their communities for building an effective partnership to meet students' educational needs and community expectations of the schools. Both parties should enter into the relationship and nurture it as though they might be together forever, while knowing this will not be. If either party starts the relationship with reservations and thoughts of *I can always quit or we can always fire*, efforts to forge a real partnership will fall short.

Change will occur. In this day and age, most superintendents will not stay in a single school district forever. Many may move on to new or different professional challenges. Or, a school board and/or a superintendent may realize at a certain point that changed community circumstances or school system needs have rendered ineffective what was a good match and an effective partnership. School boards change and may be elected to change much of what a superintendent has instituted. In such situations, a superintendent may leave, even if not asked to do so, if his or her professional integrity is threatened. But, boards and their superintendents owe their communities and the students a mutual commitment to make every effort to be effective partners during the duration of the relationship.

REFERENCES

Danzberger, J.P. (1994, January). Governing the nation's schools: The case for restructuring local school boards. *Phi Delta Kappan,* 367–373.

Danzberger, J.P. (1998). [Information about the IEL school board effectiveness program]. Director of Governance Programs, IEL, 1001 Connecticut Avenue, NW, Washington, DC 20036.

Danzberger, J.P., Kirst, M.W., & Usdan, M.D. (1992). *Governing public schools: New times, new requirements.* Washington, DC: Institute for Educational Leadership.

Immerwahr, J. (1994). *The broken contract: Connecticut citizens look at public education.* New York: Public Agenda.

Institute for Educational Leadership. (1992). *Critical problems of superintendents.* Washington, DC: Institute for Educational Leadership.

Institute for Educational Leadership. (1986). *School boards: Strengthening grass roots leadership.* Washington, DC: Institute for Educational Leadership.

Institute for Educational Leadership. (1993). *A framework for redefining the role and responsibilities of local school boards.* Washington, DC: Institute for Educational Leadership.

Johnson, J. (1995). *Assignment incomplete: The unfinished business of education reform.* New York: Public Agenda.

National Commission on Excellence in Education. (1983). *A nation at risk: The imperative for educational reform.* Washington, DC: The Commission, U.S. Department of Education.

Spring, J. (1984). The structure and power in an urban school system: A study of Cincinnati school politics. *Curriculum Inquiry, 14,* 419.

CHAPTER 10

Communications: Illusions and Realities

Dolores Boylston Bohen

George Bernard Shaw said it best: The greatest problem of communication is the illusion that it has been accomplished. Even the most visible and articulate leader, with the most extensive and sophisticated communication plan, is frequently advised to "improve communications" (a standard recommendation in consultants' reports), or is confronted with complaints from those who claim never to have heard what the leader has been saying repeatedly for at least a year to everyone who was willing to listen or read. The frustrating reality is that no amount of communication reaches everyone and, even if it did, not everyone would be tuned in to the message. Communication is a two-way process, an ongoing two-way process. It is also an essential survival skill for today's school superintendents, most of whom were hired and are evaluated (at least partially) for their ability to communicate effectively.

A superintendent sets the tone, the style, and the philosophy of a school system's organizational approach to communication. Superintendents need to have public-relations expertise at their fingertips, and, without apology, they must commit resources to managing community relations or public affairs. (Those who think too much money is being spent on printing and postage are often the same people who complain about the lack of communication.) Educators' ambivalence about public relations is apparent in the variety of titles and positions used by school systems to avoid the distasteful commercial stigma of so-called Madison Avenue PR. Unfortunately, in this age of cynicism about government agencies, even the term *public affairs* is tainted with a negative connotation. *Community relations* seems to be the least offensive term and the most commonly used by school systems. Fearing criticism during tight budgets, school systems often hesitate to give the same organizational prominence and resources to public relations as they give to the "nuts-and-bolts" of the organization. That is a mistake because, in today's school systems, public relations *is* part of the nuts and bolts.

Those of us in education value the *public* and value our *relations* with the public, but put the two words together and we flinch. When public relations is defined as "persuasive publicity," it conjures up images of commercial advertising and product promotion, which seem far removed from the noble mission of educating children. However, it is also defined as "influencing public opinion," which is certainly a legitimate responsibility of school superintendents if they want taxpayer support for schools. Neither persuasion nor influence is inherently evil. Even more jarring to educators' sensibilities than the term *public relations* is the growing use of the term *marketing*—as in *marketing your schools*. Ironically, while some educators continue to cringe at these allegedly crass concepts, the marketing metaphor is positively promoted by those outside the profession—for example, by those in the business community who say schools would improve if they placed more emphasis on such business shibboleths as bottom lines and customer service and by those who believe that public school choice will improve education because schools will be forced to survive in a competitive marketplace. When various segments of the public are expounding on the great value of market forces to education reform, why do educators hesitate to embrace these forces? Too many educators harbor illusions that obscure the realities of communicating in today's world.

Illusion: America's historic commitment to public schools is alive and well; just reminding people of the public imperative is enough to get taxpayer support.

Reality: Much of the public has lost faith in the ability of public schools to fulfill their historic mission of ensuring an educated citizenry.

Educators, more than people in most professions, are imbued with an idealistic faith in the righteousness of their work. After all, the education of the young is commonly linked to the future of our democracy, the economic survival of our nation, and the transmission of American values and traditions. This historic ideal, which binds American public schools to the nation's social, economic, and political goals, can sometimes delude educators into thinking that the nobility of their mission guarantees public support. It can blind them to the tough realities of today's world in which public confidence must be earned and mobilizing public support for schools requires more than improved communication. It is not enough to simply quote Thomas Jefferson or remind people of the imperative of public purpose that echoes through national reports. It is not enough to simply find better ways to reach the 70% of citizens in most communities who have no direct contact with public schools, unless they are reached with a meaningful message that energizes their commitment to public education in their own community.

David Mathews, president of the Charles F. Kettering Foundation, poses a disquieting question with the title of his book, *Is There a Public for Public Schools?* (1996). He presents compelling arguments, based on more than a decade of research projects on the American public's relationship with public education, to support his premise that America's historic compact with its public schools is eroding. He believes that one reason for the failure of education reform efforts is the approach taken by many educators. "This approach to reform seems to take for granted that the long-standing commitment to public schools is still intact; that the contract remains in force and needs only to be invoked; that schools have merely to demonstrate legitimate needs in order for citizens to respond with financial support. It is assumed that the public can be rallied through the standard means of publicity and marketing: The buyers are out there waiting to be told the benefits of the product. Any trouble between school officials and the public is simply a failure to communicate" (Mathews, 1996, p. 17). The world is full of frustrated superintendents who skillfully pursued sound communication plans to no avail because they based their approach on an eighteenth-century premise that is shaky at best as we enter the twenty-first century.

Public Agenda's opinion research report, *First Things First: What Americans Expect from the Public Schools* (Johnson & Immerwahr, 1994), also documents a growing distrust and dissatisfaction with public schools. The authors ask education leaders to give greater attention to the public's concerns and priorities rather than dismissing them or attempting "to manipulate people by paying lip service to their ideas. . . . People are not likely to be persuaded just because leaders put a better spin on the same old messages" (p. 39). The report recognizes what successful superintendents must never forget—that the exercise of real leadership often requires building a constituency for visionary ideas that are not yet widely accepted. That is the essence of leadership. At other times, however, the public's views reflect misunderstandings that call for more effective communication. This does not mean a "slight repackaging of the old communications plan with the latest public buzzwords thrown in. It means an authentic, well-thought-out, and continuing communications effort to help people understand what is happening in the schools and what reform is all about—a communications effort that starts from the public's concerns and priorities" (p. 38). If superintendents want to honestly assess the merits of public concerns, they should use every market research tool available to learn what their publics are thinking. Technology is making it easier every day to tap into the thinking of a community or a segment of a community without conducting a massive and expensive survey. After being inundated for more than a decade with rhetoric about education reform and failing public schools, Americans have understandably changed their attitudes and expectations. Presumptions from the past are precarious.

Illusion: Better marketing strategies will dispel public skepticism.

Reality: Better marketing can help if there is a worthwhile product to market.

Marketing is not about making bad schools look good. Glossy brochures proclaiming excellence and quality education will not help if school programs are weak and student performance is poor. In fact, they will contribute to the community's distrust and cynicism and will undermine the superintendent's credibility. Superintendents must have the insight to recognize what needs to be fixed in their schools, the intestinal fortitude to admit it, and the skill to fix it. Too often, the honest assessment of school problems is followed by a strenuous campaign to conceal them, rather than by a concerted effort to involve the entire community in solving them. Candor is high on the list of indispensable qualities for a superintendent.

When the superintendent's personal credibility is high, it is much easier to dispel unfounded negative perceptions of schools and to shape positive public perceptions that are based on factual information about the school system. The best way to get that factual information out to the community is by using the same standard communication (or marketing or public-relations) strategies that are used throughout the private and public sectors. On one level, at least, strategies for garnering public support are the same for schools as they are for other institutions or organizations. However, superintendents must know when and how to use them effectively. For example, a campaign to "sell" a bond referendum or a new school program calls for standard communication strategies, but superintendents must recognize that convincing citizens to vote for a bond or to support a specific program at a specific point in time is not the same as building sustained public support for public education. Superintendents who become too euphoric about winning a battle may lose sight of the long-term strategies needed to win the war.

American schools are public institutions operating in a public arena and supported by public funds. Public scrutiny comes with the territory. The good news is that the nation is paying serious attention to education; the bad news is that the nation is paying serious attention to education. The intense public interest generated by national and state officials has forced schools to be more open and accountable; it has also subjected them to greater criticism and distrust. In the 1960s and 1970s, many new programs were tried and some failed, contributing to the crisis of confidence that led to the 1983 publication of *A Nation at Risk* with its charge that our schools were drowning in a tide of mediocrity. Since then, despite more than a decade of rhetoric about national education-reform efforts, public confidence continues to erode and interest in alternatives to public schools continues to increase. Political interest in charter schools, vouchers, home schooling, and other variations of educational choice have put pressure on educators to change or be changed. Within this national context, thoughtful superintendents cannot afford to portray themselves as the great defenders of the status quo. Today's superintendents must aggressively and enthusiastically direct the changes, not deny the need for them.

> *Illusion: A superintendent's clarion call for change will reverberate throughout the school system and mobilize employees.*
>
> **Reality: The strongest message will die unless echoed by employees who understand and share the vision.**

Directing fundamental changes in public schools does not alter a superintendent's role as a champion for children and chief advocate for public education. It does, however, change the nature of the advocacy. Superintendents must be advocates who can admit the need for change without becoming defensive, who can spearhead changes without weakening anyone's faith in public education, and who can articulate a vision that clearly and intelligently encompasses the changes. Too many educators in recent years have responded to public scrutiny by complaining about having more challenges and less money, by denying a decline in student achievement or behavior, by blaming any decline on social forces beyond the control of the school, and by denouncing the critics and the media who give voice to the critics. Any or all of those responses might be accurate and appropriate in any given circumstance, but they sound like the defensive responses of people under siege. Superintendents who want to adopt a proactive public posture that really advances a school system's education-reform agenda must help their employees shed the siege mentality and recognize the need for change. That's the tough part—defining a stable vision and a dynamic action plan that makes believers of those who must make the changes work. Without those ingredients, the strongest message will be empty rhetoric.

No matter how positive the voice or the message from the superintendent's office, its effectiveness will be diminished by contradictory voices from beleaguered or bewildered employees. Employees are the heart of those referred to in marketing textbooks as an organization's "internal publics" and "key communicators." School employees are those who must implement the ideas and programs that emanate from the superintendent. They are the people whose lives are affected by changes that implicitly convey the negative message that their professional standards or patterns of behavior are no longer good enough. They are the people who must be helped to believe that change is an exciting and essential challenge, not a personal indictment of them. Changing education means changing people's attitudes and beliefs; that's why systemic change is hard and slow. Establishing routine communication channels that keep employees well informed is relatively easy, although it can be difficult to stay ahead of today's rapid information flow. For example, employees may feel betrayed if they learn something that directly affects them from the media instead of from the superintendent; yet, decisions made at Monday night's school board meeting may well be in Tuesday morning's newspaper or even on Monday night's late TV news. Anxieties can be eased and rumors stifled by keeping employees in the information loop about pending decisions and by using an internal electronic mail system or school system Web page to quickly confirm (or deny) what appears in the media. If considerable time is spent correcting misinformation or refuting false charges, something is wrong with the routine networks. Nothing strengthens a superintendent's message more than the voices of a knowledgeable work force that can articulate the school system's goals with pride and confidence.

Outside of their working hours, employees—especially teachers—have great informal influence on how the school system is perceived by their friends, families, and others whom they casually encounter in their neighborhoods. People logically assume that since these individuals work for the school system, they should know the inside story! Yet, in the not-too-distant past (when schools got away with saying, "Leave education to the educators"), many teachers valued "strong" administrators who buffered them from complaints and defended them against parental challenges. If administrators are "protecting" teachers from the real world outside of the classroom, those teachers are unlikely to be the effective key communicators that today's teachers must be and that superintendents need. The culture of insulating teachers so that they can concentrate on teaching their students is a condescending remnant of a patriarchal organization that had little respect for teacher professionalism. Teachers who appreciate their professional roles and responsibilities are the best spokespeople for public education; insulating them refutes everything we claim to believe about the importance of teacher involvement in education reform.

Effective communication must permeate every classroom and corner of the school system—and it must flow two ways. More messages from the superintendent that simply "tell" teachers and principals what is going on will not elicit their professional involvement or energize them to become key communicators themselves. Keeping teachers well informed is easier than getting them involved in new ways for which they have little preparation or experience. Unfortunately, the same thing can be said about principals, who are also front-line representatives of public schools, but who have little training in the kind of public relations that is rooted in a philosophy of customer service rather than in bureaucratic authority. Superintendents who want to succeed in the twenty-first century must help principals and teachers to understand how societal changes have changed the public's expectations of schools. They must also provide principals and teachers with opportunities to acquire the basic skills of Public Relations 101 that will enable them to communicate effectively with the general public. No educational jargon. No authoritarian airs. No bureaucratic shoulder-shrugging and buck-passing. Too often, these barriers to effective communication are the conditioned responses of school system employees.

Illusion: If ideas are explained often enough and clearly enough, they will eventually be accepted by virtually everyone.

Reality: "Everyone" is a theoretical nonentity; messages must be targeted to specific audiences that have a meaningful way to respond.

Unless they have had their heads in the sand for the past decade, today's superintendents know all about reaching out to nonparents, to the business community, to senior citizens, to minority groups, to civic associations, to church leaders, to elected officials, and to any other group of people who are willing to read or listen to the superintendent's message. Sending targeted publications takes less time than meeting with many groups, but no communication is as effective as personal contact—especially personal contact that allows interaction with the superintendent.

An obvious drawback in any but the smallest school systems, of course, is the impossible demand on the superintendent's time. According to one survey (Ledell, 1996), school district leaders spend 30% of their time communicating with supporters, 65% with critics, and only 5% with the 70% of the community that everyone talks about trying to reach. If good communication networks are in place for supporters, the 30% is probably somewhat higher than necessary; if the critics represent a small passionate group who will never be dissuaded from their negative views, much of the 65% is probably wasted time. Even though the percentages will differ in specific situations, the point is well made that superintendents should allocate their personal communication efforts to audiences that are high on their priority lists. And those on the priority list should be carefully and deliberately identified.

Targeting messages to specific audiences is common-sense market research. It makes more sense to run beer commercials during football games than during Saturday morning cartoons. Ted Koppel's viewers are probably not the best audience for *Barbie* doll commercials. Market research simply means taking the time to learn something about your audience. Know their interests and their concerns. Given the diversity of groups that superintendents routinely address, it is foolish to think that they all have the same interests and concerns about schools. A smart superintendent finds out what those interests and concerns are; a brave superintendent has the courage to confront them honestly instead of dismissing them. While consistency of message is an indisputable virtue and an essential asset for public leaders, it can become an Emersonian hobgoblin if the same message is relentlessly delivered without regard for the specific audience. It can become mind-numbing educational jargon that no longer conveys anything meaningful.

Today's information technologies have already accustomed people to relatively customized information both at home and in offices. Busy people expect to be able to scan quickly—whether documents, computer screens, mail, magazines, newspapers, or school newsletters—for information that is most immediately relevant to them. They value brevity, directness, and clean design—attributes that are not always found in school publications or presentations. Desktop publishing and the Internet make it easier and cheaper than ever for school systems to target various elements of a community with specific, pertinent information and to produce publications designed for the particular audience. Like it or not, we live in a sound-bite society that will digest a superintendent's messages better one bite (or byte) at a time. The trick is to formulate messages and themes that truly reflect the school system's vision, that resonate with the community, and that are woven throughout the superintendent's communications.

Reaching the public is not synonymous with engaging the public. Today's superintendents know the frustrations of struggling for greater community involvement through advisory councils, blue-ribbon commissions, task forces, citizen committees, public hearings, and endless meetings. Too often, the results are meager and highly predictable, with the usual allies and the usual critics providing the usual input. Sometimes the result is an exciting infusion of new ideas that energizes the staff and community and becomes a springboard from which the superintendent can launch needed changes. To those who encounter the first scenario, David Mathews (1996) would say that educators have trouble engaging the public because even their well-intentioned efforts have been superficial, with the public's being used for the school system's predetermined ends. When schools start with a particular purpose for which they want to demonstrate community support, Mathews believes that people feel manipulated rather than empowered, become cynical about the process, and withdraw from productive participation. He thinks that school systems, whether consciously or unconsciously, often shut the public out by using perfunctory processes and language that obfuscates the education issues. However widely these criticisms do or do not apply, they deserve thoughtful consideration by superintendents who are struggling to get meaningful public involvement.

People must believe that their substantive input is more important than the process. They must believe that someone (the superintendent) is listening with an open mind and that the school system is genuinely receptive to new ideas and (possibly) radical change. Superintendents who want to change the status quo should remember Margaret Mead's observation that nothing has ever changed the world except a small group of thoughtful, committed citizens. Superintendents should find the small group of thoughtful citizens in their communities who are willing to become committed (with the right motivation) and who will give them the leverage needed to initiate change. These citizens may or may not have official status in the community, but they should have influence. They may be vocal critics of public education. They may be business leaders motivated by economic concerns. They may be editors or columnists who write about education. Determining which citizens to seek out will take care and knowledge of the community's formal and informal power structures because the first people to clamor loudly will almost surely be the usual special-interest groups.

Illusion: The media are the problem because they deliberately distort school news and look for a negative spin; ignoring them is the safest strategy.

Reality: The media are essential to any communication plan because they have the power to shape public perception; ignoring them is suicide.

Most people, especially those who are neither parents nor teachers, learn about schools from the media. And the more remote an individual's personal connection to schools, the more likely that his or her impressions will come from national news coverage of school problems, which may or may not bear any similarity to local school realities. Local news that raises public awareness of schools is usually about contentious issues such as budget fights, election campaigns, and crisis situations. When average citizens are asked what they have heard about their schools recently, they are likely to recall such headlines as: "Superintendent Wants To Increase Taxes," "School Board Split on Sex Education Curriculum," "Eighth Grade Test Scores Fall." These predictable kinds of news stories are less likely to dominate the press coverage of schools if they are balanced by a constant managed flow of information to the public through the media. A superintendent's worst enemy is the public's lack of information; someone else will fill the vacuum. Communication plans that include the press only for major events or in crisis situations are doomed; the press is an indispensable part of the plan.

Educating the press—not only reporters, but also editors, columnists, TV news directors, radio commentators, and anyone else who influences education news—

is an important part of a superintendent's job. It comes with the territory. Whether these people are more often part of the problem or part of the solution usually depends on the professional working relationship established by the superintendent and other school administrators. That relationship has to be predicated on a reasonable appreciation of journalists' professional responsibilities; they are not paid to make the school system look good by reporting only positive news. Once that fallacious expectation is laid to rest, it is possible (in most instances) to set mutually agreeable guidelines for a mutually productive working relationship—not necessarily comfortable or easy, but productive. The way to begin is by knowing the individuals and their news organizations. Meeting with them personally, when there are no immediate hot issues to discuss, offers an opportunity to understand one another's interests and priorities. It is important to find out what they know (and don't know) about the school system, what they would like to know, and what the school system can do to help them do a good job of reporting. Implicit in this dialogue is recognition that the participants need each other. Both have an obligation to inform the public. The media need the superintendent's information, and the superintendent needs the media's access to the public.

Personal contact and persistence are needed to dispel (at least partially) the almost instinctive distrust between educators and reporters. A recent (May 1997) national study conducted by the Public Agenda Foundation for the Educational Writers Association documents and enlightens this attitude in its report, *Good News, Bad News: What People Really Think about the Education Press.* The three groups of people included in the study were educators, the press, and the public. Educators' attitudes toward the press are consistently more negative than the general public's, even when there is some level of agreement on the particular topic: 91% of educators believe that the press covers education news according to what sells, while only 69% of the public agree; 86% of educators say the press unfairly dwells on conflict and failure, while 65% of the public agree. While all responses are critical of the press, the differences in the numbers suggest that the public's healthy skepticism about what they read borders on paranoia for educators. Even when the perceptions of the public and the press are relatively similar, educators' attitudes remain more negative: 77% of the public and 67% of the press think that news organizations generally do a good job of covering education issues and events; only 40% of educators agree. On a similar question, the public and the press are even closer together: 69% of the public and 63% of the press think that news organizations usually do a good job of explaining important education issues to the public; only 36% of educators agree. Any superintendent pondering these numbers must raise serious questions about educators' expectations of the media, especially since half of the educators surveyed were public school superintendents.

The opinions of reporters and educators diverge most sharply on issues that suggest the placing of blame. The statement: *Educators often unfairly blame the press for negative publicity when reporters are simply reporting the news*, elicited a predictable 93% agreement from reporters and a meager 33% agreement from educators. Interestingly, the general public's response of 79% agreement was considerably closer to the views of reporters than to the views of educators; placing blame does not appear to be a strategy that wins many points for educators. A similar survey statement has even broader implications: *Much of the decline in public confidence in public schools is the result of negative press coverage.* A mere 21% of reporters agree compared to 76% of educators; the public was down the middle with 55%. The disparate views of the three groups reveal a chasm between reporters and educators on an issue as vital and basic to educators as the erosion of public confidence in public schools. If most educators really believe that the media is to blame for that erosion, it is no wonder that they feel hostile toward the press. And, if the press is the enemy, denouncing them is easier than building a productive working relationship intended to improve their access to information, their depth of knowledge about education issues, and the accuracy of their stories. It is also easier than objectively confronting the possibility that the public has some legitimate concerns about public schools. To whatever extent the media have contributed to the public's concerns (and they surely have!), they did not create them.

Journalists, like people in every other profession, come in all varieties of the human species. A relative few are unscrupulous and dangerous; some are idealistic adherents to journalism's constitutional roots and to freedom of the press; most are ordinary working people with a job to do, who take personal pride in trying to do it well. Most (like most educators) believe in the nobility of their profession, as indicated by the 95% positive response to the statement: *News organizations perform a valuable public service by keeping a watchful eye on what school officials do.* While only 53% of educators agree with the statement, 71% of the general public agree that the press plays a valuable role in our democratic society. When educators recognize the value of that role and accept the natural tension that it creates, it becomes easier to work with the idiosyncrasies of individual reporters and news organizations. It also helps to remember that both a free press and a free public education are generally considered to be essential elements of our democracy. Journalism, like teaching, attracts many idealistic young people. These inexperienced reporters deserve, and will usually appreciate, all the help a school system can give them. They can't provide the context for a story if they don't understand the context; they can't give two sides of a story if they hear only one because school officials won't talk to them, or they don't know where to find a second source. Whether schools are dealing with a green young reporter or a crusty old editor with entrenched ideas and opinions, educators have a vested interest in educating the media. After all, educating people is our business.

A public-relations office that is designed to function as the key source of public information for reporters, as well as for other members of the public, will be dealing with reporters every day. It will not just respond to requests, it will proactively funnel the right kind of information from the schools to the appropriate news outlets that cover the district. Large daily newspapers have different interests and deadlines than weeklies or community newspapers; the more the office understands and accommodates the different needs, the better. The electronic media, especially television, have different needs and interests than the print press. All of them should be on a continually updated distribution list for disseminating a steady flow of newsworthy information via phone, fax, mail, and e-mail. Regular news can be press releases, media advisories, reports, letters or memos, meeting notes or summaries, calendars and schedules, agendas of pending events and programs, and any information that provides reporters with story leads or the contextual background for a current education issue. In other words, the public-relations or community-relations office must be the most reliable, knowledgeable, and accessible source for the media.

Depending on the size of the community and the local press corps, establishing a credible and competent reputation demands a serious investment of time and energy by a superintendent's spokesperson or other staff members who share media responsibilities. They must be perceived as trustworthy conduits to and from the superintendent, not as bureaucratic barriers or mindless mouthpieces, and they must be available at all times. News happens at night and on weekends. Two important tasks that are well worth the time invested are orienting new reporters and training school personnel, especially principals. When both reporters and principals are operating under common guidelines and expectations about press coverage of schools, misunderstandings will be minimized. The trick is to balance the media's right to know under freedom of information laws and the principal's responsibility to maintain an orderly learning environment for students. Simple procedures that are known to the press should be printed and provided to school personnel at workshops and training sessions. The intent of the procedures should be to expedite the gathering of news for reporters without disrupting the school's instructional rhythm, intruding excessively on a principal's time, or invading student or teacher privacy. It is possible. A savvy spokesperson can develop mutually acceptable guidelines that make everyone's life easier and, when necessary, mediate between a reporter's needs and a principal's priorities. He or she must earn the respect and trust of principals by helping them in every way possible and by being a readily available resource.

Protecting schools from haphazard onslaughts by the media is one side of the coin; the other side is helping schools to funnel their good news to the media. In large school systems particularly, a news liaison network is an invaluable way to get press coverage of local school news. Each school designates an individual as its news liaison. That person is trained by the community-relations office to recognize what is considered newsworthy by the various local papers, who the reporters are, how to reach them, and how to write press releases that will get their attention. Inviting reporters to the news liaison orientation is a good way to establish personal contact and initiate some discussion of mutual interests and needs. In Fairfax County Public Schools (Virginia), where the network has been in place for 15 years and includes over 200 schools, the information from the school liaisons arrives daily in the community-relations office, where it is distilled and distributed weekly to the press in a newsletter called *Media Tips*. It is a popular and well-regarded resource for reporters. The news liaison network is one proactive, mutually advantageous way to include the media in a school system's strategic communication plan.

Superintendents who are searching for school stories that will interest both the press and the public might find clues in the surprisingly similar responses of the press, the public, and educators to two questions in the report, *Good News, Bad News: What People Really Think about the Education Press* (1997). When asked if they saw a need for more stories about how well schools are doing, 91% of educators (of course!) responded affirmatively, with the public not so far behind at 84%, and the press with a relatively high 70%. All three groups expressed high agreement with the need for more stories about ideas and programs that are potential solutions to education problems: educators, 88%; the public, 79%; and the press, 86%. These ratings certainly suggest the possibility of a productive collaboration between school systems and the press to produce news that sells. Specifically, the public would like more information about academic standards, curriculum, school safety, and the quality and training of teachers—topics that reflect the nature of the public's concerns about public schools.

> *Illusion: The media are to blame for negative headlines about crisis situations.*
>
> **Reality: The crisis situation is to blame, and it *is* news.**

Situations most likely to generate negative headlines are seldom about educational issues. They are more likely to be circumstances related to safety (asbestos or gas leaks, faulty playground or heating equipment), serious misconduct by employees or students, and other incidents involving the police. These things happen. They are inevitable. There is no excuse for not having a well-established crisis plan, including a communication strategy and a designated spokesperson, ready to activate when necessary. The key is to signal the superintendent's control of the situation, whatever the situation is, by stating clearly and quickly what happened and what actions are being taken to deal with it. The quicker, the better, to shorten the lifespan of the story. It is important to protect the privacy rights of individuals who are involved, but the school system should not feel responsible for the fact that employees and students are ordinary human beings who occasionally do things that are dangerous or dumb or even illegal. Realistic superintendents resist the inclination to be overly defensive or apologetic. On the other hand, it is a mistake to minimize what others perceive as serious. Perception is reality. If the community thinks there is a crisis and the media thinks there is a crisis, there is a crisis.

The indispensable communication link in crisis situations is with the police or other public-safety officials in the community. Police reports are the usual source of public information about crime and violence involving school employees or students. Assaults, graffiti, threats, weapons, drugs, theft, molestation, and similar offenses that are investigated by the police are also defined by the language in the police reports that are released to reporters. Because police reports provide the context for reporters' questions and the public's impressions, they should also provide the context for a school system's public responses. Why deny something that the police have already confirmed? Why try to minimize a situation that is already defined as a felony or some other serious crime? The safest way to avoid looking foolish and defensive is to have a well-established, hand-in-glove, working relationship between the police public-relations people and the school system's public-relations people. A good way to strengthen that relationship is by conducting joint crisis-management workshops for school administrators before any crisis occurs.

An advantage of such a relationship is that the credibility of both the schools and the police is heightened when they are not publicly contradicting one another; the community will be less inclined to think someone is hiding something. School officials will not be blindsided by police reports if they know what is being released to the public and when. Every jurisdiction has its own laws and regulations regarding the release of public information, and schools should know exactly what governs police procedures in their own community. Are there any circumstances in which juveniles are identified? Are public officials, including school employees, always identified when they commit a crime? At what point in an investigation are the police willing to make specific details of a crime public? When do they want the schools to help by distributing descriptive information about a suspect or a vehicle? Knowing the answers to these kinds of questions will help superintendents to make informed decisions about what the school system should or should not say publicly.

Generally speaking, when a crime is involved, the police determine what is or is not public information. The police should be answering reporters' questions about the police investigation. Schools should be answering questions about what schools are doing, not about what the police are doing. If an employee is arrested for selling drugs or molesting a child or robbing a bank, the school system response should be that the employee has been placed on administrative leave or suspended without pay or whatever other action is appropriate. Citing school system regulations that apply is not a comment on the individual's guilt or innocence; it is a comment on the system's procedures for handling such situations. Such a straightforward statement of fact does not violate any privacy or due process rights, and it is more reassuring to concerned citizens than an official "no comment." (Superintendents should almost never respond with "no comment.") When a student is involved, the same privacy and due process rights apply, in addition to the special protection afforded to juveniles; these are not violated by citing applicable student behavior codes. The message is simply that the schools have appropriate procedures in place to handle certain behaviors. The community deserves to be reassured that students who bring weapons to school or put pipe bombs in lockers will be suspended or expelled. The identity of juvenile offenders often becomes public because there is nothing to stop other students or parents from speaking to reporters. Even when this happens, however, schools should avoid making official public statements that characterize individual students or employees who are in trouble with the law.

The rapid and routine exchange of information between schools and the police can help the school system to be proactive rather than reactive in criminal situations. If police reports are provided (by fax or e-mail) to the school system as they are about to be released to the press, school officials have a little time to verify basic information and to assess the level of anxiety that the situation is likely to arouse in the school community. Neither parents nor school board members like to be surprised by news media accounts of serious school situations. Calling board members immediately (before reporters get to them) is easy to do, as long as superintendents have a prior understanding with the school board about when, how, and in what circumstances they want to be informed. It is harder for a principal to get a good letter to parents written, reproduced, and into the hands of students by the end of the school day (or as soon as possible), but it is worth the effort if time permits and the facts have been verified by the police. No matter how unpleasant the facts may be, they are usually less sensational than the rumors that swirl about when there is an information vacuum. Good letters that honestly inform and reassure the community are an art form that school administrators must master in this age of information. And, sadly, it is an art form that gets little, if any, attention in the preparation or training of school administrators.

Illusion: The superintendent's role is to be an education leader in the school community who defends schools against critics and keeps education out of the political arena.

Reality: The superintendent's role is to be a public leader who is an equal partner with other public leaders in the community and who is able to integrate education into the political, economic, social, and cultural fabric of the total community.

Events of the last decade of the twentieth century have permanently popped the protective bubble that has isolated education from the mainstream of community concerns and interests. Most citizens, today, realize that schools are not simply the concern of parents and parent teacher associations (PTAs). Most citizens now understand how the quality of their public schools affects—for better or worse—their community's economic stability, property values, cultural values, civic pride, and, in general, their quality of life. That understanding escalates citizens' concerns about poor-performing schools and lessens their tolerance for low academic achievement. They want better schools, better teachers, and better student performance. If the superintendent can't deliver—if, year after year, nothing really changes or improves—these citizens are willing converts to the charter school movement. Why not? The message of that movement is persuasive: Give others a chance to find new ways to provide the same things that district schools have promised, but failed, to provide—high academic standards, excellent teachers, small classes, innovative curricula and instruction, parent involvement, and successful students. There are no surprises in this list of what people want in schools. Public patience is waning, and the momentum for change is growing. In this climate, superintendents will find it hard to sell a status quo message.

According to Bruno Manno, a senior fellow of the Hudson Institute and co-author of two national studies about the charter movement in the United States, "The genius of the charter school concept is that it demands academic results, unlike many conventional district schools where teachers and administrators often spend as much time and energy conforming to bureaucratic requirements as they do on boosting pupil achievement" (Manno, 1997, pp. C1–C2). Manno describes a number of charter schools that he considers successful in different parts of the country and says: "Charter schools have unleashed the imagination of at least three groups of people: educators, parents, and outside organizations, all of whom want to do things differently, all of whom are frustrated by the bureaucracy of conventional schools" (1997, pp. C1–C2). Such statements resonate in the souls of those Americans who are deeply cynical about the ability of government bureaucracies and large corporations to shed the rigidity of a regulatory culture and to function efficiently in a world that now values flexibility, choice, responsiveness, and results. Business and community leaders who have been forced by economic or social pressures to adopt these new values can be a super-intendent's best allies if they perceive the school system as an integral part of a changing community, not as the last bastion of past practices.

As school superintendents formulate their public messages, they should not succumb to Manno's implication that genius and imagination are qualities reserved to those outside of the education establishment. And it shouldn't take either genius or imagination to understand why the charter school message has receptive audiences or why 29 states have now adopted charter school laws. Manno, who believes that charter schools were designed to improve public edu-cation, concludes: "They offer exciting choices for their students, welcome pro-fessional opportunities for their teachers, educational progress for their communities, and a genuinely promising reform development for the states and the nation. They are helping the nation to reinvent American education" (Manno, 1997, pp. C1–C2). In most communities, superintendents and school boards can-not only make these same promises, they can also deliver on them. Whatever continues to occur at state and national levels, local school superintendents and school boards already have the power to make meaningful reforms if they have the conviction, the will, and the citizen support to do so. The school board pro-vides the political power base from which a strong, visible, and articulate super-intendent can build the community-wide coalitions needed for successful change. When a school board and a superintendent are in concert about long-term educa-tion goals, virtually anything is possible.

Broadening and strengthening the superintendent's leadership in the total com-munity can be risky, especially if school board members perceive that position to be a threat to their own power or prerogatives. Only a superintendent with superb personal communication skills can assuage those fears. And only to a limited extent. Like our communities, today's school boards are more diverse and more likely to bring diverse opinions and arguments to the board table. Elected board members often represent ideological factions or special-interest groups with a preconceived political agenda for schools. Now that education is a prominent issue, running in a school board election is often a first step on the political ladder for those with political ambition but no long-term commitment to education. These are not new phenomena on the education landscape; indeed, they are his-torical governance issues for American education. However, they are greatly intensified by the national interest in education. In today's climate, elected school board members are more likely to compete with the superintendent (and with one another) for the sound bite on the evening news or the headline in the morning newspaper. Disputing individual board members who misrepresent the collective voice of the board or the official position of the school system is an internal board problem for the board president, but it certainly complicates a superintendent's public communications.

Despite the messy aspects of our democratic processes and the tensions resulting from our tradition of local control of education, school superintendents are in the best position to influence public discourse about American education. Unlike elected officials, they can provide stable leadership and continuity toward long-term education goals—and the constant messages that hold community coalitions together. Thoughtful and intelligent school board leaders recognize this. They know that the short average tenure of superintendents is a serious detriment to education reform. They understand that when they advertise for a superintendent who is a risk-taking, proactive leader who can articulate a vision of change for the entire community, they must believe their own words.

REFERENCES

Educational Writers Association. (1997, May). *Good news, bad news: What people really think about the education press.* New York: Public Agenda.

Johnson, J., & Immerwahr, J. (1994). *First things first: What Americans expect from the public schools.* New York: Public Agenda.

Ledell, M. (1996, November). Common ground: A way of life, not a checkoff item. *School Administrator,* AASA, pp. 8–11.

Manno, B. (1997, August 31). Charting a new outlook. *The Washington Post,* pp. C1–C2.

Mathews, D. (1996). *Is there a public for public schools?* Dayton, OH: Kettering Foundation Press.

National Commission on Excellence in Education. (1983). *A nation at risk: The imperative for educational reform.* Washington, DC: The Commission, U.S. Department of Education.

CHAPTER 11

Hardware, Software, Vaporware, and Wetware: A Cautionary Tale for Superintendents

Michael S. Radlick

INTRODUCTION

I have had a foot in both the world of education and the world of technology over the past 28 years of my career. My varying positions as teacher, school administrator, researcher, director of technology services for the New York State education department, and most recently as a technology consultant have all involved the opportunity to link technology with education. Throughout this career, I have been involved in all aspects of planning, designing, and implementing technology systems in schools. My work on technology has involved my working closely with superintendents, school boards, technology coordinators, teachers, parents, business leaders, industry representatives, and other community members. I have dealt with instructional and administrative technology systems, as well as classroom, building-level, district-wide, regional, and statewide networking projects ranging from single building districts to all the 1,400 schools in New York City. This experience has provided me with many insights into the philosophical, educational, political, technical, and practical issues associated with implementing technology for teaching and learning. I am currently using this experience to provide technology consulting services to over 50 school districts that my firm has as clients. We provide assistance in developing district technology plans, or taking an existing plan, and then developing the technology infrastructure design and implementation plan that districts need to move forward.

As I have explained many times to district clients, my role as their technology consultant is assisting the district in translating its technology plan into reality. Our ultimate goal is to help districts be successful with technology in their teaching and learning environment. I will share my experience in this chapter, highlighting some of the same questions and issues that I typically discuss with superintendents, technology committees, and school boards as I move them through this metamorphosis from vision to reality. In my role as consultant, I try to get superintendents to look critically at technology and then to base their technology initiatives on solid empirical and practical information about where and how technology can benefit students. Without this kind of critical examination and planning, a superintendent will not be successful in his or her attempt to harness technology for the benefit of education.

There is little question that school superintendents face ever-increasing pressures in meeting the demands of their jobs. On the one hand, they are pulled by the new challenges of school reform and systemic change initiatives. On the other hand, superintendents are pushed by the day-to-day conflicts presented by school finances, taxpayer initiatives, school disciplinary problems, community controversies, and the management demands of aging facilities and staff. As if these challenges were not enough, superintendents must face the incredible hype and the many pitfalls—educational, technical, and professional—that technology presents to them every day. It is no secret that failure to harness technology can even destroy a superintendent's career.

Despite the potential importance of technology to all the key players in the educational system—including students, teachers, parents, the community, and the superintendent—more frequently than not, school districts move into a technology project unthinkingly without clear understanding or a plan. After 28 years of working to apply technology in the educational process, I am convinced that technology can make a difference for students and teachers when it is carefully thought out and carefully planned. Conversely, when technology is adopted for the wrong reasons, in an approach that is not based on curricular needs and is not systematically implemented, then that district's implementation of technology will ultimately be a failure. Too often, superintendents (and the members of the community from both inside and outside the school) approach technology as a given. They start from a position of implicit acceptance, unquestioningly trying to implement technology in their schools. It is my belief that this uncritical perspective is a recipe for disaster.

Instead of starting from the perspective of technology, it is my belief that as educators, we must concentrate on teaching and learning and examine technology within that context. Superintendents, and their entire educational teams, need to stay focused on the fundamental questions—those related to learning. In addressing technology, one key question to ask is: "What can technology do well and what can't it do well to improve learning?" A related question is: "What evidence do we have to support the use of technology in our schools?" Identifying an appropriate role for technology in the educational environment is essential to a superintendent's success. Superintendents, as well as other staff in a district, need to fight against the allure of technology for its own sake. The judgment of many educators seems to be impaired by technology in the same way that a scuba diver on a deep dive is caught up in what is called the "rapture of the deep." How else can we explain the unquestioning acceptance, and often advocacy, for technology without any critical thought? The judgment of generally levelheaded educators is clouded, or even suspended, by the delirious euphoria of technology. This "rapture of technology" as I call it, results in an effort to push technology unthinkingly into classrooms.

It is a fundamental premise of this chapter, based on extensive experience and hard-won successes, that a superintendent, along with all the members of the educational team, must take a very critical view of how, where, and why to apply technology in the schoolhouse to help students grow. Although technology clearly has the potential to reshape the way we all live and work, and yes, also to reshape the ways we learn, that doesn't mean we suspend our judgment as soon as we come across the next "gee-whiz" technology gimmick. As educators, it is necessary to inoculate ourselves with the antibodies of reason and critical thought in order to fight against the marketing hype of vendors and the pressures of the technology bigots inside and outside education. Being drawn into the rapture of technology does not serve our students and community well.

CHARACTERIZING A SUPERINTENDENT'S APPROACH TO TECHNOLOGY

In my contacts with hundreds of superintendents in New York State and across the country, I have observed a wide range of perspectives held by superintendents toward the use of technology. These perspectives are grounded in a superintendent's experience, understanding, and personal predisposition toward technology. Superintendents appreciate their vulnerability with respect to the implementation of technology. In fact, technology is often seen to hang as a sword of Damocles over a superintendent. The potential impact of his or her decisions about technology can overshadow many other equally important educational decisions because of the high public visibility and large costs associated with the infusion of technology into a school district. Some superintendents can be seen out front, leading the charge for technology in their buildings. In many districts, however, superintendents have remained withdrawn from the technology discussions, leaving to staff the leadership roles of planning and implementing technology.

Without question, the potentially contentious issue of technology implementation in a school can prove a threat to the educational leadership and community support needed by a superintendent. For some superintendents, the motivation for technology is the opportunity to have a large-scale impact on their district, to leave a legacy that will remain long after they have left the district or retire. Technology is frequently associated with the perception of being on the cutting edge, so superintendents will focus on some aspect of technology, any aspect, in their efforts to enhance this view of themselves and their superintendency. This focus on the cachet of technology rather than its underlying nature and benefits often leads districts to push for technology implementation without planning for the integration of that technology into the overall educational program. These "heat-seekers," as I call them, or pursuers of technology for its own sake, want to implement technology because of the excitement and high visibility that it provides. The ranks of superintendents are filled with technology heat-seekers. These superintendents are often the driving forces behind a district's rapid incursion into a technology implementation effort. But pursuing technology for its own sake will do nothing to ensure that it will successfully meet the needs of students and teachers.

Because of the long-term period it takes to successfully demonstrate significant educational effects with technology, superintendents often pursue a high-visibility approach, gaining the salutary career effects associated with the initial implementation of technology. These same superintendents then leave their district and start the technology implementation as superintendent in another, often larger, district before they are required to demonstrate any substantial educational impact. In lieu of a well-thought-out approach based on educational needs, these superintendents focus on technology as a media event. In this scenario, teaching staff, parents, and the community at large will frequently come to question the efficacy of the effort, with the result being less and less support for any technology in the district in the future. The residual negative impact of a heat-seeking superintendent remains long after he or she has left the district. Indeed, this is not a good legacy for an educator, particularly for many superintendents who entered education wanting to have a positive impact on the lives of children.

I have characterized as heat-seekers this group of superintendents who are out in front of the pack in terms of using technology as a vehicle for higher district and personal visibility. There is another group of superintendents that can be characterized as "technology-reluctant" or "technology-avoiding" superintendents. These individuals come to avoid technology implementation in their district for a variety of reasons, ranging from fear all the way to having a philosophical aversion to any changes in the educational delivery system, particularly change based on technology. The technology-aversive superintendent typically has some understanding of the tremendous power of technology and most particularly the power that technology can have over his or her career. However, technology-aversive superintendents are often driven by their fear of action in the high-cost, high-stakes arena of technology implementation. Sometimes superintendents are left in a state of inaction because they don't understand the technology and want to avoid making a fatal career decision. A superintendent can also become *technology shy* or even technology aversive just trying to understand the rapidly changing technology components. There is no doubt about it; technology is a complex business. Witness the alphabet soup of technology acronyms (e.g., ISDN, LEDs, ADSL, VRML, ATM, SONET, TCP/IP, HDTV, DVD, WWW, HTML) and rapidly evolving technologies (e.g., cable modems, digital compression, spread spectrum wireless, server push, network computers, and thin clients) that can make a superintendent feel totally inadequate. This situation of complex technologies can often push a superintendent into a state of *analysis paralysis* as he or she tries to make a decision about what to buy or how to implement. Large-scale, high-visibility, high-cost technology projects directly expose a superintendent to tremendous criticism, not only from staff, but also from both the school board and from the community. Urging a district to wait for some soon-to-be-announced technology can buy a superintendent more time—sometimes enough time to even get to retirement without making a technology decision. How much easier to avoid any criticism by avoiding any decision about technology! More later about technology trends and what superintendents should do to address the rapid changes underlying technology.

Superintendents must face the paradox inherent in any consideration of learning technologies. At the present time, schools do not typically have widespread access to current technology, or at best, access to current technology is limited to a few teachers or a few classrooms. Creating ubiquitous access to technology is a prerequisite to having a widespread impact on learning in a district and requires a large-scale infusion of technology. The need for this large scale of implementation increases, by its very nature the cost of implementation of, and concomitantly, the superintendent's risk factor in undertaking the implementation. When a superintendent asks the district's community to support a large-scale bond issue for technology, he or she is making an implicit statement that the investment of community funds is justified by the benefits provided. Even the most forward-thinking superintendent may hesitate when forced to justify an investment with clear curricular benefits aimed toward students, which he or she is not comfortable supporting. The underlying motivation of superintendents is avoiding criticism that comes from whatever source from within the school community. This desire to avoid criticism makes the decision to push for technology that much more difficult. Superintendents want to build consensus among staff and the community, and they work to avoid anything that threatens this homeostasis. Acting slowly and cautiously (translate—emphasizing a very limited technology-implementation approach) may preserve a career, but it won't allow technology to demonstrate significant systemic benefits. When we take into account the typical short half-life of a superintendent's contract, the problem is exacerbated. The superintendent can often remain caught in the paradox of technology implementation—never taking action, or taking such limited action as to never have any impact.

Rather than expose the superintendency to a variety of criticisms related to technology, some superintendents would defer or deflect technology initiatives arising from staff and sometimes even from the community. Only if the community pressure is high, typically in highly affluent communities or those communities with a high concentration of technology-skilled professionals, will a superintendent feel forced to move forward with a large-scale technology project in spite of any predisposition to avoid technology. Even under community pressure, reluctant superintendents will typically pursue only a very slow, incremental approach to technology implementation to minimize risks. Under these conditions, some superintendents will go so far as to withdraw themselves from the discussions and to leave critical policy making and planning in the hands of their staff. This third-party observer role guarantees that if the project turns out badly, for whatever reason, they are not directly linked to it. It also will result in a less successful project because the full commitment and support of the superintendent is lacking.

There is a third type of superintendent who is more ideal from my perspective. The characteristics of this superintendent lie between that of rabid technology advocate and risk-aversive technology avoider. This third position is reflected in superintendents who bring all their critical and analytic powers to bear in understanding the power of technology and how technology can be applied beneficially within the school. These same superintendents will not single out technology alone but will analyze all instructional strategies, resources, and tools that help their students learn more, for learning is their primary focus. In the ideal case, these superintendents have probably experienced and used the technology themselves, as well as seeing first-hand situations where it can significantly benefit teaching and learning. At the same time, these superintendents appreciate the shortcomings of technology, and look as critically on technology as they do other educational solutions. A dose of healthy criticism on the part of the superintendent, applied to technology as it is to all other educational initiatives, will help to ensure that simplistic, empirically untested, and overly expensive approaches will not become the focus of a district's efforts. The ideal superintendent is constantly looking at the curricular, instructional, assessment, and staff productivity needs of the district and then trying to determine how powerful technology applications can be applied within the teaching and learning environment. This mix of understanding and criticism is very important in assisting superintendents as they move their districts forward into the twenty-first century. The bottom line is that superintendents cannot avoid technology—they need to embrace it, but not as a religion or ultimate goal. Technology is a powerful tool that can assist students and teachers, as well as the wider learning community, to function better. Technology is nothing more and nothing less.

The remainder of this chapter will provide support to superintendents who pursue this middle ground. The chapter will offer a systematic and rational view of technology and how it can be successfully implemented in school districts. This approach to technology can allow superintendents to leave "their mark" on their students and their districts in positive ways—providing true educational results. To do this requires superintendents who can present a strong rationale for why they believe technology should be used in their schools—a rationale based on learning.

WHY USE TECHNOLOGY?

There is a range of answers to the question: Why use technology? Each of these answers focuses on a slightly different perspective, but each is important in helping to clarify why schools should go through the political, fiscal, and logistical problems associated with technology implementation.

In order to reap the maximum benefit from technology, superintendents need to begin with a well-thought-out, systematic process that examines technology in the context of learning. I would ask the same question of superintendents and others reading this chapter as I have used to challenge scores of district technology planning committees, superintendents, and boards of education: Why use technology? Unless individually and collectively as a group, district representatives formulate an explicit response to this question and then convince staff and community that the answer makes sense, any quest for this Holy Grail of technology in the district will be fruitless. I have heard the mantra of technology chanted many times in discussions with superintendents and technology committees. They will argue that it is time to get something done, or to spend some unspent fund balance. With little or no thought, school representatives will argue that they need or want technology because it will improve student performance, provide better instruction, and increase student scores. Two other interrelated arguments are used to rationalize a district's investment in technology. First, advocates argue that the rest of the world has technology and students need technology skills to function in that competitive world. Second, advocates suggest that their district needs to get on the technology bandwagon. They argue that they must keep up with neighboring districts if their district is to remain competitive and attract new members to the community. There is a level of truth in these arguments. However, deep down, I believe that most of us, including superintendents, feel uncomfortable about justifying the return on investment that an extensive, high-cost technology initiative requires. The arguments based solely on these generalizations come up hollow and unsatisfying as a rationale for large-scale budgetary investments. However, when implementing technology means going to the district taxpayers with multimillion dollar requests for funding support, more convincing justification is essential if a technology plan is to ever see the light of implementation.

In working with schools, I generally have the technology advocates examine two general categories of arguments that address the question: why technology? One group of arguments reflects the use of technology to improve (reform, restructure, or transform) teaching and increase student learning. The other group focuses on the essential role of technology in developing the skills students will need to function successfully in the twenty-first century. I have assembled below an extensive list of supporting answers to this question, covering both of these categories.

Technology, when planned and implemented appropriately, allows schools to do many things.

First, technology changes and supports the learning environment and allows educators to better focus on improving curriculum, instruction, and assessment. The use of technology tools, technology software applications, and technology delivery systems allow educators to change the teaching-learning environment. Underlying this view of technology as a change agent is the entire school reform perspective. Whether we talk about it as restructuring, reform, or transformation, the essence of this view is that schools are not being as successful as they need to be in preparing students, and therefore, they must be changed if our students are going to be successful citizens of the twenty-first century. The use of technology to transform schools has been an integral part of many school-reform discussions. In fact, some have argued that the kind of transformation being sought for schools is only possible through the revolutionary application of technology in the school (Darling-Hammond, 1994; U.S. Department of Education, 1993). Thus, technology is seen as a vehicle for changing practices and supporting organizational changes that will extend learning.

Second, technology allows schools to meet new, more rigorous curriculum standards by:

- increasing student motivation through the use of engaging technology tools that challenge students as they interact with content; these are the same tools that students have grown up with and that have become part of the cognitive and social context, at least in the homes of many students—all based on the underlying argument that motivation is an important precursor to learning
- increasing learning time through enhanced, varied, and more targeted learning opportunities and resources that can be directed across all subject areas

- supporting direct teaching through graphical presentation capabilities and increased teacher productivity
- increasing literacy and communications skills including reading and writing as well as presentation in traditional and multimedia modes
- increasing research skills, including search methods, evaluation of information quality and sources, and selection of information as a result of access to global information resources
- empowering learners to take a more active role in their own learning, and to get engaged in analyzing, synthesizing, and communicating information— what would generally be considered higher-level thinking skills
- providing opportunities as well as the means to focus learning on the individual characteristics and needs of each student through individualized instruction starting with existing student competencies and increasing learning by allowing instruction to focus on specific student learning needs, as well as be based on instructional approaches that take into account a student's predisposition or preferences for learning
- creating learning experiences for students that go beyond the four walls of the classroom and that involve more authentic, real-world problems and participants by motivating and challenging all learners, young or old, because participating in more authentic experiences ensures that learning is multidisciplinary and more cognitively complex than learning tasks assigned from a discrete-skills approach to learning
- preparing students for their future role as information or knowledge workers by using technology-based information tools that help prepare students for the world of the future by giving them the information-handling, problem-solving, and decision-making skills they need to work competitively in the global marketplace of the twenty-first century technology, which is an integral part of our society and will be a critical aspect of our students' lives in the twenty-first century

Estimates suggest that a large proportion of the jobs that exist now, and that will increasingly be available in the next two decades will require technology-based information skills (U.S. Department of Labor, 1991). Technology, especially the computer and networking, is an implicit part of businesses as well as higher education. In order to be successful in the global information society, students need regular access to and experience with technology to develop these information-handling skills, so that after graduation and college, they will be able to successfully compete for jobs.

Third, technology allows students and teachers to experience aspects of continual, life-long learning in the context of interdisciplinary projects that involve students, teachers, scientists, and other real-world practitioners. These experiences model the processes and personal traits involved in life-long learning.

Fourth, technology allows students to interact with, understand, and influence their local community, as well as the global community, through real-world projects that involve communications and the social construction of knowledge using technology tools. By being involved in real projects involving not only students and teachers but also real-world practitioners, students have an opportunity to explore complex problems and to be a part of a solution.

Fifth, technology develops a greater understanding of different cultures and perspectives by exposing students to the world through global communications. Global understanding, as well as participation with students from all over the world is possible through computer networking and the Internet. Multinational projects on the Internet help to build a kind of collaborative environment that fosters social interaction, discussion, and acceptance of diversity.

Sixth, technology provides multimedia, interactive learning experiences that engage students in a wide variety of learning modes in addition to text. Students are acclimated to multimedia experiences. Students' exposure to technology in their homes (e.g., computers, CD-ROMs, the Internet, and Nintendo) may have created a different kind of learner, with different expectations and cognitive processing approaches. Technology expands the options for learning.

Seventh, technology allows students and teachers to become information and knowledge creators, not just consumers. Again, active engagement in learning (which includes the higher-level functions of analysis, synthesis, and evaluation of information) not only increases motivation, but also allows the learner to establish the explanations and patterns that help them to create meaning in their environment.

Eighth, technology enables discovery learning experiences where a student can experiment, identify patterns, and then form hypotheses through the use of technology-based simulations and other applications such as virtual environments. These experiences allow students to explore virtual environments that would be too difficult, expensive, or dangerous for students to experience in real life. These virtual environments, whether they are a biology lab or an artificial world, can be re-created and reexperienced many times, allowing students to explore complex alternative situations and solutions. These simulations allow students to apply the critical-thinking processes of evaluating and decision making. Classic computer applications such as SimCity2000, SimAnt, and other similar types highlight how students can work at different levels to influence and understand a complex environment. The integration of science probes and other computer-based laboratory tools provides further opportunities for students to collect information, form hypotheses, and then make decisions about that data.

Ninth, technology allows schools to address issues of resource equity by making access to information resource independent of geographic location. Technology, particularly computers and networks, can close the gap between wealthy and poor schools. Although there appears to be a widening division between the technological "haves" and the "have nots" in many regions across the country, technology access offers a way for students of all economic levels to get beyond the limitations of time and space that tie them to a particular school with a particular set of learning resources.

These arguments present a rationale for technology. I have heard and, in fact, used many of these same arguments in working with schools. However, a critical question to raise at this point is: What empirical evidence do we have that supports these arguments for the use of technology in schools? These points may define the promise of technology, or dare we say the "hopes" of the technology advocates. But do we have hard evidence that technology works? The detailed answer to this question is complex, and beyond the scope of this chapter. However, the simple answer is "yes." There is a wide range of empirical studies (from a variety of research sources over the past few decades) documenting the positive impact and effectiveness of different technologies on student learning. These studies focus on both the more traditional computer-assisted instruction (CAI) implementations and other more technology tool–focused research. There is strong evidence that technology improves students' basic skills mastery, scores on tests, communication skills, and motivation in school. For example, Khalili and Shashaani (1994) reviewed 36 evaluations in a metaanalysis of technology studies and found that the instructional use of computers did increase the academic achievement of students. The Office of Technology Assessment (OTA) in its *Teachers and Technology: Making the Connection* (1995) found that "technology can be a powerful tool for helping teachers with all the different parts of their job: enhancing instruction, simplifying administrative tasks and fostering professional growth activities" (p. 54). This report goes on to indicate that technology in the classroom can have a positive impact on learning in terms of achievement in selected subject areas, development of critical skills, and improvement of attitudes toward school. The OTA report also includes references to a number of other evaluation studies supporting the positive impact of technology. Two other long-term research projects that have documented increases in student learning, as well as other positive changes are the Apple Classroom of Tomorrow (ACOT, 1996) research and the Computer Curriculum Corporation (CCC, 1996) research studies conducted by Pat Suppes and more recently Mario Zanotti. In the references at the end of this chapter I have identified a few Internet Web sites that have assembled many of these studies. These Internet Web sites were created to provide a stronger empirical basis for justifying the use of technology in schools. Probably the single most comprehensive (and useful) of these sources documenting the impact of technology on learning is the Impact of Technology portion of the mid-continent Regional Educational Laboratory (McREL) Web site, which includes links to many of the studies referenced here.

The research and evaluation literature is replete with studies that document how technology is as effective or more effective than other methods such as the traditional classroom in producing increases in student learning. However, this empirical evidence supporting the positive impact of technology on learning is confounded in at least two significant ways—the underlying perspective of technology that one uses in the research, and the underlying assessment approach that is used.

First, the perspective of technology underlying the study can have an impact on the results. Technology can be perceived from at least three different perspectives: (1) as a vehicle for professional productivity; (2) as a medium or delivery system for instruction; and (3) as a tool for analyzing, communicating, and presenting information. Each of these perspectives can influence the outcomes of the evaluation. Looked at historically, the majority of educational research on technology's impact has been driven from the view of technology as a delivery system. The delivery-system perspective of technology implicitly assumes that well-designed, technology-mediated instruction can improve learning and even overcome the poor performance of teachers. Much of the research on technology approaches technology from a delivery-system perspective, and then attempts to compare one or more delivery systems. This research attempts to justify (or at least legitimize) technology-based systems as effective instructional vehicles. The research on CAI and other technology-mediated instructional approaches (including television, distance learning, and, most recently, World Wide Web–based lessons) has provided evidence that under particular conditions students learned as much or more than more traditional, nontechnology-mediated instruction. This research is often used to bolster the use of technology in a district as a means to increase student learning. The perception, although often unarticulated, is that because teachers are poorly trained, ineffective, and incompetent technology-based delivery systems should be used for instruction.

There is also a significant body of research that has found no significant difference in the effectiveness of technology-based delivery systems and more traditional approaches. Russell (1997) has an entire Web site devoted to documenting this "no significant difference" phenomenon. Comparing the impact of technology on the achievement of learners, with the achievement of learners in traditional teacher-based classroom settings, frequently shows that neither environment necessarily produces a significant difference in learning. This seems to be true regardless of the content, the levels of the students, or the technology delivery system involved. Of course some would argue that the lack of difference could either be an argument for investing in technology (since technology delivery can be as effective as a teacher) or an argument for not investing in technology systems because they are no more effective and typically cost more to implement.

Ironically, the largest fiscal investment in an instructional delivery system outside of the classroom teacher, specifically the textbook, often has had little empirical evidence to support its efficacy. The reality is that research from the perspective of a delivery system is not the best approach for justifying the use of technology in a school district. The delivery-system perspective involves the consideration of too many teaching and learning variables that are not identified or measured, such as instructional-design characteristics, content characteristics, delivery methodology, assessment tasks, and interaction with the learner's traits, that favor particular media for particular learners. Implementing a technology infrastructure that has no significant impact on student learning is not an advisable approach for a superintendent to take.

While this research perspective of technology as *delivery system* has declined, the perspective of *technology as tool* has gained ascendancy during the past 10 years. Conceptualizing technology as something to be used by the learner, rather than the medium for learning is being driven, in part, by the technology itself. The development of new applications for communicating, analyzing, and presenting information in a variety of forms including text, graphics, video, and sound has provided students and teachers with new ways to take advantage of technology across every subject area and learning situation. Recent evaluation studies have shifted to questioning how technology-based tools facilitate learning particular things in particular ways—a shift to a level of greater specificity. This emphasis on specific learning approaches, processes, tasks, and outcomes makes it easier to link technology and identify its impact on curriculum, instruction, and assessment.

It is important to note that this *raison d'être* for technology use as a tool can be built, to a large extent, although not exclusively, on a constructivist perspective of how technology and learning interact. In fact, a nonconstructivist viewpoint of technology would typically focus on *technology as a delivery system* of factual information. As discussed in the preceding paragraph, this viewpoint historically has emphasized how we could use technology to deliver information to students and get it there more efficiently. The conceptualization of technology as a delivery system explicitly brings with it a focus on the large-scale, undifferentiated delivery of teaching and implicitly on the justification of the time and money to accomplish this. The constructivist notion of technology views technology primarily as a tool used by the learner. By working with technology tools in more authentic contexts, learners have the opportunity to model expert-thinking processes and to receive collaborative stimulation and support of their work. Students can create and interact with virtual environments that allow them to "test" their thinking and decision making. Global networks allow students to communicate with fellow students as well as adults. These same tools and network capabilities allow students and teachers to share their ideas in hypermedia format and to receive criticism and encouragement from a wide community of electronic colleagues.

Thus, constructivist approaches are not teaching centered but rather learner centered. Unlike traditional tools that leverage physical labor, current technology tools (such as networks and multimedia computers with their associated application software packages) help the learner to leverage mental work. They can be conceptualized, accordingly, as mind tools that help us do the same things faster and with less effort, but also help us to do completely new things. Some cognitive psychologists (Collins, Brown, & Newman, 1989; Resnick, 1987) have proposed that the important skills of thinking, reasoning, decision making, composition, and experimentation are not acquired through the transfer of factual information but rather through the learner's interaction with real-world content. This notion is at the heart of a constructivist perspective. It appears that while constructivism is not an absolute requirement for technology implementation, it does support the current movement in technology—the model of technology as a tool—much better. This is not to say that technology provides no benefits to teachers or to their use of direct, didactic teaching approaches, because it does.

This notion of technology as tool is at the same time naively simple and profoundly powerful. In his book *Silicon Snake Oil*, Clifford Stoll (1995) criticizes educators for the headlong push to implement computers and other networking technology in classrooms. He suggests that schools want the technology so that they can bring more information to students. Why, he asks, do we need to do that when students already have too much information and are unable to deal with it? From my perspective, Stoll fails to recognize the powerful role that technology can play in a school as a tool for analyzing and processing information. While expanding network technologies actually complicates the issues of information access, as Stoll highlights, technology tools are also available to select, organize, and present information. Placing multimedia, networked tools into the hands of students and then requiring them as a part of their learning experiences to identify, analyze, select, organize, and present information is the essence of an engaged, thinking, challenging learning environment. It also can be very motivating and empowering as well.

In his 1997 *Atlantic Monthly* article titled "The Computer Delusion," Todd Oppenheimer decried the increasingly popular push toward implementing technology in schools, despite what he believed was the lack of evidence supporting technology's efficacy. His well-written argument against implementing computers in schools without a thorough and well-founded rationale for their use should be read by every superintendent. Many of the concerns about technology raised in this article (e.g., creation of artificial experiences, pressures of business to use technology, lack of development readiness of students, isolation of students created through electronic communications, and shifting of expenditures to technology and away from other important curricular areas) underlie the questions raised by school board members and the community whenever a large-scale technology initiative is discussed. A superintendent must anticipate and prepare specific responses to address the many valid criticisms that Oppenheimer and Stoll raise. The fundamental consideration to keep in mind in reading a critical article like Oppenheimer's is that technology, and particularly the computer, is not a magic elixir that will cause students to learn. The "why," "how," and "where" of implementation will determine its success. Although there are articles in the popular press that point out the deleterious effects of technology on all aspects of our society, including schools, writers like Stoll and Oppenheimer force us to clarify our own thoughts about where technology can be applied in order to affect teaching and learning. We must argue cogently and choose our applications wisely if we are to be successful.

As a direct rebuttal to the positions of Stoll and Oppenheimer, I suggest that nowhere is the power of technology as a tool that can improve learning clearer than in the convergence of computer, network, and multimedia technologies reflected in the evolving Internet. The Internet (and most specifically the converging hypermedia environment of the World Wide Web) provides at least four things that are important to teaching and learning, and that when used in a well-planned, educationally focused technology implementation, can improve student learning. First, the Internet offers access to an unprecedented range of resources and information. This information comes in all forms, including text, graphics, animation, video, and sound, as well as human contacts and experts. Second, the Internet offers the ability to interact and communicate with individuals and groups all over the globe, allowing all of them to build knowledge through their engagement and exploration. This communication can occur regardless of location and regardless of the ages of the participants. Third, the Internet offers a vehicle, as presently reflected particularly in the World Wide Web (and its associated Web development and server hosting tools), to create knowledge bases for sharing and for continued collaborative development. There is a wide range of real-world projects dealing with science, social studies, literature, history, mathematics, the environment, and many other areas in which students and teachers have worked to develop as a research project or thematic unit and then placed on the Internet. This project information provides a worldwide means for access and comment that models the kinds of dialogues expected in the best university classes. Fourth, the Internet provides a flexible delivery system for instruction and curriculum materials. In short, the Internet as a global resource offers the opportunity for a dramatic shift in the worldview of educators.

Although much of the ACOT research looks at technology as a tool, an evaluation study by the Center for Applied Special Technology (CAST, 1996) titled *The Role of Online Communication in Schools: A National Study* expands this evolving perspective of technology as a tool. This study identified positive effects on student learning in the classroom, including isolating the effect of online telecommunications on literacy and presentation skills. Studies such as this that examine specific curricular outcomes and student skills such as literacy, communications, research, and presentation provide stronger support for the role of technology. Reginal Grégoire, Inc. (1996) provides an extensive review of how technology contributes to teaching and learning. This review looks at the effect of technology on the process of learning, as well as at the specific technology environment that is implemented by teachers. This research includes both formal assessments and essays discussing technology. It provides a range of positive evidence on specific student learning, the increase in student motivation, and the ways teachers plan and assess learning.

The second confounding factor in the review of empirical evidence supporting the impact of technology is the underlying assessment that is used. The use of multiple choice, norm-referenced achievement tests as the outcome measure for a delivery system frequently makes sense. However, as a measure of tool use, these kinds of instruments are woefully inadequate. When there is a mismatch between the assessment instruments and the curricular objectives any results must be questioned. Unfortunately, the numbers and quality of instrumentation available to assess the growth of student knowledge and skills with respect to the communications, analysis, research, and presentation skills we often focus on, along with the use of technology tools are very limited right now. Instruments that can track the learning process and measure products well enough to accurately identify differences are not widely available. Over time, technology may be able to assist in the assessment process itself, making it easier to create valid and reliable measurements of student learning on and through technology tools.

FACTORS OF SUCCESSFUL TECHNOLOGY PROJECTS

As noted at the beginning of this chapter, technology can have a positive impact on teaching and learning. Both research and experience support this viewpoint. Throughout the process of technology planning, design, and implementation management, superintendents and school boards are encouraged to keep in mind seven factors of success if they want to implement a successful technology program in their district. These seven factors are based on first-hand review of successful technology projects in schools across New York State, the country, and beyond in well over 200 districts. Because I serve as a national technology advisor to the National Science Foundation and the Department of Defense Education Agency, I am also involved with technology implementation in schools across Europe. I have seen many common problems that cut across these technology implementations, and based on those experiences, I have identified what I call the common factors of successful projects. These factors reflect both my experience and a review of many empirical studies examining technology's impact on learning.

Frame whatever you do with technology in your district to be certain that you address each and every one of these seven factors.

> **1. Success requires a clear, shared vision of technology that is based on the educational benefits of technology, along with a multiyear plan and detailed budget for implementation.**

We can think about planning approaches in two fundamental ways. The first is based on an assessment of the present discrepancy between what currently exists, and what is desired—that is, a needs-based planning approach. The second is vision-based, and works backward from a vision of the future and then defines the steps necessary to implement the vision. Understanding present needs is important. However, with respect to technology, the vision-based approach appears to be the more effective in helping schools to implement systems that will let them take maximum advantage of technology. Typically, I encourage visioning in two areas—technology and learning. The technology vision describes what technology capabilities will be available to teachers and students in classrooms, libraries, computer labs, and other locations throughout the school. The technology vision must reflect both current and emerging technologies with at least a five-year viewpoint. The learning vision describes what students and teachers could do with the technology that is envisioned. The learning vision should consider current educational trends and approaches to curriculum, instruction, assessment, and research. There are at least two keys to this visioning. The first is exploring a wide range of different visions before formulating your own district vision. The second is building consensus to ensure that all key district members share the vision. Visiting other schools, reading, and discussing various options within the context of a representative group (some sort of technology committee) all help to ensure that you have an expansive vision and also help to solidify the many possible visions of learning and technology into one comprehensive vision. The Web site for the National Center for Technology Planning (1997) is one resource that districts should use during this process to review other visions and plans. You should also encourage a wide divergence of visions at the outset to prevent you from being harmed by the "You don't know what you don't know" challenge. In addition, since shared vision is important in gaining support for implementation, having one or two school board members on the technology committee during the entire visioning-planning process will pay dividends in the future adoption of the plan.

It is important to identify the benefits of technology in terms of both student learning and staff productivity. The rationale for technology needs to be explicitly defined as the vehicle for supporting the vision of learning generated by the district. Technology's rationale is support of the learning environment, not technology for its own sake. For many years, schools have made at least limited investments in the administrative productivity advantages of technology. There are many potential productivity advantages inherent in technology systems designed to support administrative and teaching staff, and schools generally can understand those benefits. Although schools have invested in administrative technology to increase staff productivity, those investments are at a significantly lower level than the investment levels of business and industry. Likewise, the investment of schools in learning technology has been very limited. In a comprehensive analysis of the technology expenditures of all public schools within New York State (Radlick, 1994a), it was determined that the average percentage of a district's total budget spent on all technology (including hardware, software, network, staffing, and operation) was only 2.4%. This is two to three times less than the estimated amount that business and industry spend. Despite these investments, neither information nor learning technology is widely available to those who could benefit from it—students, teachers, and administrators.

Only recently has the focus of expenditure shifted to learning technology. Experience in industry has shown that applying technology to solve problems through automation of existing processes does not really capitalize on the inherent power of technology. The real power of technology lies in exploring ways of doing new things in new ways, not only in doing the same things faster and with less effort. Likewise, in education we need to look at new ways of using communications and information technology to better support our overall goals, including both administrative and educational functions. Again, this is where the tool perspective of technology can help significantly. If we are going to use the business model of return on investment (ROI), it is important to establish the critical educational outcomes we want to accomplish upfront in the process and then measure the impact we have on those outcomes with technology. We should also be very careful to select potential areas of impact that are both important and also likely to be influenced by technology. To do otherwise will doom you to failure.

A district technology plan needs to translate the vision into a concrete set of implementation steps and required resources, while the detailed budget that accompanies the plan provides the projected costs for the plan. I have frequently seen districts organize a representative technology committee, work hard to develop a shared vision and more detailed implementation plan, and then languish without ever arriving at the implementation stage. The rubber really hits the road when you begin translating a technology plan and vision into reality by identifying real technology components and real costs. Gaining consensus on the vision is important, but equally important is getting consensus on the items that support that vision.

I have had extensive experience with technology cost modeling at the district and state levels (Radlick, 1994a, 1994b). Based on that work and on subsequent experience in implementing large-scale infrastructure projects in a number of districts in the Northeast, I believe it is critical to identify all the items of cost (i.e., capital and operational costs necessary over a five-year period) to implement a technology plan. Successful cost modeling looks at all the items of costs to plan, design, implement, support, and extend technology in the district. The cost model must include not only hardware, software, and networking costs but also staffing, technical support, training, maintenance, and operational costs. The perspective in the information-technology industry is that organizations must plan for technology's total cost of ownership (Gartner Group, 1996) in order to both implement and sustain a technology-based project. I agree with this perspective. While school boards may be intimidated initially by a comprehensive cost model, they will be more likely to support a plan that they know has no fiscal surprises implicitly hidden in the project budget.

---

2. Success requires an infrastructure to support teaching and learning as well as to provide a reasonable level of access for all.

Infrastructure in schools used to be thought of as bricks and mortar. However, in the information age, technology infrastructure must be conceptualized as the total foundation on which the technology-enhanced teaching and learning environment is built. Infrastructure is a critical investment area for a school because it includes all the networking, hardware, software, and system components required to support the interconnected learning environment described in the vision. In my view infrastructure also includes the support structures, policies, and procedures necessary to ensure that the system works smoothly. The infrastructure provides the means of ensuring a reasonable and consistent level of access for all students and teachers in the school. It is a fact that the productivity and learning possibilities of technology cannot be realized without implementing the technology. Likewise, technology cannot be integrated into the curriculum without allowing students to have regular access to technology tools. The infrastructure supports this access across each building and each district, typically through a high-speed Local Area Network (LAN) and high-speed connections between the district buildings (Wide Area Network, or WAN), with access to the network resources from within almost all rooms anywhere in the district. In addition, an Internet connection provides all workstations throughout the district with access to the regional or global network. The district network infrastructure often will integrate voice, video, and data communications to provide the widest level of access to information and resources both inside the district and outside of it.

If technology is to have a positive impact across a district, it must be ubiquitous and, therefore, easily accessible by all teachers and students when and where it is needed. Otherwise, there is no way that the technology can be a dependable instructional resource that can be fully integrated into the course of daily instruction. For teachers to regularly use technology, they need to have easy access to it. Having to schedule a computer or a television set for a lesson almost guarantees that only the most dedicated teacher will use that technology as a regular aspect of instruction. Likewise, expecting all students to use computer tools to research a topic or to write a report without sufficient access to the technology is like asking students to write a composition via a shared pen. The process will take a long time to complete and only the most intrepid will undertake the process when access is limited. For example, many school districts across the country have computers available to teachers and students. Nationwide the average ratio of students to computers is reported as being approximately 10 students to each computer (Quality Education Data, 1996–1997). However, a more in-depth review of the data shows that by far the majority of those computers are first-generation workstations such as the Apple II, which are incapable of running the most current multimedia applications. While these older computers can be used for keyboarding and other simple applications such as simple text processing, the powerful, multimedia tools we have discussed (including the Internet) are not accessible via this outdated technology.

Another significant consideration in planning infrastructure is flexibility and expandability. Designing and implementing an infrastructure that will be flexible and robust enough to support teaching and learning well into the twenty-first century is key. Networking designs need to be able to support high-speed connections via both existing and projected networking standards. Districts don't want to have to reinvest in networking infrastructure for a long time. Nevertheless, districts need to have a plan for reinvesting in new workstation technology on a regular basis to ensure that they can use the most current multimedia applications, where appropriate. Leasing hardware as well as establishing a regular budget allocation for new systems and software are both important strategies to avoid the present situation in which schools find themselves, where the majority of workstations and software being used are at least ten years old.

> **3. Success requires integration of technology into curriculum, instruction, and assessment. Integration into the curriculum contrasts with an emphasis on using technology only sporadically as a supplement in the classroom.**

Building technology-enhanced lessons into the curriculum as well as using technology tools as a vehicle for inquiry, analysis, and problem solving across all the disciplines will help to ensure that the technology initiative is successful in your district. Employment of technology as a supplement results in diffused, unfocused utilization of expensive resources with limited or no guarantee of educational impact. From a simple business perspective, the return on investment for technology cannot be justified when technology is implemented and used in a haphazard manner that is not tied to the district's essential curricular and instructional goals. Integration of technology by teachers into their teaching is clearly dependent on the access provided by a robust infrastructure that can expand and be adapted to meet evolving educational needs.

It is also important for districts to identify the areas where technology can make the most significant contributions. This process necessitates a review of the present strengths and weaknesses of the district's educational program. For example, a district or a building could identify problems in the area of student writing or problem solving based on test data. They could then link those needs in the areas of writing and problem solving with possible technology applications and tools. Finally, teachers could design new lessons and involve students in new ways of experiencing writing and problem solving. A good example of how a district can tie technology to curriculum is the Web site for the Bellingham School District in the state of Washington (Bellingham, 1998), or the Oswego City School District Web Site in Oswego, New York (Oswego, 1998).

> **4. Success requires administrative leadership and community support for the technology initiative.**

Districts are more successful with their technology initiatives if two important leadership conditions are addressed. The first condition requires the superintendent to work with district staff, the board of education, and the community to convince them of the value of investing in technology. The second condition requires that the superintendent present the shared technology vision that links the application of technology with instructional improvement and increases in student skills. The vision of technology and learning that the superintendent (and other key administrators) communicates to the district has to be "owned" by many other people in order for the district to obtain the fiscal and emotional commitment necessary for making their plan a reality. No superintendent can carry a technology plan solely on his or her own shoulders for very long, regardless of knowledge, enthusiasm, or dedication.

---

5. Success requires changes in organizational and teaching structures across the district.

There is a link between the use of technology and school-reform initiatives. Technology provides a vehicle to change what happens in schools—to change the time, place, organization, and forms of learning to take advantage of its power. For example, classroom space can be changed, with the implementation of computer technology, into classroom clusters rather than solely in labs. To take advantage of the technology, teachers need to change the way they organize instruction and to modify their teaching strategies. If teachers try to implement technology in the same ways they have implemented other instructional programs, without taking into account the unique requirements and opportunities presented by technology tools, they will not be able to capitalize on the strengths of these powerful tools. The adoption of innovations requires more than just assimilation of technology. To take maximum advantage of technology within education requires accommodations or changes in every aspect of the teaching-learning environment. For example, some schools continue to teach writing with a computer and word processing in the same way as with more traditional approaches. They use the computer essentially as an electronic typewriter. When schools do not use the many software prewriting components (for outlining, idea organizing, and brainstorming) and the postwriting tools (for grammatical checking and collaboration, including electronic publishing on the Web), then the computer will never have a significant impact on student learning. The integration of word processing and other tools along with the Internet allows students to communicate in new ways with their peers as well as to collaborate with other learners at all levels.

Classroom management procedures also need reexamination when technology is implemented in a classroom environment. Managing physical space where technology is being used can be a challenge for teachers. Schools are typically not designed to accommodate the spatial requirements of computers and other technologies. So, too, implementing organizational procedures that allow individuals and groups of students to effectively use technology located in the classroom (without disturbing others) requires planning and changes in both teacher and student activities. Another instructional space that requires both physical as well as operational restructuring with the introduction of technology is the library-media center. With automated library circulation, Internet, and a range of

CD-ROM resources, along with video and satellite programming now available in the library, educators need to consider new approaches to using the library-media center as an integral part of classroom learning. In all cases, the real power of technology is increased when it is used to do new things in new ways. What is done should capitalize on technology's ability to link media, to communicate, and to share information. Computer labs are the third major area in the school that need to be reexamined in terms of restructuring space and instruction. Providing sufficient quantities of workstations to accommodate an entire class of students for training or to complete a project is a continuing aspect of why schools use labs or computer classrooms.

---

6. Success requires ongoing staff development to ensure that staff understand and can use technology tools in their teaching.

In order to address two of the critical factors discussed above—the need for restructuring and changing teaching strategies, and the need to integrate technology tools into the curriculum—districts need to establish ongoing staff-development programs. Successful staff development programs are not "one-shot" type courses but rather provide progressive, hands-on training that will move teachers from wherever they are at on the computer-skills continuum forward. This continuum can be thought of as having three major levels: (1) computer awareness, (2) proficiency in the use of technology tools, and (3) integration of technology tools as an integral part of teaching and learning.

Any ongoing staff development program has to be supported explicitly in the multiyear budget. Most sites establish some sort of rule for the total five-year training costs as either a percentage of the hardware and software costs (20 to 30%) or as a percentage of the total technology budget (5 to 10%). Because the staff development requirements of a particular district can vary, establishing an exact percentage of the total budget for staff development is difficult. The exact percentage is less important than ensuring the implementation of a well-planned training program that assesses skills, and then moves teachers and other staff from where they are at with respect to technology skills to where they need to be. Establish training costs based on the identified proficiencies of the staff, as identified by a survey. Because of its cost, districts frequently attempt to downplay the need for staff development, focusing instead on the hardware and software components. Ignoring the requirements for ongoing staff development will guarantee that expensive technology systems will lie in closets unused and gathering dust.

Successful training also includes budgeting for release time, superintendent days, and after-school programs. Awarding continuing education credits can also be an important strategy for a successful training program. Training may be delivered via in-house staff, including teachers, as well as from outside trainers, or via CD-ROM, Web-based, and satellite distance-learning courses. Some districts use a combination of in-house and outside training courses with the option for teachers to get approval (and often funding support) for a wide range of outside training when a teacher can demonstrate the course will benefit the district educationally.

Any training has to include hands-on opportunities and the provision of adequate time to practice and use newly learned skills. No one can learn new skills without training, time to practice, and support and encouragement to try new techniques in the classroom. Districts need to ensure that they implement mechanisms for teachers to get support from key technology staff, as well as to help each other experiment with technology. Face-to-face and electronic discussion groups can be good approaches to supporting staff growth.

Taking home district computers during the summer, as well as using district-owned notebook computers increases the probable success of the training. Another good approach is a district-organized and -supported purchase program to help teachers get computers for their homes. Having a home computer, even when it is used for personal applications, tends to be a good indicator of use in the classroom. Also, since teachers have little time during the day to prepare technology-enhanced lessons, they really need to have a computer at home. In planning training, it is important to keep in mind that teachers generally learn best in situations that involve real, classroom-specific lessons that offer tangible lesson plans and materials that are of real benefit to teachers. Peer teaching can also be very successful and can create healthy competition among peers. All these approaches must be designed to get teachers to become more adventurous in their use of technology in the classroom. Your success or failure in the implementation of your technology vision will depend on the ongoing support of teachers.

---

7. Success requires technical support to address the ongoing "care and feeding" of the technology system.

All technological systems require technical staff to address the ongoing maintenance requirements as well as to provide for trouble-shooting and problem resolution. Complex network systems require additional levels of technical support to keep all components operating and to help users address the myriad problems they face. If systems are not available and in good working order, the probability of their use declines because they are not seen as something dependable on which to build instruction. For example, a teacher cannot build the Internet into a lesson if he or she doesn't have the confidence that it will reliably be available for the lesson. To ensure dependable instructional technology infrastructures, districts typically need to structure help desks and a hierarchical problem resolution and support structure with the staff to maintain all their systems. Trying to get staff to wear two or three "hats," or bootlegging teaching staff out of their classrooms to support a large-scale infrastructure will be paramount to disaster. In addition, to maintain a high level of technical support with the ever-evolving range of software applications' technical-support requirements, staff must participate in regular technical training. Because technical support is an ongoing operational cost, many districts want to downplay or ignore this important cost area. However, any technology implementation that lacks a strong technical-support structure will not be able to sustain itself over time. Investing in staff is important, but districts also must be realistic about how long they can hold on to technical staff. Given the limited funding in schools and the tremendous competition for good technical staff, it is likely that a district will have to regularly bring in new technical staff as existing staff use their experience as a stepping stone to advancement in the more lucrative commercial sector.

As noted earlier, the technology industry has recognized the importance of technology support by emphasizing the total costs of ownership as a part of budgeting during technology implementation. The point is that the purchase of hardware and software is only a part of the total cost of ownership for systems. Technical support, maintenance, staff training, and operating costs are the other important parts of the cost equation. Districts need to staff appropriately to support their technology infrastructure. Other options to provide this support are outsourcing to other firms. Other ongoing operational costs too often ignored include hardware maintenance, software upgrades, electrical costs, paper and toner for large printers, and insurance.

CRITICISMS OF TECHNOLOGY

Despite the potential of technology for learning, not all school districts and students are taking advantage of what technology can offer. Educators have, for too long, looked for simplistic solutions to the challenge of educating young people. Education has suffered through a Sisyphean history of hope and subsequent frustration with technology. Educators seek out simplistic educational technology solutions that they propose as the latest panacea for the ills of education, only to end up castigating their colleagues for adopting an unproductive instructional approach. Computers and the Internet are not the first innovation presented as the best way to reform education. Motion pictures, radio, television, and programmed learning were all there ahead of computers and the Internet. Both educators and noneducators alike have presented evolving technologies as the best and ultimate solution for schools and their students. Douglas Noble, in his *Edu-*

cational Leadership article "Mad Rush into the Future: The Overselling of Educational Technology" (1996) highlights some of these past experiences with technology in education. He notes that many of these expensive, high-technology solutions were marketed to education without clear educational requirements or business analyses driving them. The major focus of commercial technology marketing initiatives in schools is clearly not about using technology in the service of education. Noble's advice in closing his article is very much to the point.

> Educators, therefore, need not keep abreast of every innovation for fear of losing ground or falling behind. Leave the experiments to the technophiles. The rest of us, unashamedly and with renewed integrity, should follow our own sense of sound educational practice, using proven technologies when applicable. There is no need to join the mad rush into the future or to gamble with our students' education. (p. 23)

As we have discussed, educators should not be afraid to raise questions about technology systems and approaches. First and foremost we are educators, and the needs of student learning should have primacy in our review of any technology. Rather than becoming enraptured with the technology of the moment, we need to assess thoughtfully how a particular technology could help us accomplish our curriculum, instruction, and assessment goals. Any technology that helps us teach better should be sought out and encouraged. Conversely, any technology that does not support teaching and learning should be ignored as a solution for education.

OTHER IMPORTANT ISSUES RELATED TO TECHNOLOGY

This chapter has reviewed technology and its role in education from a number of perspectives. Before closing, it is important to address a few technology issues that can significantly impact a superintendent's technology initiative.

Technology Vendors

As a superintendent, you should be skeptical of the claims technology vendors present in marketing their products. Make no mistake about it, educational technology is big business, and the educational market represents big profits to vendors. In some cases, vendors will try to market directly to a superintendent, hoping to gain credibility and conceptual commitment without dealing with other district staff. This makes it easy for the vendor but can create conflicts among staff who have input into the decision-making process.

Hardware and software vendors do offer many donation programs and special grants as a part of their educational programs, although the present business climate in which we operate has produced fewer direct donations and partnerships than ten years ago. As altruistic as a corporate partnership program may appear, it ultimately has to support the mission of the company, which involves making a profit and staying in business. This is not to say that you should avoid involvement with vendors or that helping education conflicts with the vendor's mission. Creating school–business partnerships can create situations that are very beneficial to both the school district and the vendor. I know from personal experience. I negotiated and brought over $17 million of technology partnerships (in hardware, software, and services) to New York State schools during the early to mid-1990s. I believe that if schools work with vendors to identify specific projects that match the resources of each partner, a partnership can be worth the effort. However, if schools are only looking to get something from a vendor and don't envision the partnership as involving both mutual benefits and mutual responsibilities, it is unlikely that they will even be able to convince a vendor that the partnership is worth establishing. Conceptualizing these kinds of mutually beneficial partnerships is difficult but not impossible. There are opportunities out there for schools to take advantage of in implementing their technology plans. Superintendents can use technology vendor partnerships to create better environments for learning. However, these partnerships must be well thought out and carefully established to protect the district's interests.

Technology Trends

As technology-using educators, we should have a general understanding of the current complement of technology systems and tools available to us, as well as a basic sense of the technology trends for the future. Reading journals and other technology publications, watching television, and using the Internet can keep a superintendent more up to date on technology developments and future technology possibilities. It is clear that certain technology trends are having, and will have, a significant impact on education over the next decade or two. These include: multimedia interactive technologies, cable modems, the Internet (and particularly the World Wide Web), high bandwidth global networking (including HDSL and ATM technologies), personal communications systems and personal data devices, satellite systems, artificial intelligence and software agents, new imaging and printing technologies, and large screen display technologies, such as flat screen liquid crystal displays (LCDs). During the next decade, we will continue to see the evolution of computers, with processor speed and memory doubling approximately at least every 18 months. New technologies such as digital versatile (or video) disk (DVD) and cable modem connections to the Internet are just now becoming widely available to schools. While these reflect the most current options, these options will change over time as new capabilities are established.

Superintendents need to review their strategy for workstation acquisition. Recently there have been many questions about thin client or network computers (a variation on the mainframe and the dumb terminal) and how they could reduce the total cost of ownership. In addition, questions about leasing versus buying and the platform issue of Windows versus Macintosh are two common themes that must be considered from the standpoint of educational need as well as financial impact. One software issue is whether to standardize on tool applications such as Claris Works or Microsoft Office to reduce licensing fees and to limit software support and training cost. Another issue is whether to select an Integrated Learning System (ILS) such as Computer Curriculum Corporation (CCC), IBM's School Vista, or Jostens within the district's instructional program. Costs, linkages with instructional objectives, and unique district needs will all drive these important decisions. Technical support costs and the cost of ownership are other considerations.

Infrastructure questions abound as well. Fiber or copper cabling, shared versus switched networking segments, connections per classroom, backbone and classroom connection speeds (e.g., 10Mb Ethernet, 100Mb Ethernet, 1Gb Ethernet, FDDI, ATM, and so forth), wireless options, and appropriate Internet connection speeds are all important questions for schools. Choosing between telephone companies, cable companies, and other providers for connectivity services will be a particularly challenging issue over the next few years, given deregulation and the FCC rulings on the Universal Service Fund and the E-RATE Program. The integration of voice and video into the data network infrastructure is another area of investigation for a district to pursue during this period of service options.

Obviously, all the questions about technology can create a great deal of confusion for a superintendent and a school district. To resolve this confusion, a superintendent must look both internally and externally. It is important to encourage district technology staff to explore options. Likewise, it is important to seek outside consulting help to make the best decisions. The nature and requirements for a technology consultant will vary a great deal, depending on the needs of the district. Whoever is chosen should have knowledge of technology and experience with schools. No educator can be an expert in all these technical areas and expect to be an educational leader as well. The superintendent needs to maintain the technology and learning vision for the district and seek outside consulting help to assist the district in objectively reviewing all the technical issues that could impact the district's vision. Consultants can help your district sort through the technology issues. Although they can help in the process, keep in mind that technology consultants will not be able to define your educational objectives. Only you can do that. You need to drive the process from the perspective of learning, not the perspective of technology.

CONCLUSION

Over the past few decades, educators have been both tantalized by and contributors to the exaggerated promises articulated for technology applications in schools. Hopefully, this chapter has reaffirmed the transformational power of technology for learners. But because it can make a difference in teaching and learning doesn't mean that technology always lives up to its promises. Superintendents and school boards need to keep the seven factors of successful technology projects in the forefront of their minds as they initiate their technology planning. If they do, then their efforts will be rewarded with a technology implementation that addresses the learning needs of students and supports the productivity of staff across the district. In short, they will succeed in improving teaching and learning. If they do not address those factors, they will waste taxpayer money, potentially harm students under their charge, and also do serious damage to their own careers. It is futile to waste time and funds on technology that doesn't get used, or gets used only for games and trivial applications that divert the time of the teacher and the student. What we need is to get students thinking more comprehensively, communicating more clearly, and adapting to the challenges of the world more flexibly. Technology tools can be an integral and important part of that learning. It is essential that superintendents and others in the school community plan and implement technology solutions in a more analytical manner, always critical of the promises and the hype associated with technology. Our challenge as educators is to identify where technology can help us to do more and to do it better. We need to harness the power of these tools to our purposes. Welcome to the biggest educational challenge of the twenty-first century.

REFERENCES

Apple Classroom of Tomorrow (ACOT). (1996). *Changing the conversation about teaching—learning and technology: A report on 10 years of ACOT research.* Apple Computer, Inc. http://www.info.apple.com/education/acot.menu.html.

Bellingham Public Schools Public Web Site. (1998). http://www.bham.wednet.edu/

Center for Applied Special Technology (CAST). (1996). *The role of online communication in schools: A national study.* http://www.cast.org.

Collins, A., Brown, J.S., & Newman, S.E. (1989). Cognitive apprenticeship: Teaching the crafts of reading, writing and mathematics. In L. B. Resnick (Ed.), *Knowing, learning and instruction: Essays in honor of Robert Glaser* (pp. 453–494). Hillsdale, NJ: Lawrence Erlbaum Associates.

Computer Curriculum Corporation. (1996). *SuccessMaker evaluation summaries.* New York: Simon & Schuster.

Darling-Hammond, L. (1994). Interview with Linda Darling-Hammond. [Agency for Instructional Technology (AIT)] *Technos Quarterly for Education and Technlogy, 3*(2).

Gartner Group Consulting Services. (1996, February 9). *Total cost of ownership: Reducing PC/LAN costs in the enterprise—Evaluation of IBM.* Gartner Group Publication.

Khalili, A., & Shashaani, L. (1994). The effectiveness of computer applications: A meta-analysis, *The Journal of Research on Computing in Education, 27*(1).

National Center for Technology Planning. (1997). Mississippi State University.
http://www.netp.com

Noble, D. D. (1996). Mad rush into the future: The overselling of educational technology. *Educational Leadership, 54*(3)

Office of Technology Assessment. (1995, April). *Teachers and technology: Making the connection.*

Oppenheimer, T. (1997, July). The computer delusion. *The Atlantic Monthly,* pp. 45–62.

Oswego City School District Web Site (1998).
http://www.oswego.org

Quality Education Data, Inc. & Malarkey-Taylor Associates, Inc. (1995). *Education technology survey.* [Survey conducted on behalf of the National Educational Association, the National Association of Secondary School Principals, the National Association of Elementary School Principals, the American Association of School Administrators and Cable in the Classroom.]

Quality Education Data, Inc. (1996–1997). *Technology in public schools.* QED's 16th Annual Census Study of Public School Technology Use. Denver, Colorado.

Radlick, (1994a). *A cost model: Implementing technology in New York state schools.* New York State Education Department.

Radlick, M. (1994b, December). *Technology cost modeling.* Paper presented to the Rand Corporation and the U.S. Department of Education, Washington, DC.

Reginal Grégoire, Inc. Bracewell, R., & LaFerrière, T. (1996). S*chool net—The contribution of new technologies to learning and teaching in elementary and secondary schools.* A collaboration of Laval University and McGill University.
http://www.tact.fse.ulaval.ca/fr/html/impactnt/html.

Resnick, L. B. (1987, December). Learning in school and out. *Educational Researcher, 16*(9), 13–20.

Russell, T.L. (1997, April). *The no significant difference phenomenon.* Durham: North Carolina State University. Office of Instructional Telecommunications.
http://teleeducation.nb.ca/phenom/

U.S. Department of Education, Office of Educational Research (OERI). (1993). *Using technology to support education reform.*

U.S. Department of Labor, Secretary's Commission on Achieving Necessary Skills. (1991). *What work requires of schools: A SCANS report for America 2000.*

Stoll, C. (1995). *Silicon snake oil: Second thoughts on the information highway.* New York: Anchor Books.

CHAPTER 12

Issues for the Future

Robert R. Spillane and Paul Regnier

I've seen the future, and it's a lot like the present, only longer.
—Dan Quisenberry, Kansas City Royals

You bought this book to find out what you need to know to be a superintendent of the future, not the past or the present. So what about the future? Isn't most of the book about the past and present? Well yes, but . . .

Much that is in the chapters of this book concerns the world as we know it—the present. This is because survival, for the superintendent, is the first law of nature, just as reelection is for the politician; without it there is no future. Only those leaders who have survived the twentieth century will lead their institutions into, and in, the twenty-first century. The problem that many leaders have (especially in education) is not that they are not ready for the future but that they are living in the past. Knowing how to deal with the school systems of the present will allow you to lead them into the future.

Besides, the most important thing to keep in mind about the future is that we do not know what it will bring. We can extrapolate from the present and from what has happened in the past, and that can be very helpful, but to a large extent preparation for the future means preparation for the unexpected. It also means focusing on enduring values that will help you to make decisions about the unexpected. Probably the most important of these enduring values are academic achievement and intellectual development—in the traditional academic subjects for all students at all times—and the welfare of the individual child. Remembering these values will help the superintendent of the future do the right thing in the future—whatever the future may bring.

It is also true that, as a wise person once said, the best preparation for the future is knowledge of the past. Thus, for instance, a knowledge of the history of special-education law will help a superintendent to understand the purposes of

267

current requirements and therefore to meet them more creatively and effectively. More strongly stated is George Santayana's comment that "those who cannot remember the past are condemned to repeat it" (Santayana, 1981). Thus, those who forget the failure of half-baked, under-researched, yet glitzy innovations of the past are more likely to adopt innovations with similar characteristics in the future. This is why some of the chapters provide historical background. All of this is necessary for the superintendent of the future.

But, as you already asked, what *about* the future? What do we know about the future and how do we know it? We remember reading in *Popular Mechanix* magazine in the 1950s about what some "futurists" predicted would be the world we live in today. Among the predictions were a helicopter in every garage and nuclear power that would supply all our electrical needs and be safe and clean and too cheap to meter. Today, futurists are more prominent than they were in our youth and willing to predict not only technological but also social developments. Many of today's futurists use much better tools than those of yore—mostly better demographic and other kinds of statistical projections—but their crystal balls are still often filled with snake oil.

Unfortunately, personal charisma is often a substitute for thoughtful projections. Predicting the numbers of students in your school system year by year over the next five years, for instance, can be much improved with modern statistical techniques, but predicting the work force needs or lifestyle changes that our sixth graders will encounter after they graduate is unlikely to be any more accurate now than it was 40 years ago. For instance, the currently predicted deschooled communities—with people learning on their own schedules from wherever they happen to be—or instruction that is individualized according to brain function may end up being the ubiquitous helicopters and free, safe nuclear power of the future. We recommend that you be as careful with your futurists as you are with your education researchers.

The future is ultimately unknown, whatever the futurists say. What we can do is to make some judgments about the likelihood of some developments based on present trends. The most important thing that a superintendent can do to prepare for the future is to become familiar with the state of the world (including the history of how it got there) beyond the education business. Most of what happens in education is a subset of things that are happening in the wider world and cannot be adequately understood in isolation. One example of this is the fairly recent burgeoning of interest in alternatives (such as home schooling and education vouchers) to public schools. Interest in and political action to realize these alternatives are part of a larger movement to de-emphasize and even delegitimize government action in general. The use of the term government schools to describe public schools shows this connection. This antigovernment movement, especially in the United States is, in turn, a response to changes in the global economy. As economic competition becomes more universal, and *where* work is done becomes less important, the economic interest that the upper and upper-middle classes have in supporting services (including schools, but also including police protection, public transportation, and welfare payments) for other groups declines; the upper and upper-middle classes are increasingly motivated to have their own, "privatized" services, rather than to subsidize such services for other groups. Gated communities, private-security services, reduced subsidies to public transportation, and calls for privatized education are all reflections of this larger development. Educational leaders who do not understand such connections are likely to engage in holding actions to protect public education instead of changing the nature of public education to meet the developing new realities that will be the future. Both of us are strong proponents of public education, which serves a social good for the entire society as well as the good of individual children and parents, but we also recognize that the survival of public education, supported by taxpayers, depends on recognition by public educators and other policy makers of the larger realities that affect our enterprise.

As we said in the introductory chapter of this book, there is no substitute for a superintendent having a strong general education (e.g., having a general understanding of history, math, literature, and science) and keeping up intellectually through reading. Context is the key to understanding whatever comes along, especially to understanding it at a relatively early stage, and context can only come from being generally well informed.

Let us look at some of the developments that we anticipate will make life interesting for the superintendent of the future. The watchwords for superintendents in the next 20 years will be: higher and higher standards for all, accountability at all levels, and choice.

Many educational leaders over the past 20 years have acted as if the term *world-class standards* is meaningless. This is a head-in-the-sand view of a very significant concept. Our students must meet world-class standards because they will increasingly be competing with those in other countries who do. And by "other countries" we do not mean only the other industrialized countries of Western Europe and Eastern Asia, but we also refer to those elites in countries, such as Brazil, India, Egypt, and Russia who do meet those standards. (As we noted above, where people live is increasingly less important in the world economy, and what people do for how much pay is increasingly more important.) Let us be more specific about what the term *world-class standards* means in U.S. terms. The standards for entering a university in most competitor countries can be defined by a program that is found in few American high schools—the International Baccalaureate (IB) program, which was set up to prepare children of Western Europeans living abroad for university entrance in their home countries. This program uses external exams (graded in Geneva) to determine readiness for university study. Some American high schools that have the IB have found that some IB courses are roughly equivalent to Advanced Placement (AP) courses, so that the homegrown AP exams can be seen as roughly approximating world-class standards for the college bound. This means that if all our college-bound students are to meet world-class standards in their high school education they will be able to pass (e.g., get a grade of 3 or higher on) five or six AP exams. This is a fairly clear example of a world-class standard. In most developed countries, between 20 and 30% of young people in the age group meet this standard; smaller percentages of the age group meet this kind of standard (and enter universities) in less-developed countries.

What of the non–college bound in these other countries? This varies much more. In many of the developed countries (e.g., Germany, Japan) the non–college bound are held to very high, but different standards, and this is true in some less-developed countries, such as South Korea. These countries have highly educated populations, which means highly educated work forces, although a much smaller percentage of college graduates than in the United States. Other less-developed countries (and some developed countries, such as the United Kingdom) give much less attention to the non–college bound.

Overall, education is becoming increasingly important in the world economy, and, as we have said, where workers actually reside is becoming less important. Technology is the main reason, but there are others. This means that the educated, wherever they live, are the economic winners. Educated (as we use the term here) means to be thoroughly grounded in basic skills and knowledge plus able to use those skills and knowledge in both anticipated and unanticipated ways. A K-12 education system (such as that in the United States) that dumps into colleges and universities large numbers of students who need remedial work on basic skills while in other countries *all* university students start out achieving at the level of a small percentage of ours is not effective or efficient. Nor is a K-12 system that graduates large numbers of students into the work force with minimal reading and math ability.

A major question is whether the United States wants to go the way of countries that do not ensure all youngsters meet high standards or whether we do want to ensure this. An alternative, of course, is to continue on the present course, which has served us fairly well over time. Unfortunately, it is likely to be increasingly less successful as the economy becomes increasingly globalized. While some percentage of the U.S. population (approximately 20 to 30%) will be participants in any foreseeable global economy, the rest will be increasingly less so without imposition of world-class standards. And remember that this elite of world-economy participants will be much less dependent for their own economic well-being on the economic well-being of the rest of society than have U.S. economic elites in the past, who depended for their economic well-being on, for instance, the factory workers in their own cities or other U.S. cities.

This is why national standards and national assessments are necessary if our country (beyond the 20 to 30% elite) will be able to compete in the world economy of the future. Such assessments should not be required by the federal government but should be available for all school systems to use and to make scores available to colleges and employers. As we write this, the idea of national standards has been politicized to the point that the actual arguments pro and con get lost in a fog of hot air. But promulgating national standards and assessments based on them could easily be seen as one of the most important events of our time when the history books are written.

What this means to the superintendent of the future is that national standards and assessments (and the necessity for school systems of preparing their students to meet and pass them) are a wave of the future. Embrace it, prepare for it; adopt the equivalent (such as the IB or a strong AP program) in the meantime. One relatively easy thing a school system could do is to adopt a goal for increasing the percentages of its high school students who take AP exams and the percentage of such exams that achieve a grade of 3 or higher. Part of this objective would be to increase percentages of minority students who take and score high on the exams. This would motivate everyone in the high schools (and the parents) to recruit more students into AP classes and to work hard on preparation for the exams, which could be touted as the equivalent of world-class performance for the college bound. A step beyond this would be for a school system to create a new diploma called the "college-bound diploma." This would require meeting all the requirements for the highest-level state diploma plus scoring 3 or above on four or five AP exams. Of course, instituting the whole IB program (which requires training and approval from an international organization) for all college-bound students would be the best way to implement world-class standards for this group.

For the non–college bound, there are no easily available off-the-shelf options. What needs to be done here is to demand strong academic achievement plus some kind of transition into the work world. Guaranteeing that all graduates have at least math to the level of algebra, geometry, and trigonometry, two years of solid high school level science (biology, chemistry, physics), and English and history at what is now the college-bound level plus up-to-date professional technical courses that prepare the student for the workplace of the future is what we need to be shooting for. Actually, this group is more important to our nation's economic future than are the college bound, and we need to work hard on clear standards for the work-transition aspect of the requirements for this group, including integrating academic with professional technical instruction and the latter with actual work experience.

School-leaving standards and assessments are a necessary first step that will affect all levels of schooling down through the grades. Assessments at various levels in each of the major subjects (e.g., a test midway through elementary school and in middle school in each major subject) will be part of this. The entire question of promotion and retention will be opened up on a more objective basis using assessments throughout the years of schooling and the necessity to prepare every student for school-leaving exams to ratchet up achievement at all levels of schooling; superintendents will need to find new ways to ensure that students progress academically at a reasonable rate. Once the assessments are in place, students (and teachers and parents) can be held to more objective achievement standards and be provided with all opportunities necessary to achieve them *before* going on to the next level of learning. Some students may suffer under this system, and their needs must be met, but overall achievement will increase substantially. Our society cannot let the individual case (even many individual cases) hold back the ratcheting up of standards forever. As we write this, the Chicago schools are implementing a program to end social promotion, something that presages the high-accountability public school of the future.

Getting students to meet these standards will require substantial changes in perspective, not only in the education perspective but in the larger community. Let us first comment on the larger community—parents and those without children in school—and students. One reason that our students are not meeting world-class standards is that our communities have not demanded it, parents have not demanded it, and (many educators would say) students have not wanted it. Most teachers, principals, and superintendents can remember many cases in which the parents of a student have told the school they want their child to be held to high-achievement standards and then have backed off when the student resisted demands. These cases are the tip of an iceberg of parent ambiguity about the priority of achievement in a world in which part-time jobs, sports, social life, television, and many other things compete for student (and parent) attention. The schools will be hard put to raise achievement without parent and other community support, but that kind of support is growing. One very interesting recent finding comes from a Public Agenda survey (Bradley, 1997) in which two-thirds of students surveyed said they could do much better in school if they tried, and three-fourths said they would pay more attention to their studies if they were required to learn more and pass tests. The students understand they are coasting and know what will get them going, if only their parents, teachers, and everyone else involved is willing to put on the pressure.

But are we as educators ready to raise and enforce high standards? One of our problems is that we do not have among us enough people who are truly educated in the academic disciplines that are taught in our schools. One thing that public education needs is much more influence—at all levels of the "education establishment"—of people who are learned in these disciplines, conversant with developments in these disciplines, and able to make sense of these disciplines in terms that students of various ages and grade levels can understand. With more people like this preparing teachers and providing staff development, leading K-12 professional organizations and writing for education journals, serving in federal and state departments of education, and writing textbooks and other educational materials, those teachers and administrators who actually make and implement decisions in schools and school systems will have the intellectual wherewithal to help their students meet high academic standards. There is one area in particular in which such people should predominate—curriculum development. Those who develop curricula should be highly qualified (probably the Ph.D. level with publications in an academic field, such as mathematics, physics, history, literature—*not* in math ed. or any other kind of "ed." and especially not in "curriculum and instruction"); they should also be able and willing to make sense of subjects they know at the highest level for students at the lowest grade level. Recruiting such people will be difficult but not impossible and is one of many ways that K-12 education and universities (not their schools of education) can work together. Curriculum is one important element, and having these kinds of people in charge of curriculum will make a big difference, but instruction is another important element, and here what needs to be done is even more radical.

What needs to be done in instruction (i.e., the methods used to convey the curriculum to the students) is to very carefully examine the claims of all instructional methods in terms of actual findings of actual research. Much work needs to be done to expose bad research on learning and discover good research that then, of course, needs to be implemented. Broad-scale implementation will not be easy but there is research on this. Research in the Memphis schools, for instance, indicates that "reform strategies that work are curriculum based, have extensive and ongoing professional development that helps teachers deal with classroom instruction, and have clear goals that are well matched to school goals" (Olson, 1997).

Increasingly, the intellectual foundations of the K-12 educational enterprise will be open to criticism from scholars outside this enterprise (such as E.D. Hirsch, whose latest book, *The Schools We Need and Why We Don't Have Them* [1996] is the most important single book on education in the last 10 years) and from those inside the enterprise. These critics will demonstrate that much that is promoted in K-12 education (e.g., brain-based instruction, holistic, thematic, student centered, interdisciplinary whatever) has little or no conclusive basis in research. Superintendents had better get outside the standard sources of information and into research and commentary by the critics if they are going to defend what they are doing and change it when necessary.

The struggle between the education establishment and the "outside" world will not only be fought on intellectual grounds. Another battleground will be teacher certification. This battle will be between those supporting the existing ed-school-state-government system that we all came through and those who value subject expertise (combined with a willingness and ability to make the subjects understandable to youngsters) and want to recruit bright college graduates and to change the atmosphere of schools so that this kind of teacher will flourish. "Teach for America" is just the beginning of a movement to recruit and retain a new type of teacher.

Accountability will be tied to high standards and assessments, but there is more to it than that. Schools will be under the gun for years to come, and the only response is to raise the level of accountability—at all levels and for everything—as high as possible. This means fiscal accountability based on cost-effectiveness, program accountability measured by rigorous program evaluation, personnel accountability based on evaluation of all support personnel, teacher accountability based on teacher evaluation that is at least partially tied to student achievement, and student accountability for their own work and achievement. What we have left out here are parent accountability and the accountability of the community to adequately fund and support education. We are not sure how to get to these. But all of this depends on the assessments of student achievement that define the results that everyone we have mentioned is trying to achieve.

And effort to achieve accountability cannot consist only of sticks; we will need carrots too. In the Fairfax County Public Schools, both of us have been through what is probably the most extensive implementation of teacher merit pay in the past 30 years in U.S. public education. For a few years, in the late 1980s and early 1990s, over 2,000 (out of around 10,000) Fairfax County Public School (FCPS) teachers were receiving substantially higher pay than other teachers in the system based on a very credible performance evaluation system (about 100 teachers per year were also losing their jobs based on this system). When the FCPS merit-pay program was eliminated by the school board, a new teachers' organization (mostly made up of those who had qualified for the merit pay) rose from the ashes and has since flourished in FCPS. Teacher merit pay (perhaps eventually based, at least partially, on national certification) is one of those waves of the future that we see lapping at the shores of our profession.

Increasing productivity will be one of the critical accountability issues. Increasing productivity requires: (1) defining the results desired (i.e., student achievement standards), (2) establishing measures of those results (i.e., school-leaving exams) and monitoring them, and (3) implementing incentives (e.g., merit pay) for producing results. Public schools have never operated this way, but we will be increasingly expected to do so in the future. There are good reasons why it is difficult for schools to operate this way (e.g., greater difficulty—compared to private industry or other public agencies—in establishing what results schools should be responsible for and how to measure them), but just citing these difficulties rather than working to overcome them will no longer be an option.

Choice—like it or not—is another wave of the future, and parents are going to have choice whether public schools offer it to them or not, so those of us who strongly support public schools had better figure out ways to offer choice within public school systems. This makes the United States different from most of the rest of the world, where centrally planned curriculum and instruction predominate. In any case, setting the standards with national assessments while allowing schools maximum freedom to teach as they will seems to be the new American way. The best way to develop schools of choice is to let them bubble up from the grass roots, each community developing the school, based on research, that will best meet the needs of its children.

Schools of choice will proliferate within public school systems to provide flexibility as achievement standards and accountability mechanisms are put in place. Schools will be expected to provide programs that appeal to parents' and students' particular interests and needs while ensuring high academic achievement.

Schools of choice are not exactly a new idea. For instance, a few school systems have provided "traditional" and/or "progressive" elementary schools as a choice for parents who have wanted an alternative to one or the other. Other elementary schools have provided "partial immersion" programs, in which students are taught in a particular foreign language during part of the school day; FCPS currently has 13 such schools, each offering either French, Japanese, Spanish, or German. There are many other examples of existing special-interest schools. Special-interest high schools, such as schools for the arts (e.g., the Duke Ellington School in Washington, D.C.), or schools preparing students for particular careers (e.g., Aviation High School in New York City), or those emphasizing science, math, and technology (e.g., Bronx High School of Science or FCPS's Thomas Jefferson High School for Science and Technology [TJHSST]) receive more attention than special-interest elementary schools and usually limit entry based on exams. But special-interest elementary schools are becoming more common and will become even more common in the near future.

Elementary schools of choice are not for everyone. The most significant objection to them is that elementary schools should be neighborhood schools. In many cases this objection can be met. For instance, in the FCPS foreign language partial immersion schools only some students (those whose parents have chosen the program) are in the partial immersion program; all students in the attendance area are served in the school, but parents still have a choice, while some parents from outside the attendance area can enroll their children in the immersion program. Another example of maintaining neighborhood schools while offering choice is that of underenrolled schools that offer an enhanced program to all students and allow students from outside the attendance area to attend. In FCPS, Bailey's Elementary School for the Arts and Sciences (BESAS) enrolls about 100 students from other parts of the county who are attracted to Bailey's program and bring native-English-speaking ability to a school that is otherwise 80 percent nonnative-English speaking. This way, those who want to attend their neighborhood schools (including those in the magnet schools' attendance area) may do so, while those who are willing to send their children outside their neighborhoods to a special program have that option. In the case of elementary schools of choice, the desire for neighborhood schools will always be an issue.

A connected issue is transportation. One solution is to make it clear to parents that they will need to provide transportation for any students who attend schools of choice outside their attendance areas. This approach has worked well in partial immersion schools. Another solution is to figure out ways to provide transportation for students attending these schools; in FCPS, this has been done by integrating transportation for BESAS magnet students into an existing transportation system for students at a nearby school. Neither of these two solutions is ideal, and planners should be aware that parents are likely to ask for transportation to a magnet school even though they have been told it would not be available.

It is not easy, but creating schools of choice is worth the trouble because it allows parents the opportunity to obtain something special for their children's well-being and to do it within the public schools. All of us who have struggled to involve parents in school planning and governance know the value to parents of making their own choices for their children. Parents are more likely to support whatever school program their children are in (including the "regular" academic program, which most of them are likely to choose) if they have been given a choice. In any case, some kind of choice is in the future for public education, and school administrators ought to be exploring ways that choice can be provided.

The first step to providing choice is developing alternatives to the regular program. Every elementary school ought to be looking at alternative ways to ensure that every student meets high academic standards. There are many alternatives out there but not all are useful. To some extent, study of research and program results can help those looking at alternatives to avoid choosing one that offers little promise. Unfortunately, inflated "research" claims and other sorts of hype are not uncommon in our business, so *caveat emptor* is good advice here.

Any alternative needs to be carefully chosen by the school's community, including parents and other community members as well as teachers, the principal, and other school staff. Usually, an alternative first gets the attention of teachers or the principal and is then discussed with the larger community, which can start with the parent teacher association (PTA) but should eventually include a larger community representation, including local school board members and other local notables with a stake in the school. As the community looks at and discusses the alternative, the principal will get a sense of whether there is strong support for it. If there seems to be fairly strong support, the principal should start to consider the percentage of parent support that the particular alternative would need to be implemented effectively. If the alternative would not include the entire student body (as with foreign language partial immersion), a simple majority or even less might be sufficient, although even in this case, the program is likely to have some effect on the rest of the students (e.g., the partial immersion programs can lead to larger class sizes for "nonimmersion" students in the upper grades of a small school). If the alternative will substantially affect most or all students and/or teachers, not to mention altering the parents' vacation and child-care schedules, a supermajority ought to be considered. An example of such an alternative is an extended school year alternative, which will put students in the school on a different year schedule than those in the middle and high schools in the same pyramid. In cases like this, in which the alternative will have strong effects on those in and outside the school, the school ought to consider offering parents alternative placements in nearby schools that will not offer the alternative. In any case, such a strong change calls for a percentage of parental support (and, of course, staff support) that is substantially higher than 50%. How much higher is a decision that the principal must make him- or herself, but the percentage required should be decided before surveying the parents.

Once a school has adopted an alternative, the first priority is to make it successful for the students in the school. In some cases, the alternative will include students from outside the attendance area from the beginning of its implementation, and in other cases (such as the extended year described above) students in the attendance area will be offered placement in other schools, or both in- and outplacement may be part of the alternative from the beginning. However, probably in most cases, the alternative will first be implemented for the students in the attendance area. We call these special schools "focus schools." A successful focus school can operate indefinitely for only the students in its neighborhood.

One of the big differences between education now and education 15 years ago is that then all that was needed to continue a program was a high rating on the "smile index"; if everyone (students, parents, teachers) liked it, it was successful. Today, our communities ask for evidence of effectiveness, and this will increasingly be the case in the foreseeable future, especially among the increasingly large percentage of our population that does not have students in our schools. Taxpayers (including parents) are less interested now in how happy children and parents are and more interested in whether academic achievement is high and the schools are operating cost effectively—and the taxpayers are right. Evaluation of the achievement of students in the alternative program is crucial to a program's continuation. The evaluation should assess not only the academic goals of the particular alternative (e.g., are students learning a foreign language in the partial immersion program) but also general academic achievement (e.g., reading and writing in English). In many cases, the primary goal of the alternative program is to improve performance in reading, writing, arithmetic, and other basic academic subjects. Whether or not the alternative's primary goal is improvements in these subjects, student achievement in them should be assessed as part of any alternative's evaluation.

Once an alternative has been proven successful with students from the school's attendance area, it is likely to attract attention from other schools in the school system and elsewhere. These other schools may then consider the possibility of offering alternative programs, especially if they can consider a number of different alternatives. It is possible, though unlikely, that every school in a system might offer an alternative.

Focus schools may remain focus schools indefinitely, but some will become magnet schools, offering alternatives to families from other areas. Magnet schools are true schools of choice, and if several magnet schools are available, families can have a wide variety of choices for their children. One place that has provided complete choice to parents is a community school district in the East Harlem section of Manhattan. Principals and teachers were encouraged to develop alternative types of schools, and parents were allowed to choose their children's schools. Much success was reported from this "public schools of choice" system in a very low socioeconomic area. In most cases, however, not all schools or communities will want to become magnet schools; in fact, not all schools and communities will want to become focus schools. More often, schools will become magnet schools because of issues that are particular to the specific school and community. An example of this is BESAS, in which an underenrolled school with an 80% limited-English-proficient student body and neighboring schools with similar demographics sought to provide an enhanced program for students from its attendance area, and to bring in native-English-speaking students from other parts of the school division.

Planning for the future means, among other things, planning for alternatives and for choice. There are many alternative programs "out there"—some excellent and some not so excellent. Principals should be aware of these alternatives and should be discussing them with their staffs and communities. Critical to this planning is ensuring that any alternative improve the basic academic achievement of all students. Schools of choice will be part of the future of education, and those principals and superintendents who thoughtfully explore choices will lead all of us into that future.

Besides this trilogy—higher standards, accountability, and choice—a number of other items will be hot issues in the near future. Among these will be special education, values education, and multiculturalism.

Special education is likely to become the hottest topic in education outside the more general standards and accountability issue. Special education is currently approaching a crisis: On the one hand, you have special-education advocates (sometimes split between inclusionists and noninclusionists), and on the other hand, are those trying to downscale special-education referrals for educational reasons or to save money. It is hard to see how this one is going to come out, but accountability is likely to play a large role in the debate. Also, there is new federal legislation, the Individuals with Disabilities Education Act (IDEA). Watch out for this one.

Values education has had more said about it and less action than almost any educational issue in the past 20 years, but many people remain passionate about it. We are not sure what is going to happen with this, but it is likely that the issue will continue to arise from time to time in the foreseeable future. Taking a strong intellectual approach, involving philosophy (Mathew Lipman's *Philosophy for Children* is an excellent problem for elementary school students), literature, history, science, and other disciplines is critical in this area, Peter Greer's summation of the four areas that need to be attended to in what he calls "Teaching Virtue" provides a good overall approach. Greer's four areas are: "grounding teachers in the study of ethics, including the entire teaching community, integrating study into every aspect of school, and providing a framework for students' understanding of what they are learning" (Greer, 1998).

Multiculturalism is another education issue that is connected to changes developing outside the world of K-12 education. It has both a concrete material aspect and an intellectual aspect; it has become an issue in education because of a combination of demographic and ideological changes. The demographics have pushed school systems to make decisions, and the new ideologies have affected those decisions. As schools in many countries include increasing numbers of students whose families have religious and cultural practices that increasingly diverge from those of students who have previously constituted the student bodies in those schools, teachers and school administrators are increasingly forced to decide the extent to which they will acknowledge that the divergent practices are integral to the new students' identities. While, in the past, schools were more likely to ignore the divergence and insist on a high degree of cultural homogeneity, they are now more likely to acknowledge, or even celebrate, diversity. This conflict between insisting on cultural homogeneity (with or without a high degree of *individual*, as distinct from cultural-group-mediated, freedom of behavior) on the one hand, and recognizing or celebrating cultural heterogeneity, on the other hand, is not at all an easy one to resolve, as is evident in recent cross-cultural conflicts in many developed countries. For instance, the conflict over whether to allow Muslim girls to wear veils in French schools has split both left and right in that country and can be seen as a conflict either between individual rights and group control (on the left, for instance) or between cultural imperialism and recognition of cultural group freedom (on the right) (Johnstone, 1990). The most significant quality of the multiculturalism dispute is that it raises many difficult and fundamental questions (such as the relative value of group rights, individual rights, and national solidarity in a modern democracy) that require learned, reasoned, intellectual discussion. Many superintendents have been pushed into making political decisions about such issues or decisions based on vague slogans (such as "embrace diversity" or "American values") without thinking through the very complex issues involved. In fact, neither the idea that only the perspective of the individual's ethnic group is valid for him or her nor the idea that ethnic-cultural differences are superficial is adequate to such decisions. This is one of many areas in which the superintendent of the future will need to be well educated, up to date, and thoughtful in areas beyond K-12 education.

What can be done now? Most of what we suggest that superintendents could do right now to move into the future is discussed above. Pushing for world-class standards using AP exams for the college bound and increased graduation requirements (especially in math, science, and English language plus professional technical preparation) for the non–college bound will have the greatest immediate (i.e., over the next five years) effect. Superintendents should also strongly support national standards and assessments, which may be crucial to saving public education. Using disciplinary experts (e.g., professors of math, English, and sciences from your local university) to look at the curriculum and at the extent to which students are learning what is in it would help improve the rigor of what is taught in your schools and build bridges between your teachers and administrators and scholars in the subjects your schools are teaching. Superintendents who have some schools that are performing below standards should convey the message that teachers will be recognized and rewarded for teaching in these schools and improving achievement there. Moving teachers who are expert in methods (such as Socratic seminars) that encourage student thinking into classrooms with high levels of students from traditionally underachieving groups while encouraging a return to direct teaching, memorization, and drill and practice when appropriate for all students (so that there is a mix of appropriate instructional techniques for all students) is likely to improve instruction across the board. Merit pay for teaching excellence will come again, and superintendents who develop plans and get stakeholders (including teachers' unions) on board now will be ahead of the game. As important as anything here is to get a personal handle on research—good, bad, and indifferent. Contact practicing cognitive psychologists and ask about the actual research support for some of the instructional strategies being promoted in your school system; you may be very surprised.

These are some things that superintendents can do now in their schools, but equally important in the long run is doing something for yourself. We have mentioned a number of times the importance of strong intellectual preparation and continued reading—both in education and in other areas. Every superintendent needs to determine his or her own program for getting and staying current, but we thought it might be interesting to readers to have a start. Therefore, here is one way to start.

Read four books about education that are probably not on your local school of education's reading list but that (in our very humble opinions) deal very intelligently with four extremely important issues that superintendents need to know about.

- E.D. Hirsch, *The Schools We Need and Why We Don't Have Them.* This is a systematic critique of the intellectual foundations of the K-12 education enterprise in the United States. It is very perceptive and very thorough, but those who have too much of a stake in things as they are (and seem always to have been) in our business won't like it. We think it is one of the two or three most important books about K-12 education published in our lifetimes.
- Laurence Steinberg, *Beyond the Classroom.* For all the educators who say that there is only so much that the schools can do given the rest of society, this book describes some significant research about just how that society affects students and their achievement.
- Eric Hanushek, *Making Schools Work: Improving Performance and Controlling Costs.* Hanushek is an economist, who has written on many non-education topics. Recently, he has done research and has written on making the educational enterprise effective and efficient, and this book deals with that research. Superintendents need to know about this work if they are to defend the cost-effectiveness of their schools.
- Harold Stevenson, *The Learning Gap.* Stevenson, a psychologist, also comes to research on education from an "outsider" perspective. This book relates the findings of many years of research comparing schooling in the United States with schooling in Japan, China, and Taiwan. You may be surprised with what he has found.

NEW! Diane Ravitch of New York University and the Brookings Institution's new book *Brookings Papers on Education Policy* has just been released. It includes articles by some of the most significant scholars of learning and education in the U.S. (most of whom are mentioned in the book you are holding). It is published by the Brookings Institution Press.

OK, this will get you started with some important issues in education, but what about the bigger picture, which is equally important. Far be it from us to say that no one can recommend books to someone he does not know. Here is a semirandom list of recent books that should pique your interest: Steven Pinker, *The Language Instinct: How the Mind Creates Language;* George W.S. Trow, *Within the Context of No Context;* Robert Hazen and James Trefil, *Science Matters: Achieving Scientific Literacy;* Paul Kennedy, *The Rise and Fall of the Great Powers: Economic Change and Military Conflict from 1500 to 2000.* Any of these will get you started thinking and probably reading more about an important subject outside the education enterprise.

But these are all nonfiction. Does literature have any place on a superintendent's reading list? You bet! We tend to accept the truth (although not in a simplistic sense) of the comment by Kenneth Burke, one of twentieth-century America's most important literary and cultural critics, that "literature is equipment for living." You may well have your own fiction "to read" list already at hand, but, if not, one way to get started is to read some of the works required in your high schools' English classes. If you have already done this, or don't believe literature is equipment for living, try this experiment (based on an "Intellectual Life of Schools" institute that P. Regnier directed recently). First read Jane Austen's novel *Emma;* then view the video of the movie based on the novel's plot— but *not* the costume drama starring Gwyneth Paltrow in the eponymous role; instead, view *Clueless,* which takes place in today's Los Angeles, features teen life, and is filmed, to a large extent, in school, but whose plot is based on Austen's novel. We leave the rest to you, but you may discover a closer relationship between life and art than you had expected.

There is a lot for the superintendent of the future to learn, but none of us would be in this business if we didn't like to learn. Learning from life is important, but the more and the more broadly we read, the better we can understand what happens in the very real life we deal with every day. We hope that this book helps our readers make those connections—between the life of the mind and the life of the classroom and corridor—that will make the difference between the pedestrian superintendent and the excellent superintendent of the future, because it will be a struggle of ideas, as much as anything else, that will shape our profession in the twenty-first century.

Mastering the details and being able to think through the ideas are the skills you will need. We hope that this book helps you to develop both of these skills and the ability to connect the two. We remain optimistic that great superintendents will become even more involved in the educational policy decisions of the new millennium.

REFERENCES

Austen, J. 1996. *Emma.* New York: New American Library.

Bradley, A. (1997, February 12). Survey reveals teens yearn for high standards. *Education Week.*

Burke, K. 1973. *The Philosophy of literary form.* Los Angeles, CA: University of California Press.

Greer, P. (1998, February 4). Teaching virtue. *Education Week.*

Hanushek, E. (1994). *Making schools work: Improving performance and controlling costs.* Washington, DC: Brookings Institution.

Hazen, R., & Trefil, J. (1991). *Science matters: Achieving scientific literacy.* New York: Doubleday.

Hirsch, E.D. (1996). *The schools we need and why we don't have them.* New York: Doubleday.

Johnstone, D. (1990, January 24–30). In "great kerchief quarrel" French unite against Anglo-Saxon ghettos. *In These Times.*

Kennedy, P. (1987). *The rise and fall of the great powers: Economic change and military conflict from 1500 to 2000.* New York: Random House.

Olson, I. (1997, April 30). Teachers need nuts, bolts of reforms, expert say. *Education Week on the Web.* http://www.edweek.org; accessed February 1998.

Pinker, S. (1994). *The language instinct.* New York: Wm. Morrow & Co.

Steinberg, L. (1996). *Beyond the classroom: Why school reform has failed and what parents need to do.* New York: Simon & Schuster.

Santayana, G. (1981). *The Life of Reason.* New York: MacMillan.

Stevenson, H. (1994). *The Learning gap: Why our schools are failing and what we can learn from the Japanese and Chinese education.* New York: Touchstone.

Trow, G.W.S. (1981). *Within the context of no context.* Boston: Little Brown.

Index

About the Editors

Robert R. Spillane is a Regional Education Officer for the United States Department of State in Washington, D.C. From 1985 to 1997, he was the Superintendent of Schools in Fairfax County, Virginia, and before that, Boston, Massachusetts. He has also held the post of Deputy Commissioner for Elementary, Secondary, and Continuing Education in New York State, and served as Superintendent of schools in New Rochelle, and Roosevelt, Long Island, New York, and Glassboro, New Jersey.

Paul Regnier is the Coordinator of Community Relations for Fairfax County Public Schools, in Fairfax County, Virginia. He also directs the Intellectual Life of Schools Project sponsored by George Mason University. Previously, he worked for the New York State Education Department, first as Assistant to the Deputy Commissioner for Elementary, Secondary and Continuing Education, and then as Coordinator of Special Program Development. Before that he taught English in New York State high schools.